The Koran

by Shaykh Muhammad Sarwar and Brandon Toropov

ALPHA

A member of Penguin Group (USA) Inc.

To Stephen Toropov, the pre-eminent reader of great books.

ALPHA BOOKS

Published by the Penguin Group

Penguin Group (USA) Inc., 375 Hudson Street, New York, New York 10014, USA

Penguin Group (Canada), 90 Eglinton Avenue East, Suite 700, Toronto, Ontario M4P 2Y3, Canada (a division of Pearson Penguin Canada Inc.)

Penguin Books Ltd., 80 Strand, London WC2R 0RL, England

Penguin Ireland, 25 St. Stephen's Green, Dublin 2, Ireland (a division of Penguin Books Ltd.)

Penguin Group (Australia), 250 Camberwell Road, Camberwell, Victoria 3124, Australia (a division of Pearson Australia Group Pty. Ltd.)

Penguin Books India Pvt. Ltd., 11 Community Centre, Panchsheel Park, New Delhi—110 017, India

Penguin Group (NZ), 67 Apollo Drive, Rosedale, North Shore, Auckland 1311, New Zealand (a division of Pearson New Zealand Ltd.)

Penguin Books (South Africa) (Pty.) Ltd., 24 Sturdee Avenue, Rosebank, Johannesburg 2196, South Africa

Penguin Books Ltd., Registered Offices: 80 Strand, London WC2R 0RL, England

Copyright © 2003 by Beach Brook Productions

International Standard Book Number: 978-1-59257-105-5
Library of Congress Catalog Card Number: 2003108342

15   14   13   20   19   18   17   16   15   14   13   12   11

Interpretation of the printing code: The rightmost number of the first series of numbers is the year of the book's printing; the rightmost number of the second series of numbers is the number of the book's printing. For example, a printing code of 03-1 shows that the first printing occurred in 2003.

Printed in the United States of America

Most Alpha books are available at special quantity discounts for bulk purchases for sales promotions, premiums, fund-raising, or educational use. Special books, or book excerpts, can also be created to fit specific needs.

For details, write: Special Markets, Alpha Books, 375 Hudson Street, New York, NY 10014.

Publisher: *Marie Butler-Knight*
Product Manager: *Phil Kitchel*
Senior Managing Editor: *Jennifer Chisholm*
Senior Acquisitions Editor: *Renee Wilmeth*
Development Editor: *Jennifer Moore*
Production Editor: *Billy Fields*
Copy Editor: *Ross Patty*
Illustrator: *Jody Schaeffer*
Cover/Book Designer: *Trina Wurst*
Indexer: *Julie Bess*
Layout/Proofreading: *Becky Harmon, Donna Martin*

Contents at a Glance

Contents

Foreword

There are many reasons to read the Koran. With the whole world fearful of a "clash of civilizations" between Judeo-Christian and Islamic societies, and especially in the aftermath of the shocking events of September 11, 2001, many Western readers demanded to know "the best book to read about Islam." For Muslim as well as non-Muslim experts, there is, of course, no better introduction to the faith of the Prophet Muhammad than the Koran.

Western readers may also be drawn to the Koran by a simpler, more innocent curiosity. But Muslims believe the Koran, which is a direct communication from the Creator, must be known in Arabic to perceive it in its fullness. Since the global majority does not know this sacred language, translations are not only legitimate, but necessary; not only worthy, but useful.

In addition, some aspects of the Koran require elucidation for the ordinary reader, Muslim as well as non-Muslim. Commentaries on the Koran are therefore as important for Muslims as they are for non-Muslims. Many Westerners mistakenly believe the Koran is not subject to interpretation by Muslim believers, but this is absurdly wrong. The Koran is not a primitive set of prescriptions; nor is it a long but simple sermon. It is a complicated discourse, stunningly beautiful in its complexity. Seeking fuller comprehension of the Koran, scholars throughout the history of the faith have celebrated difference and argument, and, with some notable if unfortunate exceptions, have shunned any attempt to impose a narrow conformity over understanding of the text.

The Koran is a holy book which, as a book, constitutes one of several symbolic links between the followers of the Prophet Muhammad and those who received the earlier monotheistic revelations—the Jews and Christians. The latter are designated in the Koran as "People of the Book," and their devotion to the Torah and Gospels unites them with the devotees of Islamic scripture.

The Koran is, however, a different kind of book. Unlike the Torah, it does not describe the history of the Arab people, as the Torah does that of the Jews. And in contrast with the Gospels, it does not relate the life of the Prophet, as the writings of Matthew, Mark, Luke, and John tell us about Jesus. Instead, it offers a message to the individual believer, as well as all of humanity, about the challenges in believers' own lives, today as well as 1,400 years in the past, when it was received.

Further, both the Torah and the Gospels are varied in their styles, while the Koran embodies a single idiom. The classical Arabic of the Koran has become the standard literary language of the Arab world, and has immensely influenced other "Muslim" languages, from the variant of Slavic known as Bosnian, through Albanian, Turkish, Persian, Urdu, the Malayan languages, and those of Saharan and sub-Saharan Africa.

In the Islamic world, the production of beautiful copies of the Koran has been a high art, comparable to the decoration of the Gospels in medieval Christendom. However, among Muslims the tradition of memorization and recitation of the Koran also remains vibrant. This, too, is an art, and an exquisite one. If there is one thing that is to be regretted when Western readers first examine the Koran, it is that they will seldom have heard the sublime voices of Koran reciters, which are encountered in all mosques everywhere.

But the words and principles enunciated in the Koran, and the light of faith that shines through even in translation, remain extraordinarily compelling and inspiring. The directness of the Koran's message is one of the sources for the intensity of faith we see visible among the world's Muslims—an intensity that many in the Judeo-Christian world find intimidating.

Shaykh Muhammad Sarwar and Brandon Toropov have accomplished a marvelous and commendable work in producing this book. Shaykh Sarwar's English translation of the Koran has been undertaken with the laudable aim of increasing mutual understanding between Muslims and non-Muslims in the West, and he has brought to it his full dedication as a scholar and outstanding religious leader.

There is one enemy for Muslims, and their non-Muslim neighbors, in today's world: fear of the other. The Koran provides Muslims with resources to overcome the anxieties they experience. Reading a guide to the Koran of this kind may help non-Muslims defeat the fears growing among them as the spectre of interreligious conflict stalks the world. The Creator has always told those who believe: Be not afraid. Muslims believe that religion was given to us to make our time on Earth easier and better, not to make our existence difficult and burdensome. All honor is due to those who assist the fearful in gaining peace, security, and tranquility in their lives, homes, and futures.

—Stephen Schwartz

Stephen Schwartz, who has studied Islam for many years, is the author of a number of books on international affairs, including *The Two Faces of Islam: The House of Sa'Ud from Tradition to Terror* (New York: Doubleday, 2002).

Introduction

The Prophet Muhammad was selected not long ago as the most influential person in history by a respected (non-Islamic) historian. This author, Michael H. Hart, took it as his task in his book *The 100: A Ranking of the Most Influential Persons in History* (Citadel Press, 1992) to compile a list of the 100 most eminent historical figures ever.

The choice of Muhammad over Caesar, Christ, Newton, Einstein, Darwin, St. Paul, and other figures more familiar to Western readers came as something of a surprise to many who read the book. Hart's argument in favor of the Prophet, however, was persuasive. Here, Hart argued, was a man who was triumphantly successful in religious, military, and social spheres, whose success was based on clear goals, and whose direct influence has endured for nearly a millennium and a half. Clearly, Hart argued, this was a career without parallel in the human chronicle.

Indeed, it has been argued that the final decade of the Prophet's life—when he rose from leader of an obscure religious sect to emperor of Arabia and head of a great monotheistic faith—reflects success on a scale that dwarfs that of any other leader. And his influence in death has grown, rather than diminished.

At the center of it all was—and is—the Koran.

Many Westerners today are curious about the specifics of the message that catapulted the Prophet and his movement to prominence—a message that is regarded by believers and unbelievers alike as a masterpiece of Arabic literature and a massively influential religious text. This book is meant to give anyone who is unfamiliar with the Koran some idea of the enduring power and dynamic force of its message—the message that formed the heart of the Prophet's extraordinary career.

What Is It about This Book?

Although there are miracles mentioned in the Koran, the book itself remains the abiding miracle for the believer.

Many contemporary misunderstandings about Islam by non-Muslims arise from the assumption that the Koran "must be" roughly equivalent to the Judeo-Christian Bible, or to the Hindu Bhagavad-Gita, or to the Taoist Tao-te Ching, or to any of the other religious texts that have influenced human society over the centuries. Muslims, on the other hand, believe that the Koran is set apart from these texts ... and, in fact, from all the literature to be found on Earth.

For those unfamiliar with the Islamic faith, this simple fact—that Muslims consider their book to be fundamentally different from other religious texts—leads to an important question. *Why* do 1.7 billion Muslims hold this book in such high esteem?

Why do they feel the guidance they receive in the Koran is uniquely, miraculously authoritative?

Is this feeling about the Koran entirely a matter of social conditioning? Is it solely the result of the influence of religious institutions? Does it have something to do with governmental regulation? Does family influence play a role? Or is there something in the *content* of the text itself that has caused one fifth of the world's population to grant this fourteen-century-old Arabic text such an extraordinary position in their lives?

These, of course, are questions that each person must answer independently. We believe, though, that these questions can only be addressed by approaching the text of the Koran itself. As a result, we have included many quotations from the Koran in this book. Wherever possible, we have introduced main topics and tried to allow the Koran to speak for itself, so that you can reach your own conclusions about the reasons for this book's extraordinary influence through the centuries.

"Allah" and "God"

The word "Allah" predates the mission of the Prophet Muhammad by a vast span of time. This word is used in the Koran as the name of the Creator. To be sure, the Koran also passes along many *attributes* of the Creator—Benificent, Merciful, All-Knowing, and so on—but it always comes back to Allah as the holy name.

Some non-Muslims, however, assume the word "Allah" to be a creation of Muhammad, or assume that Muslims, in worshipping Allah, are worshipping some separate being from the Creator. "Allah" (which means simply "the God") is not a separate deity from the Creator, but is an ancient word for the same all-powerful, all-knowing entity. To reinforce this point, we have used both words—"Allah" and "God"—in this book.

Other Arabic Terms

Of course, many Arabic terms likely to be unfamiliar to non-Muslims are likely to arise in a book of this kind.

There sometimes appear to be as many different possible English renderings of Arabic words as there are readers to encounter them. This is partly due to the fact that the English alphabet does not have equivalent sounds for many Arabic letters. In this book, we have tried to keep the spellings of these words consistent, to define them as they arise (see "Extras" below), and then to use their English equivalents wherever possible. In quoted passages, we have allowed the original author's transliteration of Arabic terms to stand.

The name for the Islamic holy book itself is rendered in various ways by various English-speaking writers: Koran, Qur'an, Quran, Kor'an, etc. For our book, we have chosen what appears to be the most common usage over the years—Koran—on the theory that that rendering will be most familiar to non-Muslims.

How to Use This Book

This book is divided into six sections, each of which explores a different aspect of the Koran.

Part 1, "The Fundamentals," gives you an overview of the key concepts, common questions, and relevant historical events related to the book and the faith it guides.

Part 2, "A Document Like No Other," offers insights into the structure, distinctive message, and unique features of the Koran.

Part 3, "Allah and Humanity," presents an overview of God's relationship to—and message for—humankind, as described in the Koran.

Part 4, "Obligations of the Faith," explores the Koran's conceptions of virtue, justice, family, and duty as they relate to believers.

Part 5, "Life on Earth and the Afterlife," shows you what the Koran teaches concerning the purpose of life on Earth, dealings with unbelievers, and what awaits us after death.

Part 6, "The Holy Koran Today," explores contemporary issues and resources related to Koranic study.

You'll also find helpful appendixes that provide you with recommended reading, a timeline, Islamic resources in your area, and a structural overview of the Koran itself.

Extras

In addition to all that material, you will find sidebars designed to make improving your knowledge of the Koran easy. These text boxes feature information you can absorb almost immediately, with little or no effort. Here's how you can spot these features:

 The Word

Here's where you'll find particularly important extracts from the text of the Koran itself.

 What's It Mean?

In these boxes, you'll get concise definitions of terms that may not yet be familiar to you.

Points to Ponder

In these boxes, you'll discover interesting points regarding the Koran and other religious and social traditions.

Caution!

Here, you'll learn about potentially troublesome misconceptions about the Koran—and about the facts as they really stand.

Spotlight on Islam

Here, you'll gain insight on the religion of Islam. Islam means "submission (to the will of God)," and this faith regards the Koran as the divinely revealed word of God; in these boxes, you'll learn about specific religious traditions, viewpoints, and practices associated with the Koran.

A Word about the Translation

Unless otherwise noted, the translation employed is that of Muhammad Sarwar.

Acknowledgments

Grateful thanks go out to Renee Wilmeth, Jennifer Moore, Judith Burros, and David Toropov, all of whom helped this book to reach the light of day.

Trademarks

All terms mentioned in this book that are known to be or are suspected of being trademarks or service marks have been appropriately capitalized. Alpha Books and Penguin Group (USA) Inc. cannot attest to the accuracy of this information. Use of a term in this book should not be regarded as affecting the validity of any trademark or service mark.

Part 1

The Fundamentals

Ready to begin at the beginning?

This part of the book gives you an overview of the key concepts, common questions, and relevant historical events related to the Koran and the faith it guides.

The Basics

In This Chapter

♦ Understanding the Koran

♦ Why translations of the Koran are no match for the original Arabic version

♦ An overview of Islam

♦ How Muslims interpret the Koran

Bismillahir rahmanir raheem!

These words are a transliteration of the Arabic phrase that opens the first chapter, or Sura, of the Koran—and all but one of the remaining 113 Suras as well. The phrase means "In the name of Allah, the Compassionate, the Merciful." It can be written in many, many calligraphic styles, some of them hypnotically beautiful. (A sample of this script appears in the next section.)

The Koran, which many regard as hypnotically beautiful in its own right, is the holy book of the Islamic faith. *Muslims,* or those who follow the Islamic faith, consider the Koran in its original Arabic to be the actual divine word of the one and true God, Whom they call *Allah,* a word that predates the Koran and means simply "The God."

It's probably worth noting here that believers consider the Koran to be the verification and completion of the revelations granted to the Jews and the Christians in the centuries before the Koran. It's worth noting, too, that Muslims consider the religious texts associated with those two traditions to have been modified and corrupted over time by human beings. The Koran, by contrast, is held to have been preserved in its original divine form.

In this first chapter, you'll get an overview of some of the essentials of the Koran and the Islamic tradition. You'll also get a sense of the purpose of the book you're now holding in your hands—and its limitations.

There Is No Substitute!

Here's what one version of the Bismillah looks like in Arabic:

The Bismillah, the opening lines of the Koran: "In the name of Allah, most gracious, most merciful." (1:1)

(Illustration [from traditional Arabic collections]: Judith Burros)

What's It Mean?

Muslim means "one who submits." **Islam** means "submission." Islam, then, is the way of submission to the will of **Allah** ("The God"), and Muslims are those who follow that way.

This script is part of the Koran. What you're reading now *isn't*. A book like this can serve as an introduction to the Koran. However, *The Complete Idiot's Guide to the Koran* should not be confused with the text of the Koran itself, which Muslims believe should be read or heard on its own terms and in its entirety. That said, this book can certainly explain the Koran—its history, its content, and the faith of its believers.

What Gets Lost in the Translation

The Koran was first translated into English in 1649, and since then dozens of people—Muslims and non-Muslims alike—have translated it into many languages. No matter how good the translation is, however, Muslims believe that every single one of them falls far short of the original.

That's because Muslims regard the Koran, as it was delivered in Arabic (more on this "delivery" later), as the *literal and divine word of God.* Any variation from that text is no longer divine, and no longer the Koran. So although a translation into English (or any other language) may be helpful and necessary for non-Arabic-speaking Muslims and others who are interested in the holy book, it should never be confused with the Koran itself.

Points to Ponder _____

You will find in this volume many English-language passages from Muhammad Sarwar's English translation of the Koran. Unless otherwise noted, that is the version quoted.

Commenting on the Koran

If translations of the Koran aren't actually the Koran, then what are they? Muslims consider translations of the Koran to be *expressions of the meaning* of the original. In this regard, Islam differs from conventional Christianity, in which translations of ancient texts, and not the ancient texts themselves, are usually the focus of belief and study.

Points to Ponder _____

There are a number of famous "obligatory principles," or pillars of Islam, outlined in the Koran. They are as follows:

- The bearing of the two-part testimony of belief: No one deserves to be worshipped except Allah (God) and that Muhammad is the Messenger of Allah (God).
- Prayer.
- Almsgiving.
- Fasting during the holy month of Ramadan.
- Pilgrimage to Mecca and Medina.
- Obedience to certain authorities besides Allah and his messenger, as specified in the Koran. (4:59)

Muslims believe that learning about these obligations by studying the Koran, or even fulfilling these obligations, are not the conclusion of one's submission to God. That is a lifelong business!

Surveying the Suras

The Koran is composed of 114 chapters, or Suras. Each chapter is composed of a number of verses, or ayats. Some of the Suras are remarkably long; some ayats incorporate paragraph-sized chunks of information. Some of the chapters are extremely short; some ayats are only a few words long.

The Koran explores three basic themes:

- God's supreme power and authority

- The accountability of individual human beings for their actions during this life

- The transient nature of our current life, and the inevitability of an afterlife

> **Caution!**
>
> In this book, you will find the spelling *Koran* used consistently in the main text (although quotations from other sources might spell it differently). This spelling is most familiar to non-Muslims. Among English-speaking Muslims, the spelling *Qur'an* is preferred.

These three powerful ideas are explored over and over again, from every conceivable angle, using a dizzying array of pronouns to establish the voice of God. The three themes are looked at independently and in all possible combinations. They are illuminated by means of a startling variety of approaches: stories of the lives of Allah's prophets, warnings to humanity, historical narratives, instructions on etiquette, legal codes, breathtaking poetry, earnest appeals to the reader's logic and reason, and many other literary forms. It all blends together masterfully, though it can be a little confusing in the early going. The Koran has been called the most beautiful book ever written. It is, in the final analysis, a multifaceted appeal to the human heart.

Frequently, the Koran will begin an examination of one of these three major themes with the word "Say." Such passages, Muslims believe, relate Allah's instructions about what the Prophet Muhammad was supposed to *say* to his audience—an audience that was frequently quite skeptical of the Koran's message. You'll be learning more about the Prophet Muhammad very shortly.

As you read this book, you'll come across many passages of the Koran that feature material enclosed in parentheses (like this). In these passages, the translator has supplied additional words in an attempt to make the meaning of the original clearer in English. The extra words are set off with parentheses so you'll know what's Arabic and what's added for context. Something very similar appears in the King James Bible, the landmark English translation of the Old and New Testaments, which was published in the early 1600s. In the King James Bible, extra words added for context were placed in *italics*.

> **Spotlight on Islam**
>
> The Koran is divided into 114 Suras, or chapters. One might expect these to be arranged chronologically, or in some story-driven narrative sequence, or in thematic groups. In fact, the Suras are arranged (roughly) in descending *length*, from longest to shortest—though there are a few exceptions to this, notably the first Sura, *The Opening*, which is extremely brief. Within this sequence, the Suras can be categorized as either *Meccan* (from the early revelations Muhammad received while at Mecca) or *Medinan* (from the later revelations he received while in Medina). Both cities are in present-day Saudi Arabia.

The Individual and the Community

The Koran (in its complete and original Arabic form) is not only a means of spiritual growth and discovery for the individual, but also the foundation of Islamic law. It is, in short, the light that guides the global community of Muslim believers. To understand the role it plays for the individual Muslim and the Islamic community as a whole, it's important to know a little bit about the Koran's history. To that end, here is ...

A (Very) Brief Overview of Islam

Muhammad—also known as the Prophet—is believed by Muslims to have received the Koran over a period of 22 years as a revelation from Allah (more on this in Chapter 2).

At the time of his first revelation, the Prophet was a prosperous merchant in Mecca, a thriving city. In those days people of Arabia were notable primarily for their economic status, their ignorance, and their moral decadence. To give just one example, they followed a cruel tradition that permitted them to bury baby girls alive if the father did not want a daughter.

Mecca's economic prominence in the region was due to the caravan trade and to the fact that it was the home of the *Ka'ba*, an ancient shrine and the site of religious pilgrimages. Many prominent Meccans, including authorities, profited from these pagan pilgrimages.

> **What's It Mean?**
>
> The **Ka'ba** is an ancient shrine Muslims hold to have been established by Abraham. It is a square structure built of black stone. According to the Koran, it marks the spot where Abraham offered to sacrifice his son in obedience to the order of God. The Ka'ba is the most important shrine of Islam; at the time of the Prophet's first revelation, it had been desecrated by pagans.

The message the Prophet shared with the residents of Mecca was (to pagans, at least) an unsettling one, and it quickly earned Muhammad several enemies.

Pagans, Be Damned!

You see, the revelations included an uncompromising demand for a new social order, one that emphatically rejected worship of anyone or anything—including the pagan idols worshipped at Ka'ba—other than the One God. Furthermore, the recitations identified the act of associating anyone or anything to the One God as a deadly sin called *shirk*.

As a consequence, the message the Prophet shared was not a popular one with the authorities of Mecca, who tried to have him killed. In 622 the Prophet emigrated to the city now known as Medina (but then known as Yathrib). This event, called the hijra, marks the beginning of the Muslim calendar. It is an extremely significant date because, in Medina, the Prophet met with some welcome support for his message and initiated the first Muslim community. He quickly gathered strong popular support, and established a truce with the leaders of the local Jewish tribes.

Muhammad's vision for Medina was that of a community guided not by idols and superstitions and misrepresentations of older prophetic traditions, but by the final revelations of God.

> **What's It Mean?**
>
> **Shirk** is the sin of associating someone or something with the One God—making something equal to Allah. It is the gravest of all sins, and is regarded as unforgivable if the person committing it dies while still engaged in it. Pagans in Arabia who worshipped many gods, in the Islamic view, were guilty of shirk.

The Movement Grows

The revelations continued after Muhammad and his followers moved to Medina. The Prophet's movement grew, and he forcefully asserted his leadership role throughout the region.

In a remarkable series of conquests, he overcame the old order in Arabia, wiped out pagan practices, and reclaimed the Ka'ba—the ancient shrine of Abraham, which had been covered over with images and sculptures of the pagan gods. Muslims regard the Ka'ba as the "first sanctuary appointed for mankind" (3:96)—the physical site marking the initiation of God's relationship with humanity.

By 632, the final year of the Prophet's life, he had forged a unified community of Arabs who acknowledged both his authority and his revelation. The text of the Koran was maintained by a number of "rememberers" who had memorized the revelation as the Prophet had taught them to recite it; it was later formalized by a committee headed by his personal secretary.

After the Prophet's death, the Arabs were led by a sequence of four caliphs ("successors"). These caliphs continued to propagate Islam, and in an astonishingly short period of time, the new faith swept from Arabia to the shores of the Mediterranean in the West, and to the mountains of Afghanistan in the East.

During his time on Earth, the Prophet launched a new kind of empire—an empire founded on submission to the will of the One God and on the notion of an Islamic community. The idea of a community of believers is and always has been important within Islam ... and this community is built upon the words of the Koran.

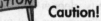

Caution!

It is common for outsiders to refer to Islam as having been "born" in the seventh century of the common era (C.E.). Muslims, however, regard Islam as the religion of submission revealed by God through his messengers—such as Abraham and Moses—at various points throughout human history.

A Message Like No Other

Muslims believe that the Koran serves as a divinely delivered guide to humanity, one that supersedes all other human teachings, including the Christian and Hebrew Bibles.

Muslims also believe that the Koran, as the literal word of God, provides authoritative answers to all questions. Some of these answers are explicit; some are implicit. In interpreting the Koran, the book itself requires that believers "ask those who know (al-Dhikr) about the heavenly Books if you do not know about this." (16:43)

It is sometimes suggested by Westerners that Islam places too much emphasis on conformity, and that there isn't enough consideration given to the rights, feelings, or interpretations of individuals. Actually, there is an abundance of diversity of interpretation within the faith, and a traditional emphasis on personal spiritual discovery and autonomy that often eludes conventional Christianity.

Points to Ponder

Muslims classify the teachings of the Koran in two ways: *Muhkamat*, which applies to statements or words that do not require any explanation, and *Mutashabihat*, which applies to statements or words that are not clear. Passages that fall into the second category require interpretation, and (fallible human) scholars are to avoid appealing to them in order to prove a legal or ethical point.

Spotlight on Islam

One important hadith relates that the Koran has, besides its (translatable) surface meanings, deeper intrinsic meanings … meanings that are not apparent to every reader, but only to a select few. Thus, the ultimate meaning of the Koran is not to be found in any translation, but in the Arabic text itself, a text that defies simple word-for-word rendering.

What's It Mean?

The **Sunna,** consists of the holy Prophet's words, deeds, and approvals. Statements issued by the Prophet himself are known as *ahadith* (*hadith* in the singular). These statements and teachings are not to be confused with the Koran itself, and any contradiction between the Sunna and the Koran is always resolved in favor of the Koran. The **Shari'a** is the codification of law emerging from Koranic principles.

There is, for instance, no figure remotely resembling the Catholic pope in Islam; nor is there an intermediary figure such as a priest to serve as a representative to God for the community of believers; nor is there any notion of a sacrificial Christ who wins salvation for the faithful. Each Muslim, individually, is accountable to God, and each Muslim, individually, is responsible for carrying out the obligations laid out in the Koran and living up to the principles it outlines.

There are scholars and cleric, who command extraordinary attention and respect from believers; the Ayatollah Khomeini would be a recent example of one of these. None of these individuals, however, claims to serve as an intermediary between God and the individual believer. Muslims regard certain individuals (notably the Prophets) as infallible individuals supported by the Holy Spirit. Ayatollahs, on the other hand, are doctors in Shari'a and strict followers of its rules.

Each Muslim is not, however, expected to become a scholar of the Koran. (This is fortunate, as the book is a work of seemingly endless complexity; one could easily devote one's entire life without reaching a full understanding of it!) In the years since the death of the Prophet, the traditions of the *Sunna,* the *hadith,* and the *Shari'a* have emerged to guide the community.

Diversity of Belief and Interpretation

To get some insight on the remarkable diversity of belief and interpretation that has characterized Islam over the past fourteen centuries, let's look briefly at an issue that is often a polarizing subject between Muslims and non-Muslims: that of the proper dress for women.

We're going to look at this issue early on—not because the issue of how women should dress is central to an understanding of the Koran, but because this issue shows how many different approaches can be taken by devout Muslims to the same verse.

To Veil or Not to Veil?

Today, many non-Muslims believe that all Islamic women are forced to wear a veil or other facial covering in order to fulfill the requirements of the Koran.

They see, on television or in newspapers, images of Muslim women wearing veils, burkahs, chadhors, or other head coverings, and assume that (a) there is a universally observed instruction within Islam that women dress this way, and (b) that all Muslims regard this instruction as coming from God.

The truth is a good deal more complicated—and a good deal more interesting. Let's start at the beginning ... with the Koran itself. The Koran has the following to say about attire for women:

> (Muhammad), tell the believing woman to cast down their eyes, guard their chastity, and not to show off their beauty except what is permitted by the law. Let them cover their breasts with their veils. They must not show off their beauty to anyone other than their husbands, father, father-in-laws, sons, step-sons, brothers, sons of brothers and sisters, women of their kind, their slaves, immature male servants, or immature boys. They must not stamp their feet to show off their hidden ornaments. All of you believers, turn to God in repentance so that perhaps you will have everlasting happiness. (24:31)

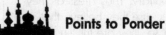

Points to Ponder

A similar, but much less commented-upon, set of instructions on modest dress for *men* immediately precedes the Koranic verse on appropriate dress for women. This is worth remembering, because non-Muslims sometimes make the mistake of assuming that the Koran does not set out obligations in this area for both genders.

Interpreting the Word

Notice that there is an instruction in the passage you just read that is open to a certain amount of interpretation: not to display one's "beauty" (or in some translations "ornaments") to strangers. What, precisely, are a woman's "ornaments"? Does the meaning of that word include the human face?

This is a question that one must resolve in order to carry out the instructions appearing in this portion of the Koran. And if we do just a little bit of exploring, we learn that it is a question that has been resolved in a variety of different ways over the centuries by various communities of devout Muslims. The question of whether or not the passage above requires a woman to wear a veil is, in fact, one that Muslim men and women have discussed earnestly, and in various countries, for about fourteen straight centuries.

In resolving the question of what "beauty" means, we find that a host of related questions wait to be considered. For instance: What did the Prophet or the members of his family have to say about the custom of wearing veils? How reliable are the surviving traditions we have about the Prophet or the members of his family that address this issue? What legal principles deriving from the Koran have evolved over the centuries with regard to female dress? What school of thought do these legal principles emerge from? And so on.

There are some Islamic countries (say, Saudi Arabia) where one will see broad cultural conformity to a single interpretation of the passage regarding whether or not a woman should wear a veil in public to conceal the "beauty" of her face. There are other countries (say, Egypt) where one will see believing women interpret the passage in a great variety of ways, and many of these women do not consider the covering of the face to be necessary.

> **Caution!**
>
> It is worth noting that the vast majority of Muslim women resent the implication that they dress as they do because they are forced by men to do so. To the contrary: They dress as they do because they believe that, in doing so, they are fulfilling the instructions of God. (Note, too, that different Muslim countries have different laws regarding dress. See Chapter 14 for a fuller discussion of women in Islam.)

So Remember ...

Three critical points are worth bearing in mind as you consider the Koran:

- Although there are five established schools of thought regarding how to follow Islam (Hanafi, Shafi, Maliki, Hanbali, Ja'fari), there is today no central authority that can determine what a given passage in the Koran "means" for all believers.

- The requirements of the Koran are open to interpretation within Islamic society, and these interpretations are shaped by the Sunna and the Shari'a.

- Although there are certainly cultural forces that influence the practice of Muslims, there is also a powerful and enduring tradition within Islam that regards each believer—regardless of gender or race or social position—as individually accountable to God's word.

What the Prophet Said About the Koran

There are a number of inspiring—and reliable—traditions concerning Muhammad's personal views on the Koran. The following is one of the most memorable:

> The Messenger of Allah said, "It is the time to complete (the task) and cut off (from this world). When mischief confuses you like a dark night you must hold to the Holy Qur'an; it is an intercessor (an associate whose association is beneficial) whose intercession will be accepted and a solicitor whose words are believed. Whoever gives it the lead, it will take him to paradise. Whoever leaves it behind, it will then drive him to the fire. It is a guide that shows the best path. It is the book that contains details and explanations, and accomplishments. It is a criteria and not a useless thing. It has face and hidden meanings. Its face meaning is law and its hidden meaning is knowledge. Its face meaning is unique and its hidden meaning is deep. It has stars and upon its stars there are stars. Its wonders do not end and its unique rare facts do not become old. In it there are the torch of guidance, and the lighthouses of wisdom. It serves as proof of veracity of knowledge (for one who wants to verify the truth of his knowledge) and who has come to know the attribute, let him brighten his eyes to reach the attribute. It saves from destruction, and protects against dangers ... (Hadith No 3431, chapter 1, hadith 2, al-kafi vol 2 of 8, part 2, the book on the excellence of the Holy Koran)

This is one example of a hadith—or "account" of the words and actions of the Prophet Muhammad. It is only one of many, of course. This particular hadith, however, is significant for our purposes, because it has guided countless believers back to the Koran, in search of its wonders that do not end and its enduring facts—about God, about human accountability, about the transience of this life—that do not become old. Such wonders and such facts are, believers maintain, in abundant supply in this extraordinary book.

The Least You Need to Know

- Muslims believe that the Koran is the literal recital of God's word; it is the basis of personal spiritual faith and harmonious community life.

- The Koran is written in classical Arabic, and only that original version is considered to be the literal word of God.

- No one can explain the Koran definitively except people mentioned in chapter 16, verse 43 of the Koran.

- The requirements of the Koran are open to interpretation within Islamic methodology, and these interpretations are shaped by the Sunna (the traditions of the Prophet).

2

The Prophet

In This Chapter

- ◆ The life of the Prophet
- ◆ The impact of his mission
- ◆ His place in history

Muhammad is regarded by Muslims as God's final Prophet—ending a line of Prophets that began with Adam and included Noah, Moses, Jesus, Solomon, and many other biblical figures. He unified Arabia, turned a previously polytheistic people into worshipers of a single God—Allah— and left a cultural, military, and religious legacy that is rivaled by few, if any, figures in history. The last Prophet's importance to Islam is summed up in the first of Islam's so-called Five Pillars: "There is no God but God, and Muhammad is his Messenger." Let's take a closer look at the life of God's messenger.

A Prophet Is Born

Muhammad was born in about 570 C.E. in Mecca, a city on the Arabian Peninsula in present-day Saudi Arabia. At the time, Arabia was less developed than other regions in that part of the world, with a political structure consisting mainly of tribes of nomadic people of shared ancestry who worked the land or engaged in trade. Each tribe was made up of clans, or extended family groups, and the blood ties of these clans constituted the primary way that people identified themselves. The man Muslims believe to be the final Prophet of Allah, Muhammad ibn Abdallah, was born into the Hashim clan of the powerful Kuraish tribe. His people were primarily traders.

He was orphaned at a young age, and was taken in first by his grandfather and then his uncle, who raised him until manhood. He grew up illiterate, but that wasn't unusual—most people at the time had no reading or writing skills. The wealthiest lady of Mecca, Khadija, entrusted him with the task of leading her caravan into Syria; she found him to be both a trustworthy employee and an excellent businessman—the caravan yielded profits beyond her expectations. Before long, she decided to find a way of making him agree to marry her; the two were joined as man and wife despite his poverty and his being disadvantaged in social circles.

Khadija was 40 when they were married, and he was 25. While she lived, she was the only woman in his life.

Receiving Divine Instructions

Muhammad was known for uprightness and fair dealing and wasn't involved in military exploits. Very little else is known about his adult life before the age of 40. We do know that he often would go to a secluded place outside of Mecca, where he would pray. During one of these visits, when he was around age 40, the archangel Gabriel (called Jibril in Arabic). Gabriel asked that Muhammad "Recite as I recite …

> Recite! Your Lord is the most Honorable One, who, by the pen, taught the human being. He taught the human being what he did not know. Despite this, the human being still tends to rebel because he thinks that he is independent. However, (all things) will return to your Lord. (96:3–8)

The Prophet recited, as he had been asked to do. In this way the apparently miraculous reading of the Koran to humanity began; it continued for a period of more than two decades.

An illiterate man, a visit from an angel, and the spontaneous recitation of what has certainly become one of the most influential books in human history—these were the beginnings of the faith.

Muhammad Shares His Revelations

With the help of his wife's wealth, and using his own insights and experience, the Prophet began his divine mission of preaching the way of life he had been instructed to call "Islam" (submission). A Sura of the Meccan period tells the early followers:

> By the declining star, your companion is not in error, nor has he gone astray. He does not speak out of his own desires. It is a revelation which has been revealed to him and taught to him by the great mighty one (Gabriel), the strong one who appeared on the uppermost horizon. (53:1–7)

He shared the message first with his close relatives. (As it happened, the Prophet's wife, Khadija, was the first convert to Islam.) He then broadened the mission gradually, expanding his preaching to other groups in Mecca and eventually to people in outlying areas. His manners of preaching were authoritative and decisive; at no time did he show uncertainty or confusion. He believed himself to be acting upon instructions from the Lord of the worlds, with the Koran and the angel Jibril on his side.

Muhammad asked his followers to commit his messages to memory and to write them down for safety and proper preservation. Thus, during the lifetime of Muhammad, the Koran was written down, and many Muslims had committed the whole thing to memory.

The Holy Teachings

The Prophet's preachings were powerful and direct. Included among them were the following tenets:

- There is no God but God.

- Human beings must submit to God in all matters.

- The nations of the world have been chastised for tormenting and ignoring the Prophets of God.

- The world will end and there will be a Day of Judgment.

In addition, the religion that the new Prophet espoused emphasized prayer, almsgiving, and pilgrimage as religious obligations. It also directed followers to fast during the holy month of Ramadan.

The Islamic movement was founded on a harmonious balance between body and soul, embracing the idea of the pious believer enjoying all good things created by God. Furthermore, Islam's call was universal. It invited all of humanity, regardless of race or origin, to join the community of believers, with the only recognized superiority being based on a person's level of devotion to the will of Allah.

Spotlight on Islam

Although the Koran limits the number of wives a man can have to four, Muhammad married nine times, and was given special dispensation to do so in the Koran.

In this early period, the Prophet attracted many opponents and only a few trusted followers. However, he relentlessly emphasized the divine message—belief in a single God, in resurrection, and in a final judgement—with a single-mindedness and a sense of purpose that has few, if any, parallels in any other "grass roots" movement in history. This one extraordinary man stayed—to use a popular current term—"on message," denouncing pagan practices and urging all who would hear him to acts of obedience, charity, and mercy.

He was mocked and abused for his efforts. His following grew slowly, and eventually his persistent attacks on polytheistic religious practices earned him powerful enemies. Such enemies fell into two groups: those whose ancestors had been worshipping multiple gods for centuries, and those who stood to profit financially—directly or indirectly—by the journeys of pagan worshippers into Mecca.

In fact, the economic foundation of the city was revenues from pagan visitors to its shrine, the Ka'ba. The greater the number of gods featured in the Ka'ba, the greater the revenues from the various pilgrims. The opposition to Islam was intense, and it resulted, eventually, in persecution and torture for the Prophet and his followers.

Flight and Oppression

In 622, having become aware of an assassination attempt, the Prophet left Mecca for the more hospitable city of Yathrib, a city that would from that point forward be known as Medina, the "City of the Prophet." (The departure from Mecca, known as the hijrah, is the beginning point of the Muslim calendar.)

The pagan leaders of Mecca issued a demand to Muhammad's beloved uncle and guardian, Abu Talib: Turn over Muhammad so that he may be put to death in Mecca. The Prophet's uncle refused, and so the leaders instituted an economic boycott against Muhammad's tribe. Great sufferings resulted, but Abu Talib refused to relent. He and the people of his tribe suffered tremendous shortages of food and resources for three long years.

It was during this period that Muhammad's uncle, protector, and virtual stepfather, Abu Talib, as well as his beloved wife, Khadija, died of malnutrition. He is said to have described this time as the most difficult of his life.

An Alliance That Never Materialized

The Prophet appears to have expected Jews and Christians to accept the revelations and to follow his teachings. They did not. What the course of later world history would have looked like had they accepted his invitation to unite in a single monotheistic faith is interesting to ponder!

After the escape of the Prophet from their assassination plot, the pagans declared looting of the properties of the Muslims in Mecca to be lawful. Muslims hard-hit by the loss of their property asked the Prophet to allow them to take compensation from the trading caravan of Meccans returning from Syria. After receiving divine permission for this, he turned his (tiny and very poorly armed) forces on the Meccans, and won an apparently miraculous victory at Badr in the face of superior numbers.

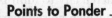

Points to Ponder

There were three major religions in West Asia during the Prophet's lifetime: Christianity, Judaism, and Zoroastrianism. The latter was a polytheistic faith that had a powerful influence on Christianity.

A series of military conflicts between Medina and Mecca marked the next phase of the Prophet's career. Having agreed to a truce arranged in the interests of religious pilgrimages, the Prophet eventually found that the treaty had been abused. In 630 he took control of the city of his birth, having encountered no military resistance in Mecca, and announced that idolatry would no longer be permitted.

The Prophet's ban on idolatry forms one of the cornerstones of Islamic belief. In Islam, artistic representation of images meant to represent Allah is forbidden; this is because nothing is like him. There is also a tradition of avoiding the depiction of living beings, because no one can actually create such beings besides Allah. (This tradition is both ancient and controversial.)

Islam's Triumph

By this point, the tribes of the Arabian Peninsula, as well as large numbers in Iraq and Palestine, had voluntarily accepted Islam. Scattered groups of Jews and Christians in the region had, as mentioned earlier, declined the Prophet's invitation to accept Islam. They were permitted to continue worshipping as they chose as taxpayers to the state that protected their lives and property. While the establishment of a tax directed at unbelievers may sound harsh to contemporary ears, the fact is that other conquerors of the day would have killed or enforced the conversion of people who held to different faiths. Jews and Christians were also allowed to exercise judicial authority over their own people.

The Prophet extended a blanket amnesty to his former enemies that was extraordinarily lenient, given the sufferings he and his people had been forced to undergo at their hands. He then saw to the consolidation of his empire and the end of pagan ways in Arabia.

In the year 632 (or 10, by the Muslim calendar), the Prophet went to Mecca on pilgrimage. There he encountered 140,000 Muslims who had, like him, journeyed to the sacred city to fulfil Islamic obligations. He gave a famous sermon to the huge crowd in which he summarized the fundamental principles of the teachings of Islam. Here's how he defined his faith:

- Belief in One God, similar to whom there is nothing

- Piety as a standard of excellence for all believers without distinction of race or class

- Sanctity of life, property, and honor

- Abolition of interest (on money lent as well as in the exchange of certain commodities), and establishment of a complete system of justice and criminal laws

- Better treatment of women

- Obligatory inheritance and distribution of the property of deceased persons among near relatives of both sexes

- Establishment of laws and guidelines for earning and spending one's wealth, to remove the possibility of unlawful accumulation of wealth in the hands of the few

Points to Ponder

Muslims don't regard Muhammad as divine, seeing him instead as a human being guided by Allah. Thus, the Koran reads: "We have revealed a Spirit to you, (Muhammad), by Our command .... You certainly guide (people) to the right path." (42:52)

Believers regard Muhammad as the most perfect model for correct conduct.

The Prophet's personal example supported all of these teachings, including that of the fair distribution of wealth. (At the time of his death, he is said to have possessed only a few items: his sword, a horse, a camel, a donkey, a staff, a jar, some cups, and a few pieces of clothing.)

Clearly, a revolution had occurred, probably the most far-reaching and influential revolution of human history. Anarchy, the worship of multiple gods, and rampant immorality had given way to a clearly ordered way of life built on principles derived from two things and two things only: the Koran and the behavior and sayings of the Prophet.

The Death of the Prophet

After making what turned out to be his final pilgrimage to Mecca, the Prophet returned to Medina, where he became ill and died on June 8, 632. After he died, his followers attempted to deify him, but his aide and close friend, abu Bakr, who was to emerge as his administrative successor, quieted the crowd with these words: "If any of you here worshipped Muhammad—he is dead. But if you worshipped God, He lives eternally."

> **Points to Ponder**
>
> Muhammad is strangely overlooked in many contemporary educational and intellectual circles, and among many historians. This may be because he is associated so strongly with Islam, a faith with which the West has yet to come to terms, or it may be because Western institutions have yet to accept his role in the development of world civilization. Here, however, is a sampling of what some of the most highly regarded non-Muslim scholars of the last century have had to say about the Prophet whom Muslims believe served as the instrument through whom God delivered Islam and the Koran:
>
> - "If greatness of purpose, smallness of means, and astounding results are the three criteria of human genius, who could dare to compare any great man in modern history with Muhammad?" (Lamartine, in *Histoire de la Turquie* [vol. II], published in 1854.)
> - "It is impossible for anyone who studies the life and character of the great Prophet of Arabia, who knows how he taught and how he lived, to feel anything but reverence for that mighty Prophet, one of the great messengers of the Supreme." (Annie Besant, in *The Life and Teachings of Muhammad*, published in 1932.)
> - "... none of the great figures of history is so poorly understood in the West as Muhammad." (W. Montgomery Watt, in *Muhammad at Mecca*, published in 1953.)
> - "My choice of Muhammad to lead the list of the world's most influential persons may surprise some readers and may be questioned by others, but he was the only man in history who was supremely successful on both the religious and secular level." (Michael H. Hart, in *The 100: A Ranking of the Most Influential Persons in History*, published in 1978.)

The Prophet's legacies were many, including the following:

- A religion focused powerfully on monotheism and on the notion of submission to God
- Civil order where there had before been chaos
- A system of humane warfare

◆ An indisputable personal example of religious tolerance

◆ Tireless concern for the welfare of the poor and the disadvantaged

◆ An ordered, reliable, and impartial system of law, where theft and corruption had previously thrived

◆ The clear enunciation of the principle that all humanity is subject to the authority and will of God

His own life and personal example was to emerge as a potent force in the development of Islam—a force second only to the Koran itself.

Timeline of the Life of Muhammad

Date	Event
circa 570 C.E.	Born in Mecca; parents die shortly after his birth; the boy is brought up by his uncle, Abu Talib.
circa 594	Marries Khadija, the wealthiest lady of Makkah (Mecca).
610	Receives first revelation at Mount Hira.
615	Followers persecuted; a group of Muslims leaves for Abysinnia.
616	Another movement of Muslims to Abysinnia.
circa 620	Active opposition from Meccan authorities intensifies.
622	Migrates to Medina, where he will establish the world's first written constitution, called the Constitution of Medina. According to scholars, it radically changed the way groups of people defined themselves. Faith, more than blood relationships, determined group identity.
624	Victorious at Battle of Badr.
625	Near-victory at Battle of Uhud is suddenly transformed into defeat when Muslim archers, anticipating victory, disobey the Prophet's orders and leave their defensive posts.
627	A huge force is arrayed against the Muslims at Medina; superior planning, effective disinformation sown in the ranks of the enemy, and an unexpected sandstorm combine to bring victory to the outnumbered forces of the Prophet. The battle is known as the Battle of the Ditch, for the (cavalry-neutralizing) trench that the Muslims dug around their city.
630	Conquest of Mecca.
632	Dies in Medina.

The Illiterate Master

The fact that the Prophet, through whom the Koran was delivered to humanity, was illiterate is well established in the historical record. He received no schooling or instruction of any kind. There was and is no evidence that he had any experience in composing even the simplest oral poetry or prose before he was called upon to recite the Koran, a work of great beauty, depth, and complexity.

Somehow, from this unlettered man, came a timeless work addressing fluently (and with timeless eloquence) such subjects as harmonious social ordering, modes of worship, etiquette, diet, angels, animals, history, astronomy, embryology, warfare, peacetime, marriage, divorce, business dealings, economic principles, astronomy, the Old and New Testaments, liturgy, prayer, and the creation of the universe—among hundreds of other topics. This illiterate man, in other words, delivered a work whose power, breadth, and mastery have been acknowledged even by non-Islamic scholars.

> **Caution!**
> Don't confuse the Prophet's illiteracy with simple-mindedness; reading wasn't a widely practiced skill during his lifetime.

Countless people who have reviewed the particulars of the Prophet's life have found themselves forced to confront some difficult questions. How did an untaught seventh-century merchant who didn't even possess the ability to read manage to hold forth with such eloquence on such an astonishing array of subjects? How is one to reconcile the sharply differing styles of the Koran and the known discourses of the Prophet? What explanation is there for an illiterate "author" from this period composing the incomparable masterwork of Arabic literature?

An answer is supplied in the following verse of the Koran:

> We did not teach him (Muhammad) poetry, nor was he supposed to be a poet. It is only the word (of God) and the illustrious Koran. (36:69)

Or to put it another way: There is no God but God, and Muhammad is his messenger.

The Least You Need to Know

♦ Muhammad was born around the year 570 C.E. in Mecca.

♦ At the age of 40, Muhammad received the first of an extraordinary series of visions, during which he is believed to have received the text of the Koran from God via the angel Gabriel.

♦ The Prophet's teachings were powerful and direct: There is no God but God; human beings must submit to God in all matters; the nations of the world have been chastised for tormenting and ignoring the Prophets of God; the world will end and there will be a Day of Judgment.

♦ Muhammad died in Medina in 632 C.E., having made a profound impact on human history.

3

Common Misconceptions About Islam

In This Chapter

◆ Roots of misunderstanding and prejudice

◆ The rise and spread of Islam

◆ Marriage and the status of women in Islam

◆ Islam's teachings concerning innocent people

Let's face it: Islam has gotten a bad rap.

In an era when it is unacceptable to discriminate against people because of their religious beliefs and it is considered a grave social misstep to ridicule the faith of fellow-citizens ... it is still "open season" on Islam and Muslims. Today religious discrimination against Muslims is rampant, and coarse attacks upon the faith of millions of Americans (not to mention more than a billion other people around the globe) is all too common.

Why?

One answer is rooted in the tragedy of September 11, 2001. Another (and perhaps more complete) answer has to do with some unfortunate and persistent misconceptions about Islam that have been pervasive in the West, and particularly in the United States, for some decades.

Anyone interested in correcting these misconceptions will want to begin with an understanding of the role of Islam in the lives of its practitioners.

Understanding a Way of Life

Muslims view their tradition not simply as a "religion," in the Western sense of the word, but as a way of life that encompasses all actions in social, political, family, and economic realms—or, for that matter, any other realms of activity.

As noted in Chapter 1, Muslims rely on two sources for guidance in the lives of those who choose to follow this way of life: the Koran and the Sunna.

- **The Koran**—the unparalleled book covering all aspects of the Islamic faith. Muslims—those who submit to the will of God and follow Islam—regard the Koran as the God's revelation to humankind. It is the most-read book in its original form in human history.

- **The Sunna**—a collection of statements, descriptions of the deeds, and approvals of the Prophet recorded in written form to refer to as the source of law for proper living. This portion of the law is preserved in larger volumes that are much-analyzed for the sake of veracity.

These two sources of inspiration are meant to be the motivating forces of human activity. Not all human beings, however, live up to the standards outlined in the Koran and the Sunna.

The point to bear in mind is simple: *If any person takes part in activities, or expresses beliefs, that clearly go against the teachings of the Koran or the authentic Sunna, then that person's activities or doctrines are not Islamic.*

Islam vs. Muslim

Islam, in other words, is not the same as Muslim. Islam is a way of living one's life; Muslim is a descriptive term for the huge group of people who aspire to follow the tenets of Islam.

Some misconceptions about the faith have arisen because of the actions of Muslims; others have arisen because of the current state of knowledge concerning Islamic principles in certain parts of the world, including the United States. And some misconceptions, including many relating to Islamic militarism, have arisen because of a combination of these two factors.

An Example from History

Consider, as an example of how misconceptions about religious traditions might arise, the many abuses perpetrated by the European (Christian) Crusaders of the eleventh through fourteenth centuries against civilian populations. These abuses included the slaughter of entire towns.

These bloody actions might, to someone unfamiliar with the ministry of Christ, seem to suggest that Christianity promoted violence against the innocent. Yet anyone familiar with Christ's teachings will understand that these historical events are, if anything, perversions of Christianity, rather than expressions of it.

Just as those Christians harmed innocent people in the name of God when the teachings of their faith made it clear that such actions were prohibited, a tiny minority of Muslims, in the name of Islam and Allah, have perpetrated similar acts of hatred against innocent people. The attacks of September 11 are one example of such perversions of Islam.

Spotlight on Islam

Unfortunately negative and wholly inaccurate stereotypes about Islam are common in the United States. Some analysts imply or say openly, for instance, that Islam is an inherently violent and intolerant system of thought—conveniently ignoring the fact that Muslim nations are remarkably free of racial strife and violent crime and that the Islamic faith's history of religious tolerance over the centuries is well documented. It is a strange brand of intolerance that yields racial harmony!

In response to incessant media reports linking Islam with violence or intolerance, many Muslims have asked—at times with some annoyance—why the most violent or intolerant actions of Jewish or Christian extremists don't result in media reports that those religions are, therefore, inherently violent or intolerant.

Here, then, are five of the most common—and potentially divisive—misconceptions about the Islamic faith, along with a consideration of the realities underlying each. In today's world, which has featured so much irresponsible perpetuation of unfortunate myths about Islam, it may be more important than ever for Westerners to take the time to address the realities behind these misconceptions before embarking on any serious study of the Koran.

A Religion of the Sword?

Misconception #1: Islam was spread by the sword, and its popularity today is because of its forcible imposition on millions of people.

Islam, like both Judaism and Christianity, has a history that includes bloodshed and religious conflict.

Like both Judaism and Christianity, Islam has, and has always had, adherents willing to die for their beliefs. The common Western notion, however, that the worldwide popularity of Islam is the result of its having been forcibly imposed upon millions of people who would otherwise have had nothing to do with it, is absurd. This idea is also more than a little insulting to the 1.7 billion Muslims of the world.

No Muslim armies battled in Indonesia (the country with the largest number of Muslims in the world today) or on the east coast of Africa (a region where the faith experienced dramatic growth in the twentieth century). And despite some of the least flattering media coverage imaginable, Islam has emerged as the fastest-growing religion in the United States over the last 50 years. There was, of course, no military campaign to impose Islam in the United States—or, for that matter, in Europe, where it has spread with similar vigor.

> **CAUTION**
>
> **Caution!**
>
> Contrary to popular belief, remarkably few people died during the 10-year period of Arabian "wars" led by the Prophet. In his *Introduction to Islam* (Centre Culturel Islamique, 1969), Dr. Muhammad Hamidullah estimates that the total loss of life for Muslims and non-Muslims alike was less than 500.

A Stark Historical Contrast

The often-overlooked truth is that, while Christian armies slaughtered Muslim men, women, and children during the Crusades, Muslim armies practiced a system of humane warfare that limited the application of violence to combatants and required respect for the religious practices of civilians. Consider, too, that Muslim leaders ruled in Spain for roughly 800 years and in India for roughly 1,000 years. In neither case were non-Muslims forced to convert under the threat of violence. (European armies, however, systematically repressed and murdered Muslims in Spain following military victory there!)

The question of whether any movement can assume global dimensions, and thrive for more than fourteen centuries by means of force, rather than by means of powerful—yet peaceful—guiding principles, is an interesting one. While we ponder it, we can consider the existence of the 14 million Arabs who today practice the Coptic Christianity of their ancestors. Islam simply cannot have been founded upon the idea of forced conversion—otherwise, Arab Christians would never have escaped annihilation centuries ago when they refused to convert to Islam.

Although Islam's initial triumphs certainly had a military dimension, just as the spread of Christianity in Europe did, the faith endured and spread because of its message, not because of compulsion and the sword. Indeed, the Koran forbids forced conversion.

In his book *Islam at the Crossroad*, historian DeLacy O'Leary writes that "History makes it clear ... that the legend of fanatical Muslims sweeping through the world and forcing Islam at the point of the sword upon conquered races is one of the most fantastically absurd myths that historians have ever repeated."

> **The Word**
>
> There is no compulsion in religion. Certainly, right has become clearly distinct from wrong. Whoever rejects the devil and believes in God has firmly taken hold of a strong handle that never breaks. God is All-hearing and knowing. (2:256)

An Arab Religion?

Misconception #2: The majority of Muslims are Arab, and Islam is an essentially Arab religion.

Among many Westerners, the terms "Muslim" and "Arab" are used interchangeably. This is a major error.

Arab typically refers to the *Semitic* people who inhabit present-day Saudi Arabia and other countries of the Middle East. It is estimated that only 18 percent—less than one fifth—of the nearly 2 billion Muslims worldwide fit this description.

The Koran is written in Arabic, but its appeal transcends any conceivable geographic, racial, political, and gender boundaries. The Koran states unambiguously that its message is universal, and that the Messenger was sent to transfer Allah's word to mankind "as a mercy to the worlds." (21:107)

> **What's It Mean?**
>
> **Semitic** means of or pertaining to the Afro-Asiatic language group comprising Arabic, Hebrew, Amharic, and Aramaic.

> **Caution!**
>
> Don't make the mistake of confusing the terms "Muslim" and "Arab." Most of the 1.7 billion Muslims are non-Arabs. Muslims are Indonesian, Iranian, American, Canadian, English ... in fact, they can be found in just about every nation.

It is worth mentioning here that the Koran's status as a document composed in ancient Arabic hasn't prevented believers of all nations from memorizing it and reciting it. Indeed, the Koran reminds us that it was created in a form that made this kind of familiarity with the text a miraculously common occurrence:

> We made the Koran easy to understand, but is there anyone who would take heed? (32)

An Uncivilized Approach to Marriage?

Misconception #3: Unlike "more civilized" faiths, Islam allows men to marry more than one wife.

Yes, the Koran does allow men to marry up to four wives, but it's also the only sacred text within any major religious system containing a passage in which a man is *advised* to marry only one wife. One may search as long as one wishes through the Bible, the Tao Te Ching, the Vedas, the Bhagavad-Gita, and the Book of Mormon without encountering such advice.

What one finds in the Koran is a carefully limited endorsement of the notion of *polygamy* (marriage between one man and more than one woman), one rooted firmly in principles of fairness and justice. The relevant passage is as follows:

> With respect to marrying widows, if you are afraid of not being able to maintain justice with her children, marry another woman of your choice or two or three or four (who have no children).

> If you cannot maintain equality with more than one wife, marry only one or your slave-girl. This keeps you from acting against justice. (4:3)

Interestingly, the Koran later advises that dealing justly and fairly with more than one wife is "very difficult." (Indeed, this is the conclusion reached by the vast majority of Muslim men today.)

If the Koran's teachings on marriage seem unfamiliar or strange to Western observers, it's fair to observe in turn that Western tolerance of adultery and promiscuity, and the saturation of the Western media with sexual imagery, is just as disorienting to many Muslims. Is it possible that these practices—evident enough even to non-Muslims—have contributed to high divorce rates, or damage to the children of the West? Many Muslims would answer "yes," and would be concerned about the long-term implications to any society of the prevailing attitudes toward marriage and sexuality in the

United States. By comparison, in the Islamic view, the Koran's teachings on these matters, which include a limited sanction of *polygamy*, have resulted in enduring social stability and a tradition of respect for the varying roles of men and women in society.

At the time the Koran was first transcribed, it was common for men to have dozens or even hundreds of wives, so the Koran can be seen as having created a more fair marriage environment for women. There is certainly no commandment within Islam *requiring* men to have more than one wife, as some seem to believe. (Consider, too, that during and after wartime, there are often more women around than men—if a certain number of men have been killed in battle—and that women in these situations sometimes face severe social and economic hardships.)

What's It Mean?

Polygamy is a marriage between one man and more than one woman—is seen as an exception, not as a rule, within Islam. The Koran sets an upper limit for men of four wives, and focuses closely on fairness and just dealing between spouses.

Points to Ponder

It's also worth noting that the Christian and Jewish biblical accounts include many stories in which a man is married to more than one woman. Solomon, for instance, had many wives.

Inherently Hostile to Women?

Misconception #4: Muslim women are regarded as inferior to Muslim men.

The complex subject of the respective roles of men and women in society deserves a fuller examination than it can receive here, and is covered at length in Chapter 14. A famous passage from the Koran, however, will make it clear how alien the idea of "inferiority" of women is from the Islamic spiritual tradition.

> God has promised forgiveness and great rewards to the Muslim men and the Muslim women, the believing men and the believing women, the obedient men and the obedient women, the truthful men and the truthful women, the forbearing men and the forbearing women, the humble men and the humble women, the alms-giving men and the alms-giving women, the fasting men and the fasting women, the chaste men and the chaste women, and the men and women who remember God very often. (33:35)

This is only one of a number of passages making clear the Koran's insistence on a gender-inclusive approach.

The following statement may touch on a subject deserving of much further discussion, but it is nevertheless beyond dispute: Muslim women have different social and legal roles than Muslim men, but men and women are—as the Koran states repeatedly and emphatically—equal before Allah.

At the same time, in the social realm, men are envisioned as protectors and maintainers of women:

> Men are the protectors of women because of the greater preference that God has given to some of them and because they financially support them. (4:34)

Consider, as well, the following passage:

> People, We have created you all male and female and have made you nations and tribes so that you would recognize each other. The most honorable among you in the sight of God is the most pious of you. God is All-knowing and All-aware. (49:13)

The Word

Any believer, male or female, who acts righteously, will enter Paradise and will not suffer the least bit of injustice (4:124).

Allah, we are instructed time and time again, grants favor based on the person's knowledge, awareness, faith in, and hope of Allah. No other consideration—race, ancestry, gender, or anything else—enters the equation (for more on women in Islam, see Chapter 14).

Indifferent to the Shedding of Innocent Blood?

Misconception #5: Islam tolerates the murder of innocent persons and, in its modern expression, encourages terrorism.

This is one of the most serious and widespread misconceptions regarding Islam. It is, tragically, a theme, both spoken and unspoken, of most Western news coverage of the Islamic faith.

Yet the Koran, without the slightest ambiguity, declares that any Muslim who takes the life of an innocent person has perpetrated a grave offense against Allah:

> The only proper recompense for those who fight against God and His Messenger and try to spread evil in the land is to be killed, crucified, or either to have one of their hands and feet cut from the opposite side or to be sent into exile. These are to disgrace them in this life and they will suffer a great torment in the life hereafter. (5:33)

A Contradiction in Terms

Any reference to "Muslim terrorists" or "Islamic terrorists" is therefore both illogical (along the lines of "Christian [or Buddhist] serial killer") and deeply offensive to believers. Yes, some Muslims do commit acts of terror (as do Christians, Jews, agnostics, atheists, and people of every other faith). But these acts are not sanctioned by Islam.

As a broader and more profound understanding of Islam and its principles becomes prevalent in the West, it may become clearer that individual Muslims who commit sins involving the shedding of innocent blood do so at peril of their souls—for Allah *will* judge them—and certainly not under the instruction of the Almighty. (The Islamic view on *jihad* is explored in Chapter 16.)

Points to Ponder

The sword of Islam is not the sword of steel. I know this by experience because the sword of Islam struck deep into my own heart. It didn't bring death, but it brought a new life; it brought an awareness and it brought an awakening as to who am I and what am I and for what am I here?

—Ahmed Holt, British civil contractor, after his conversion to Islam in 1975.

On Relations with Jews and Christians

The question of whether followers of Islam are to promote conflict or discord with Judaism and Christianity is also answered without ambiguity by the Koran, which counsels forbearance and forgiveness to those nonbelievers whose revelations derive from "the Book" (in other words, Jews and Christians):

> … many of the People of the Book would love, out of envy, to turn you back to disbelief, even after the Truth has become evident to them. Have forgiveness and bear with them until God issues His order. God has power over all things. Be steadfast in your prayer and pay the religious tax. You will receive a good reward from God for all your good works. God is Well-aware of what you do.

> They have said that no one can ever go to Paradise except the Jews or Christians, but this is only what they hope. Ask them to prove that their claim is true. (2:109–111)

This appeal to clear reason—"bring your proof!"—is typical of the Koran. Time and time again, its response to doubt, misconception, superstition, prejudice, and ignorance is to appeal to the message of Allah … and ask the reader to judge the matter for himself or herself.

The Least You Need to Know

♦ Due in large part to unfortunate misconceptions regarding Islam, prejudice against Muslims is widespread in the United States.

♦ Islam was not "spread by the sword," and the Koran explicitly forbids forced religious conversion.

♦ "Muslim" is not synonymous with "Arab." The vast majority of the world's 1.7 billion Muslims are non-Arab.

♦ The Koran doesn't require men to marry more than one wife (although it does allow them to marry up to four), and in fact advises only one wife for those who fear they may not be able to deal fairly with more than one mate.

♦ Allah grants favor based on faith, not on gender (or any other factor).

♦ The Koran explicitly prohibits the shedding of innocent blood.

Chapter 4

Twenty-One Questions (and Answers) About Islam

In This Chapter

◆ The truth about Muslims

◆ A sampling of Muslim beliefs and practices

◆ How Islam differs from Christianity and Judaism

◆ Terrorism, politics, and other complex issues

You can't turn on the nightly news or open a newspaper these days, it seems, without encountering a story about Muslims. And most of the time, those stories present Muslims negatively—if they aren't portrayed as gun-toting, turban-wearing terrorists, then they may be shown as severe-looking, women-hating radicals or Mercedes-driving, oil-hoarding princes. Images and discussions of Muslimahs (that means female Muslims) usually manage to carry the implication that they are persecuted and oppressed. Can these possibly be accurate characterizations of the majority of Muslim people? … The answer, quite simply, is an emphatic "No!"

Unfortunately, mainstream journalists seem to be satisfied with grossly inaccurate portrayals of Muslim people, leaving Westerners with many unanswered, or inaccurately answered, questions about Islamic beliefs and Muslim lifestyles. It's fair to say that there are more questions in Western pressrooms, churches, and synagogues about Islam than about any other major religious tradition. In this chapter, you will find answers to some of the most common of these questions.

Time for Some Q&A

Although many of the following points are discussed in more detail in other chapters, this question and answer format is intended to give you ready access to some of the most common questions Westerners have about Islam and its adherents.

1. What Is a Muslim?

A Muslim is someone who follows Islam—one who submits to Allah.

2. What Is an Arab?

There are two accepted answers to this question. (1) An Arab is someone whose primary language is Arabic. (2) Arabs, a Semitic group, are regarded as coming from one of three groups: the al-Ba'ida, a people of whom we have no surviving records; the al-Ariba, descendants of a figure known as a-Qahtan; and the al-Musta'riba, descendants of Ismael, the son of Abraham.

3. Was Muhammad the Founder of Islam?

Non-Muslims frequently refer to Islam as having been "founded" by Muhammad in the seventh century C.E. The Muslim view, however, is that faith in the One God has been revealed to humanity consistently from the very earliest moments of human experience, and that Muhammad was the last in a long series of Prophets chosen by Allah. It is therefore incorrect to refer to Muhammad as some kind of social, religious, or cultural innovator operating independently of Allah. It is equally incorrect, believers insist, to suggest that Muhammad, and not Allah, was the author of the Koran.

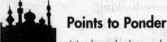

Points to Ponder

Muslims believe that Allah brought about Muhammad and the rest of the Prophets—not the other way around.

Muhammad is, from this point of view, the receiver of the final divine revelation to mankind. The religion that accompanies that revelation, however, shouldn't be confused as originating as a result of the thoughts and actions of a single man. It is eternal, and it commences with the Creation.

Furthermore, Muslims *do not* worship Muhammad. Allah is the only object of worship within Islam.

> **Caution!**
> Muhammad is regarded by Muslims as the final Prophet—not as a divinity himself. Western observers who referred to Islam as "Mohammedism" in the eighteenth and nineteenth centuries were profoundly misguided.

4. Who Are the Prophets Recognized by Islam?

Most of them are familiar to people who have studied the Hebrew scriptures of Judaism (called the Old Testament by Christians): Adam, Noah, Abraham, and Ezekiel, to name just a few.

Moving on to the New Testament, Jesus is also acknowledged as one of Allah's Prophets; far from being denigrated, as some Christians suppose, he is accorded a special place of honor in Islam. John the Baptist, too, is acknowledged as a Prophet of Allah.

Each of these figures appears (with an Arabic name) in the Koran. You'll learn more about these and other familiar figures from the Bible in Chapter 5.

The Koran also makes reference to other predecessors of the final Prophet—people who do not appear in the Hebrew scriptures or the New Testament. The Koran tells us that there have been other Prophets, as well. We just don't know who they were.

The main point to remember is that Muslims believe that their religion was handed down to humanity by means of a number of human messengers, beginning with Adam and concluding with the final Prophet, Muhammad. Each of these Prophets, Muslims believe, bore the same fundamental message of salvation—submission to the Lord—although some of the particulars of the law associated with their message were altered over time.

Believers hold that the actual revelations conveyed by Allah to the Prophets who came before Muhammad were lost, corrupted, or altered over time. The final Prophet's revelation, by contrast, is regarded by Muslims as complete, authoritative, and unchanged—and as God's final word.

The Word

The Prophet Muhammad was the latest in a long line of messengers:

(Muhammad), Say, "I am not the first Messenger. I do not know what will be done to me or to you. I follow only what has been revealed to me and my duty is only to give clear warning." (46:9)

Furthermore, the Prophet consolidated and completed the revelations that preceded him:

Muhammad is not the father of any of your males. He is the Messenger of God and the last Prophet. God has the knowledge of all things. (33:40)

5. Why Don't Muslims Eat Pork or Drink Alcohol?

The Koran specifically forbids the consumption of pork or alcohol. Alcohol and other intoxicants are dismissed from the lives of believers as briskly as gambling is:

(Muhammad), they ask you about wine and gambling. Tell them that there is great sin in them. Although they have benefits for men, the sin therein is far greater than the benefit. (2:219)

And the consumption of pork is set in an equally dark category for believers:

Believers, eat from the good things that We have given you and give thanks to God if you worship only Him. God has forbidden you to eat that which has not been properly slaughtered, blood, pork, and the flesh of any animal which has not been consecrated with a mention of the Name of God. However, in an emergency, without the intention of transgression or repeating transgression, one will not be considered to have committed a sin. God is All-forgiving and All-merciful. (2:172–73)

That pork comes from an animal that will consume virtually any form of filth, and that it is regarded as unclean in the Jewish tradition, are interesting but secondary considerations to Muslims. The fact that Allah has forbidden its consumption is reason enough to avoid it.

6. Does Fulfillment of the "Five Pillars" of Islam Mark the Completion of a Muslim's Duty to Allah?

No. The so-called "five pillars"—bearing witness, engaging in daily prayer, fasting, charity, and pilgrimage to Mecca—are an unfortunate oversimplification of a Muslim's obligation to Allah. Observing these obligations may well be described as the foundation of worship within the Islamic faith, but a building is more than its foundation. To be a Muslim, one must strive to maintain constant God-consciousness, and to submit to Allah in all the components of one's life.

7. Is Islam a Religion or a Social System?

It is both.

Islam's influence on both formal expressions of worship and the activities of daily life is a potentially confusing issue for non-Muslims. Followers of Islam view *all* areas of human activity as opportunities to serve and worship Allah, and they are instructed in the Koran to remember Allah in all they do.

Given Islam's status as a total way of life—and not merely as a set of formalized religious rituals—it isn't surprising that the Koran includes guidance, not merely on prayers, fasting, and other methods of formal observance, but also on trade, inheritance, etiquette, warfare, matrimonial traditions, travel, and many other subjects.

There are laws and rules for all activities. Any required activity undertaken, or forbidden activity avoided, as part of an obligation to submit to the will of the Lord within the course of a believer's life is regarded as worship.

8. Are There Priests Within Islam?

No.

A priest is an intermediary between a human being and God. But there are no intermediaries within Islam.

The Western mass media's eager discussions of the influence of "Muslim clerics" has helped to obscure, for non-Muslims, one of the most important features of this faith: The practice of Islam is intensely personal. One's relationship with Allah is not diverted, directed, or mandated by any other individual. The state of each believer's soul is his or her own responsibility.

There is, of course, a great body of tradition, law, and custom to be understood within Islam, and with all of this comes the role of interpretation that has emerged for Islam's religious figures. But there is and can be no intermediary.

9. What's the Difference Between the Koran and the Sunna?

The Koran, Muslims believe, is the revealed, literal word of God. The Sunna, on the other hand, is a collection of sayings, deeds, and decisions of the Prophet compiled by those who followed him. The Sunna, then, is acknowledged as a series of traditions recorded and preserved by human beings; the Koran, on the other hand, is revered as a divine revelation.

In the case of a conflict between the Koran and the Sunna, the resolution, for a believer, is simple and instantaneous: The revealed word of God is what determines the matter.

Spotlight on Islam

The Months of the Muslim Lunar Calendar

Muharram

Safar

Rabi' I

Rabi' II

Jumada I

Jumada II

Rajab

Sha'ban

Ramadan

Shawwal

Dhu al-Qa'ada

Dhu al-Hijja

Spotlight on Islam

During the holy month of Ramadan, Muslims must abstain from sex and eating during daylight hours.

10. Why Doesn't Ramadan Fall on the Same Day Each Year Within the Gregorian Calendar System?

Ramadan, the holy month of Islam, is the month in which the Koran was first revealed. It is a month-long period of fasting and purification. (See Chapter 13 for more information on this important holiday.)

Ramadan is observed as part of a 12-month lunar calendar system—the system in place at the time of the revelations of Muhammad. In this system, a new month always begins with the crescent moon. This lunar year contains 354 days, rather than 365, so the Muslim calendar is in a constant state of flux relative to the seasons of the year. (Note, though, that Muslims also use the Gregorian calendar.)

11. Do Muslims View Sex as Evil and Sinful?

Muslims don't view sex between married partners as a sin. All righteous human actions, including sexual relations within the bonds of marriage, are considered to be a form of worship of Allah. There is evidence that the Prophet taught his followers that sexual relations between a husband and wife carried spiritual rewards—because sex sanctioned by law prevented the unlawful satisfaction of carnal desire.

12. What Is the Major Difference Between Islam and Christianity?

Believers hold that nothing is similar to Allah, that Allah can be compared to no other, and that Allah can have no associates. The Koran specifically rejects the notion that God had or ever would have a son. So while Islam embraces the actual ministry and teachings of Jesus, it rejects the Christian belief that he was a human deity. (See Chapter 7 for more on the relationship between Christian and Muslim belief systems.)

Points to Ponder

The idea that God could be incarnate within any human being is blasphemous within the Islamic tradition.

13. Do Muslims Believe in Original Sin?

No. Muslims believe that human beings are born without sin. Islamic teachings hold that moral accountability for one's mistakes begins only with puberty. Islam also rejects the notion that one human being can take on the burden of the sins of another.

The very idea of Allah *needing* to implement some kind of sacrifice to overcome human sinfulness is regarded as absurd by followers of Islam. Allah is all-powerful, and can forgive whomever he wishes.

14. What's the Deal about Cutting off People's Hands?

Many non-Muslims who know nothing else of Islam have heard that the Koran has a verse about punishing a thief by means of cutting off a hand. Some people are even under the impression that Islam requires that a thief have his or her hand cut off in all cases. To understand why this is not so, one has to understand the important role of the Sunna.

The relevant verse from the Koran is:

> Cut off the hands of a male or female thief as a punishment for their deed and a lesson for them from God. (5:38)

In practice, the penalty is extremely rare, and is applied in cases where there are serious mitigating circumstances (such as a pattern of repeated theft). The penalty is even unheard of in some Muslim nations.

Does this mean that Islamic jurists are ignoring the Koran when they don't (for instance) order that a child who steals candy from a candy store have his or her hand severed? No. In the Sunna, the Prophet Muhammad offered detailed guidance on when a person's hand may be severed as punishment for the crime of theft; these include a number of important limitations. For instance, according to the Prophet, this penalty may never be imposed for the crime of stealing anything edible, or for stealing some paltry item, or in the case of a person who steals as the result of need. There are also many binding legal precedents that have been interpreted as limiting the application of this verse.

This is one of the most misunderstood verses in the Koran by both Muslims and non-Muslims. It's important to understand that imposing penalties for theft or other serious crimes is a judicial matter, and that no one other than a qualified, totally impartial judge, subject to many restrictions, may pass such a sentence.

15. What Is the Main Difference Between Islam and Judaism?

Islam rejects the Jewish notion of a "chosen people." Human beings, the Koran insists, may distinguish themselves before Allah by means of their faith and piety (that is, by means of a deep concern about the state of one's relationship with Allah). They do not accept that spiritual merit can be attained by any other means.

16. Do Muslims Believe in Heaven and Hell?

Yes. Islam teaches that, on the Day of Judgment, each individual human being will be held accountable for everything he or she has done, said, made, intended, and thought during the course of earthly life. Each person's carefully maintained record will be revealed, and then, depending on the person's good or evil deeds, the individual will be sent either to Paradise or to hell. The measure of one's good deeds, of course, is one's willingness to submit to the will of God.

On the Day of Judgment, *no one*—not even Iblis (the figure corresponding to Satan in the Judeo-Christian tradition) will want to be in hell. And *everyone* will want to be in Paradise. But only those whose records please Allah enough to warrant entry to the bliss of Paradise will be admitted there. For the rest … unimaginable torments await. Helping human beings make the decision to humble themselves, submit to Allah, earn entry to Paradise, and avoid the torments of hell is the business of the Koran.

17. What Is the Greatest Sin, According to Islam?

Worship of someone or something in the place of Allah. This sin is known as shirk.

18. When Do Muslims Believe the Day of Judgment Will Take Place?

No one but Allah knows this.

19. Does Islam Encourage or Sanction Terrorism?

"Terrorism" is generally defined as the intentional slaughtering of innocent civilians. The killing of innocent people is explicitly forbidden by the Koran:

> For this reason, We made it a law for the children of Israel that the killing of a person for reasons other than legal retaliation or for stopping corruption in the land is as great a sin as murdering all of mankind. (5:32)

There are many ahadith (traditions) recording the Prophet's reaction to military assaults on noncombatants. He doesn't sanction such activity. Once, we are told, Muhammad came across the corpse of a woman who had been slain in battle. He said disapprovingly, "She was not fighting. How did she come to be killed?"

Similarly, we are told that the Prophet forbade the killing of captives or of anyone bound; that he prohibited the killing of monks in monasteries; and that he forbade the killing of the elderly, women, and children. These instructions constitute binding legal edicts upon believers. Those who disobey them will be held accountable for their actions in the next life.

20. What Is the Difference Between Sunni and Shi'a Muslims?

Sunni Muslims are the majority group, accounting for perhaps 80 to 85 percent of believers worldwide; Shi'as are the minority. (At the global level, that is; Shi'as form majorities in specific countries, notably in Iraq and Iran.)

Both groups accept the Koran as the divine word of Allah; both accept the binding nature of the Sunna ("traditions"), from which the name of the Sunni ("traditional") school is derived; both acknowledge the obligations of daily prayers, pilgrimage to Mecca, fasting, almsgiving, acknowledgment of the oneness of Allah and Muhammad's role as his prophet, and so on.

The differences begin with how Sunnis and Shi'as view Islamic history. The word Shi'a means "follower or partisan." Shi'as, then, are followers ... but followers of what? The answer is that Shi'a Muslims are those who follow the authority of the Prophet's son-in-law, Ali, and his descendants, and believe that Ali was the divinely appointed immediate successor to Muhammad.

As a matter of historical fact, Ali was the fourth successor, or *caliph*, to his father-in-law Muhammad. Shi'as believe that he should have been the *first* caliph, rather than the fourth caliph, and that his divinely chosen line should have governed the Islamic empire. (It did not.)

Spotlight on Islam _____

Here are some common Arabic terms and their (basic) English equivalents:

- **Allah** God. (Literally, "The God"—the word "Allah" predates the Prophet Muhammad.)

- **Allahu Akbar** "God is most great."

- **Assalamu Alaikum** "Peace be upon you." (The standard greeting between Muslims.)

- **Ayah** A verse in the Koran.

- **Ayatollah** A Shiite who is learned in Shari'a, the Koran, and the Hadith, and who is known for their piety. This person is considered by his followers as the most learned person of his time period, which gives him the authority to make independent judgments.

- **Bismillah ar-Rahman ar-Rahim** The opening line of all but one of the 114 Suras of the Koran. It means "In the Name of Allah, the Beneficent, the Merciful." The verse does *not* opens the ninth of the Koran's Suras. That ninth Sura, *Repentance*, deals at some length with the fate of unbelievers.

- **Caliph** Successor to the Prophet Muhammad (as leader of the Muslims).

- **Fatwa** Legal ruling within Islam.

- **Hadith** An account or sayings attributed to the Prophet Muhammad.

- **Haj** Pilgrimage (to Mecca).

- **Imam** Leader.

- **Iman** Faith.

- **Jihad** Struggle; striving on behalf of Islam, perhaps peacefully or perhaps in a setting involving armed conflict.

- **Muslim** One who submits (to the Lord).

- **Nabi** Prophet.

- **Salaam** Peace.

- **Shari'a** Divine law.

- **Sura** A chapter in the Koran.

- **Umma** Nation. (This term is used to refer to the international body of Islamic believers).

- **Wassalam** "And peace." (Used as "farewell" or "goodbye" in English.)

Another big difference between Sunni and Shi'a Muslims involves the role of the Imam. Shi'as regard Ali as the first Imam (with a capital I). They consider his oldest son Hassan as the second Imam, and his younger son Husayn as the third Imam.

("Twelver" Shi'as, the largest group within the Shi'a movement, follow the authority of the 11 imams, or spiritual leaders, who followed Ali. The community of people known as Ismaelies is also considered to be Shi'a.)

When used in the generic sense, "imam," rendered with a lower-case "I" in English, simply means teacher. When used by Shi'as to refer to the successors of the Prophet, the word Imam describes a set of traditions carrying religious authority not unlike that which is claimed by the Roman Catholic Church through the doctrine of apostolic succession.

Other distinctive elements of Shi'a Islam include some differences in legal philosophy, including marriage and divorce regulations, a willingness to expand Shari'a law to resolve contemporary questions, the belief that the Prophet's family was infallible, and a unique reverence for certain holy sites. One of these sites is Karbala in present-day Iraq, where the Prophet's grandson Husayn and his followers were butchered by an overwhelming force loyal to the grandson of Abu Sufyan. (Abu Sufyan was the chief of the pagans of Mecca; he claimed to have converted to Islam, but could not overcome his hatred toward Islam.)

It helps, perhaps, to understand that Shi'a Islam began, many centuries ago, primarily as a philosophical and political movement in support of divinely appointed leadership claims of the Prophet's family. Today, the Shi'a movement is the only remaining alternate school.

21. How Many Muslims Are There in the United States?

At last count, approximately 5 million. This means that there are roughly as many Muslims in America as Jews. As noted previously, there are approximately 1.7 billion Muslims throughout the world.

> **Spotlight on Islam**
>
> To find out more about Islam as it is practiced in the United States, check out the Islamic Society of North America (ISNA). Their website can be found at www.isna.net.

Bonus Question: Can Anyone Become a Muslim?

Yes.

All that is necessary to become a Muslim is one's pronouncement of the testimonies of faith, known as shahada. (Private recitations are wonderful, but a public recitation carries certain social benefits.) The declaration is as follows:

Ash hadu anla ilaha illa Allah, wa ash hadu an-na Muhammad rusool Allah.

It means: "No one deserves to be worshipped (that is, no one deserves to be regarded as the absolute owner of the universe) except God, and Muhammad is the Messenger of God."

A simple ceremony is built around the recitation of these words to at least one other person. The ceremony can take place at a mosque, in a private home, at an Islamic center, or in any number of other settings.

Someone who recites these words begins a lifelong process of learning—learning about Islam, about its history, about the Sunna, and, of course, about the Holy Koran.

The Least You Need to Know

- ◆ Muslims do not worship Muhammad.

- ◆ Muslims regard their religion as having originated with Creation.

- ◆ There are no intermediaries between Allah and the believer.

- ◆ Islam does not regard the exercise of lawful carnal desires as inherently dirty or sinful.

- ◆ Islam does not sanction terrorism.

- ◆ Anyone can become a Muslim.

The Prophetic Tradition

In This Chapter

- ◆ God's other Prophets
- ◆ Traditional Hebrew and Christian Prophets who appear in the Koran
- ◆ Allah's nonbiblical Prophets

Although the Koran recognizes Muhammad as God's final Prophet, he is by no means the *only* Prophet mentioned in the Koran. As a matter of fact, the Koran points out that there were many Prophets who served as God's messengers before Muhammad. The Koran names 25 Prophets, 21 of whom appear in the Judeo-Christian tradition, and it also says that there were many more Prophets whom it does not identify. It does not specify a particular number of Prophets. In this chapter, you'll get an introduction to the Prophetic tradition.

According to Islam, a Prophet has been sent for every nation, and each of these Prophets sent warnings to humankind to follow the same religion: submission to the will of Allah. The Prophets, we read, always faced some form of opposition and sometimes endured bitter suffering, but they remained steadfast to the mission placed upon them by their Lord. Some Prophets conveyed not only warnings, but also comprehensive books of revelation (like the Taurat and the Injeel, otherwise known as the Torah and the Gospel, brought by Moses and Jesus, respectively). Muslims believe that in all cases but that of Muhammad, however, humanity tampered with and corrupted the original scriptures conveyed by Allah's Prophets. The Koran, believers maintain, stands perfect and complete to this day.

Many Prophets, One Religion

Muslims revere the messages of the Prophets—but they also believe that, as a matter of historical fact, people who *aren't* Prophets have often revised and misinterpreted the experiences and teachings of the Prophets—in some cases breaking those experiences into separate religions. In the Koran, we read that Allah doesn't want humanity to distinguish between the messages of his Prophets, but instructs people to regard them as a single faith:

> (Muslims), say, "We believe in God and what He has revealed to us and to Abraham, Ishmael, Isaac, and their descendants, and what was revealed to Moses, Jesus, and the Prophets from their Lord. We make no distinction among them and to God we have submitted ourselves." (2:136)

In this chapter, you'll learn *some* of what the Koran has to say about *some* of the Prophets who came before Muhammad. What follows is, of course, a concise summary; many dense books could be, and have been, written on this subject.

First, we'll take a closer look at what it means to be a Prophet of God. Then we'll examine the Koran's take on some of the Prophets familiar to readers of the traditional Hebrew and Christian scriptures. Their appearances—and reappearances!—in the Koran offer some fascinating points of contact between the three great monotheistic faiths: Judaism, Christianity, and Islam.

After that, we'll look briefly at some Prophets mentioned in the Koran who *don't* make an appearance in either the Hebrew or Christian scriptures.

What Is a Prophet?

We learn in the Koran that Prophets are chosen by Allah for his reasons, not ours. We learn that they are human beings like the rest of us:

> (Muhammad), say, "I am only a mortal like you, but I have received revelation that there is only one Lord. Whoever desires to meet his Lord should strive righteously and should worship no one besides Him." (18:110)

The Prophets, the Koran tells us, came complete with emotions like sadness, anger, grief for lost loved ones, and the frustration that can come when things don't go as you expect them to go. We also learn that Prophets are people who possess the highest moral values:

> You will certainly receive a never-ending reward. You have attained a greatly high moral standard. (68:3–4)

They offer, in other words, the best possible model of human behavior.

We also learn in the Koran that some of the Prophets have gifts that exceed the gifts of others.

Spotlight on Islam

The Koran teaches that of the Prophets, some had special rankings. In the same passage, it offers a related point, namely that the misinterpretation and wrangling that sometimes accompanies the mission of a Prophet arises because certain people disobeyed their commands:

> We gave some of Our Messengers preference over others. To some of them God spoke and He raised the rank of some others. We gave authoritative proofs to Jesus, son of Mary, and supported him by the Holy Spirit. Had God wanted, the generations who lived after those Messengers would not have fought each other after the authority had come to them. But they differed among themselves, some of them believed in the authority and others denied it. They would not have fought each other had God wanted, but God does as He wills. (2:253)

The ranks of Prophets may differ, yet Muslims believe that mankind must respect all the Prophets from Allah. We know a great deal about some of these Prophets; we know far less about some others. As for characteristics that unite the entire group, Muslims content themselves with the following: Allah selected certain righteous people to convey his message; these messengers were human, but guided in a special way by the Lord; they had families; they received guidance through various processes; they showed diverse personalities (due to the issues they faced) but shared the traits of enormous endurance and strength of character; and they never lost sight of their obligation to Allah. Last but not least, the Prophets were all, Muslims maintain, people whose message should be listened to.

Why Send Prophets at All?

The Koran teaches that Allah sent the Prophets for two important reasons: to bring people the good news of divine mercy, and to warn them against the torments of hell.

What's It Mean?

The Koran speaks similarly of the role of **Prophet** (*nabi*, or news giver in Arabic) and **messenger** (*rasul*, one who demands a response from those to whom he has sent a message). In translations of the Koran, both terms may be incorporated within the single English rendering "Prophet." Muslims believe that Prophets and messengers receive guidance from God, which they then pass on to other people.

A Biblical Surprise

Many non-Muslims are surprised to learn that the Koran spends a great deal of time discussing the lives and experiences of Prophets who appear in the Old and New Testaments. These Prophets aren't just mentioned in passing in the Koran—their stories are repeated again and again, as though the author of the book wanted to be certain that the lives and missions of the Prophets didn't go ignored or unnoticed. This technique of repetitive storytelling to emphasize key points is one of the distinctive features of the Koran. The technique is most obvious in the way the Koran relates the lives of the Prophets; they are mentioned in many different Suras, each time for a different reason or to reveal a different aspect of their teaching.

However, the stories the Koran has to pass along regarding the Prophets aren't always the same as they are in the Bible!

Roll Call!

Here is a list of the Prophets mentioned within the Koran. Readers of the Bible will notice that most of the Prophets identified in the Koran are also mentioned in the Bible. (In the case of biblical Prophets, both the standard English and Arabic versions of the names are provided.)

◆ Adam (Adam)

◆ Enoch (Idris)

◆ Noah (Nuh)

- Hud

- Salih

- Abraham (Ibrahim)

- Ishmael (Isma'il)

- Isaac (Ishaq)

- Lot (Lut)

- Jacob (Yaqub)

- Joseph (Yusuf)

- Shu'aib

- Job (Ayub)

- Moses (Musa)

- Aaron (Harun)

- Ezekiel (Dhul-Kifl)

- David (Dawud)

- Solomon (Sulayman)

- Elijah (also known as Elyas) (Ilyas)

- Al-Yasa' (Elisha)

- Jonah (Yunus)

- Zechariah (Zakariyya)

- John (Yahya)

- Jesus (Isa)

- Muhammad

Points to Ponder

Islam teaches that there were no female Prophets of Allah. The opinion on why this is so varies; some suggest that it's because the divinely appointed task of Prophethood often requires a degree of physical suffering that men are best prepared to endure.

Points to Ponder

The Koran states that God sent Prophets to all nations at various key points in human history. Muslims are ordered in the Koran to believe in and show respect to the messages of all the divinely appointed Prophets. This is a particularly important point to bear in mind when considering Islam's relationship to Christianity.

Unlike the Judeo-Christian scriptures, which sometimes emphasize the errors or misdeeds of some of the people on this list, the Koran presents each of these individuals as models for correct behavior. Of course, they were not divine figures—that is, they were not part of God: they often showed grief, fear, frustration, and anger, especially when they met with resistance from the people they were calling to the way of Allah. All the same, they kept to their message: Return to God and submit to him and him alone!

Islam Isn't Anti-Christian After All!

Many Western commentators blithely pronounce that
Islam is an "anti-Christian" faith. Such a statement
actually demonstrates a profound ignorance of Islam.

In fact, Muslims show great reverence for the ministry
of the Messiah, and there is a long and impressive
history within the faith of studying his words carefully.
Muslims do believe that the scriptures used by most
Christians have been altered over time (more on this
in Chapter 7), but this is certainly not the same as
believing that a Christian's faith is condemned in the
Koran! To the contrary, Muslims are specifically
ordered in the Koran to show tolerance to the faith
and belief of both Christians and Jews—the People of
the Book—and to permit them to practice their faith.

The Old and New Testament Prophets

Let's look now more closely at some of the most prominent Prophets who exist in the
Jewish, Christian, and Islamic traditions.

Adam

The first Prophet, he shared the religion of Islam with his children.

To get a sense of the way in which the Koran spreads its narratives around, and how
it demands constant examination and re-examination, consider that the life story of
Adam and Eve appears in various parts in four separate chapters, or Suras! The creation of Adam and Eve appears in the second Sura; the fall of the couple is related in
the second and the seventh; the familiar story of their two sons, Cain and Abel, and
Cain's murder of Abel, appears in the fifth; and Adam and Eve's temptation by the
proud Satan appears in the twentieth! Yet the pieces all fit together to deliver a coher-
ent narrative.

Abraham

Acknowledged as a Prophet in Genesis 20:7, Abraham is the subject of extraordinary
emphasis in the Koran. He is presented as a model for upright and pious behavior; as
the establisher of the Ka'ba, the great shrine to monotheism; as a vigorous condemner

of both idolatry and sinful behavior; as an eloquent preacher; and as a believer willing to confront the powerful—but deeply misled—idol-worshipping religious authorities of his day.

The familiar story of the sacrifice, which appears in Genesis, appears as follows in the Koran:

> Abraham prayed, "Lord, grant me a righteous son." We gave him the glad news of the birth of a forbearing son. When his son was old enough to work with him, he said, "My son, I have had a dream that I must sacrifice you. What do you think of this?" He replied, "Father, fulfill whatever you are commanded to do and you will find me patient, by the will of God." When they both agreed and Abraham had lain down his son on the side of his face (for slaughtering), We called to him, "Abraham, you have fulfilled what you were commanded to do in your dream." Thus do We reward the righteous ones. It was certainly an open trial. We ransomed his son with a great sacrifice and perpetuated his praise in later generations. (37:100–8)

Points to Ponder

Muslims believe that Abraham and Ishmael built or repaired the Ka'ba; they trace the descent of the Prophet Muhammad through this son of Abraham, and the descent of the Jewish Prophets through his half-brother Isaac.

But there is a great deal more. Abraham is regarded in the Koran as neither Jew nor Christian, and as the all-important model for future Prophets. He is cited again and again as a pattern for correct behavior. One particularly important passage reminds Muhammad to follow his example:

> Abraham was, certainly, an obedient and upright person. He was not a pagan. He was thankful to God for His bounties. God chose him and guided him to the right path. We granted him virtue in this life and he shall be among the righteous ones in the life to come. We sent you, (Muhammad), a revelation that you should follow the tradition of Abraham, the upright one, who was not a pagan. (16:120–123)

Caution!

Don't make the common mistake of assuming that all prophets must pass along predictions. Prophets might or might not make predictions about what will take place in the future. What matters is that they guide humanity to the will of God.

Lot

Having settled in Sodom, Lot warned its inhabitants to repent, learned that the city was about to be destroyed, and was warned by God to leave it ... and avoid the fate of its inhabitants.

Lot's insistence on following God's instructions, and the fate of those who ignored him, is discussed repeatedly in the Koran.

> Our Messengers said, "Lot, we are the Messengers of your Lord. They (the unbelievers) will never harm you. Leave the town with your family in the darkness of night and do not let any of you turn back. As for your wife, she will suffer what they (unbelievers) will suffer. Their appointed time will come at dawn. Surely dawn is not far away!" (11:81)

Interestingly, in the sixty-sixth Sura of the Koran, we are told that Lot's wife was punished for "betraying" her husband—not through adultery, as we might interpret the word "betray," but by ignoring his directions. There is no mention in the Koran of her being turned into a pillar of salt, but the passage above suggests that she probably "turned back," thus ignoring instructions passed on by her husband from Allah. ("Do not let any of you turn back," above, has also been translated "do not let any of you look back.")

Isaac

Readers of Genesis will be familiar with Isaac as the only son of Abraham and Sarah. The Hebrew scriptures also describe how he was tricked by his wife Rebeccah into blessing his son Jacob, rather than his other son Esau.

The Koran often seems to presume the reader's familiarity with events in both the Hebrew and Christian scriptures, so it should not be all that surprising or disorienting that it doesn't retell the Jacob and Esau story. It does, however, share the remarkable circumstances of an aged, and supposedly barren, Sarah giving birth to Isaac. The Koran stresses that God guided both Isaac and his son Jacob in extending the message (referred to as "Our guidance" in the following passage) against idolatry:

> Such was the authoritative reasoning that We gave Abraham over his people. We raise whomever We want to a higher rank. Your Lord is All-wise and All-knowing. We gave (Abraham) Isaac and Jacob. Both had received Our guidance. Noah received Our guidance before Abraham and so did his descendants: David, Solomon, Job, Joseph, Moses, and Aaron. Thus is the reward for the righteous people. (6:83–84)

Joseph

Thanks to the enduring success of *Joseph and the Amazing Technicolor Dreamcoat*, Joseph is familiar even to people who don't read very much scripture. Joseph (or Yusuf, in the Arabic form) is the next-to-youngest of the 12 sons of Jacob. His 10 older half-brothers plot against him; his sufferings are many, and he finds himself a captive in Egypt. By means of an extraordinary ability to interpret the meaning of dreams, he rises from the dungeons, correctly predicts an imminent famine, helps the Egyptians establish a successful plan to survive the famine, and becomes a favorite of the Egyptian ruler. As a powerful official within the Egyptian government, he gives grain for food to his half-brothers who betrayed him, and they realize their guilt. Finally he forgives them. In the end, Joseph is triumphant, and Jacob and his sons all settle in Egypt.

The twelfth Sura of the Koran offers a fascinating retelling of the story of Joseph and his brothers—a story that differs in significant ways from the account that appears in the book of Genesis.

For one thing, the Koran's account places an extraordinary emphasis on Joseph's decision to turn aside the illicit sexual advances of the king's wife. For another, the Joseph of the Koran is given a specific Prophetic message to relate before offering his analysis of the dreams of his fellow captives:

> Two young men were also sent to serve prison sentences (for different reasons). One of them said, "I had a dream in which I was brewing wine." The other one said, "In my dream I was carrying some bread on my head and birds were eating that bread." They asked Joseph if he would interpret their dreams. They said, "We believe you to be a righteous person." (Joseph) said, "To prove that my interpretation of your dream is true, I can tell you what kind of food you will receive even before it comes to you. My Lord has given me such talents. I have given up the tradition of the people who do not believe in God and the Day of Judgment and I have embraced the religion of my fathers, Abraham, Isaac, and Jacob. We are not supposed to consider anything equal to God. This is part of God's blessing to us and the people, but most people do not give thanks. (12:36–38)

And at the time of his reunion with his father Jacob, the Koran tells readers that Joseph gave further evidence of the faith-driven nature of his story of struggle and triumph:

> "My Lord, You have given me the kingdom and taught me the meaning of dreams. You are the Creator of the heavens and the earth. You are my Guardian in this world and in the life to come. Make me die as one who has submitted to the Will of God and unite me with the righteous ones." (12:101)

In other words, this Joseph offers divine guidance; he is not merely a trickster or adventurer, as the Joseph of the Old Testament may sometimes appear to be. The Koran's version of this story strongly emphasizes Allah's role as protector and sustainer, as well as his ability to resolve apparently impossible contradictions and challenges.

A few more observations on the Koran's extraordinary story of Joseph are worth making before we move on. First, the twelfth Sura is unique in the Koran: It is a lengthy, sustained narrative focusing on the life and deeds of a single person (Joseph). This suggests that the story is worthy of particularly close study. Second, the Sura plays an important role in Islamic history: according to tradition, it was revealed in its entirety shortly after the Prophet Muhammad was challenged by powerful unbelievers to prove the nature of his mission. Jewish tribesmen had persuaded the Prophet's Arab political opponents to humiliate him publicly by testing the divinity of his mission. They did this by posing a question they believed to be beyond his knowledge: "Why did the Israelites settle in Egypt?" The stunning, detailed answer to their question—an answer which was indeed unknown in the Arab world—is contained in this portion of the Koran.

Noah

Noah's story of warning, flood, and redemption is told, and appealed to, with remarkable frequency throughout the Koran.

Unlike the Old Testament, the Koran describes a flood that is not necessarily worldwide—and this is in agreement with modern scientific theories of a catastrophic flood in the Black Sea region many thousands of years ago.

The Old Testament's Noah is portrayed as simply carrying out the orders of his God. The Koran's Noah takes a more active role, praying to Allah *not* to allow the unrepentant, sinful people of his era to survive the flood. Noah's prayer parallels the earlier (Koranic) Prophetic mission of Abraham. Both missions explicitly condemn not just the sinfulness of unbelievers, but also their strong attraction to the sin of idolatry. In the following passage, Noah names the specific idols whom the people of his day worshipped, and laments the disobedience of those whom he has called to follow Allah's commands:

Spotlight on Islam

Some kind of reference to Noah or his people appears in 29 of the 114 Suras of the Koran.

Noah said, "Lord, they have disobeyed me and followed those whose wealth and children will only bring about destruction for them. They have arrogantly plotted evil plans against me, and have said to each other, 'Do not give-up your idols. Do not renounce Wadd, Suwa', Yaghuth, Ya'uq and Nasr (names of certain idols). They have misled many and the unjust will achieve nothing but more error." (2–24)

David

David is celebrated in the Koran as a Prophet, as a singer of God's praises, and as the bringer-forth of the Psalms, which are described as issuing from God himself.

Reference to the familiar story of David slaying Goliath appears in the Koran's second Sura; the long struggle between King Saul and king-to-be David is referred to glancingly in the same Sura—in a way that presupposes a certain familiarity with the material.

Job

Beyond citing him as a Prophet and acknowledging that the revelation of God was delivered to him, the Koran has comparatively little to say about the long-suffering Job. But what it does have to say is fascinating—emphasizing as it does the man's ultimate faith, rather than his early laments and his pointed questions about God's fairness:

> We found him to be patient. What an excellent servant he was. He was certainly most repenting. (38:44)

Moses

Moses, like Noah, is remarkable for his recurring presence throughout the text of the Koran. Of all the Prophets, his name is mentioned most frequently in the Koran.

Moses' relationship with Pharaoh, in particular, is given special, and repeated, emphasis:

> They were wicked people. When the Truth from Us came, they called it simply magic. (10:75–76)

Moses is, however, sometimes called upon to play a role very different from that described in the Hebrew scriptures. There is a remarkable passage involving Moses in the eighteenth Sura that addresses many fundamental questions concerning justice, fairness, and the inscrutable will of God:

> Moses asked him, "Can I follow you so that you would teach me the guidance that you have received?" He replied, "You will not be able to have patience with me. How can you remain patient with that which you do not fully understand?" (18:66–68)

Aaron

Aaron is the fair-spoken brother of Moses. He is usually referenced in the Koran side-by-side with his brother.

Jesus

The Koran offers a number of fascinating additions to the Gospel accounts of Jesus' life. (It describes a miracle of him speaking while still an infant, for example.) It is in agreement with conventional Christianity about many things: his virgin birth, the divine authorization of his ministry, and the failure of the people of his time to accept his message, to name just a few.

The Koran differs notably with the received texts of Christianity, however, on Jesus' own status as a divine being, the only Son of God, and on some other important points of Christian doctrine. In accordance with the Koran, Muslims believe Jesus to have been a Prophet singled out for special emphasis and glory by God himself … but a human Prophet nonetheless.

In the Koran, Jesus himself explicitly renounces any effort to portray him as God or as the Son of God:

> When God asked Jesus, son of Mary "Did you tell men to consider you and your mother as their gods besides God?" he replied, "Glory be to you! How could I say what I have no right to say? Had I ever said it, You would have certainly known about it. You know what is in my soul, but I do not know what is in Yours. It is You who has absolute knowledge of the unseen." (5:116)

In a fascinating departure from the New Testament accounts, the Koran maintains that Jesus was not killed by his opponents—but was, instead, delivered up to Allah. Those who sought to destroy Jesus, we read, only *thought* that they had done away with him, but they were mistaken.

Caution!

The Koran often refers to Mary, the mother of Jesus, as "sister of Aaron"—at least, it does so in English translations. Many non-Muslims assume that this is a major historical error. In fact, the Arabic word used here simply reflects the fact that Mary was a member of the priestly family that traced its roots to Aaron.

Points to Ponder

The Koran repeatedly instructs its readers that God alone will judge the "People of the Book"—Jews and Christians and Muslims—regarding "that in which they differ."

Nonbiblical Prophets

The Koran also features some intriguing details about three pre-Muhammadan Prophets who do not appear anywhere in the Hebrew or Christian scriptures. They are ...

- ♦ Hud, who warned the tribe of 'Ad to turn away from idolatry and sinfulness; they ignored his entreaties and were destroyed by Allah.

- ♦ Salih, who condemned the atheism of the people of Thamud, and urged them to turn to Allah to seek forgiveness. When they refused, they were struck with a blast that left them "motionless on their faces, as though they had never existed." (11:67–68)

- ♦ Shu'ayb, who warned the prosperous people of Midian to turn to Allah, abandon their unjust trading practices, abandon the idolatrous practices of their forefathers, and seek Allah's forgiveness. They rejected his mission, and were obliterated by the Lord as a result.

In all of these cases, the Koran tells us, Allah preserved the Prophets and their followers while destroying those who opposed them.

Anyone Else?

In this chapter, you've learned about some of the Prophets besides Muhammad who are identified in the Koran. Remember, though, that the Koran makes a point of informing its audience that it has not identified all of the Prophets whom Allah sent to guide humanity:

> (We sent revelations to) the Messengers mentioned to you before and also to Messengers who have not been mentioned to you. (4:164)

The Koran does not say who all of Allah's Prophets were, but we can be certain that each of them carried the same consistent message of monotheism, repentance, and salvation that Islam associates with such revered figures as Abraham, Moses, Noah, Jesus ... and, of course, the final Prophet, Muhammad.

The Least You Need to Know

♦ A Prophet or messenger is a human being who brings other humans true communication or guidance from God.

♦ Muslims believe that Muhammad was the last Prophet.

♦ The Koran also recounts events from the lives of Prophets familiar to readers of the Hebrew and Christian scriptures.

♦ There are fascinating similarities and differences between the Judeo-Christian accounts of the Prophetic tradition and those appearing in the Koran.

♦ The Koran also tells us about a number of Prophets who do not appear in the Hebrew or Christian scriptures.

Part 2

A Document Like No Other

Believers and unbelievers alike have come away from the Koran convinced that it is unique in the world's religious literature.

It's time to learn why. This part of the book offers insights into the structure, distinctive message, and unique features of the Koran.

A Document Like No Other

Believers and unbelievers alike have come away from the Koran convinced that it is unique in the world's religious literature.

It's true relate why This part of the book offers insights into the structure that characterizes and unique features of the Koran.

Chapter 6

Navigating the River

In This Chapter

- ◆ Using the metaphor of a river to describe the Koran
- ◆ Unusual textual features of the Holy book
- ◆ Why Muslims believe that the Koran is the exact word of Allah

Experiencing the Koran has been compared to navigating a wild river. It swirls and twists and turns, then doubles back from where it came ... and then, just when one thinks one knows where the river is going, it curves yet again in a new direction entirely.

That metaphor may well be an oversimplification of the text of the Koran ... although one must always remember that Muslims believe that *any* explanation of the text is an oversimplification! There are certainly some stretches of the Koran that provide what appears from the surface to be relatively straightforward warnings to humanity, narrative material, and poetry, and these are less "river-like" than other passages. Still, a great deal of the text remains, from verse to verse, entirely unpredictable and more than a little intimidating the first-time reader.

So perhaps the idea of navigating an unknown river through an undiscovered country is indeed useful to bear in mind when approaching the work for the first time. Both experiences can be a little disorienting for the newcomer, and both experiences demand that the newcomer abandon preconceptions or principles appropriate to other kinds of journeys.

In this chapter, we'll get a look at some of the unusual textual features of the Koran—and then we'll examine a few of the reasons Muslims are so convinced that this extraordinary work is in fact the divinely revealed word of God.

Navigating the River

Non-Muslims approaching the text of the Koran for the first time usually agree on one thing: It isn't what they expected.

It doesn't, to take the most obvious issue first, sound like the Bible. What's more, it isn't organized chronologically. The longer chapters (of which there are many) don't have what readers who are familiar with Judeo-Christian scriptures might consider to be traditional elements of viewpoint, narrative, or resolution. And finally, the tone and intensity of the chapters can change radically, depending, in large degree, on whether the chapter in question was received by Muhammad before or after the hijrah.

Spotlight on Islam

The Koran is divided into Suras (a term that corresponds to the English word "chapter") and ayats (verses). In this introductory chapter, for ease of understanding, the terms "chapter" and "verse" are used.

Here's a generalization that may help you as you make your way through the Koran. Chapters composed *before* the journey to Yathrib (known, you'll recall, as the "Meccan" revelations) tend to take the form of warnings to humanity. Chapters from *after* the journey to Yathrib (the "Medinan" revelations) also include warnings, but they may also address social, legal, and domestic questions.

Beyond Excerpts

The text's most startling challenges aren't as obvious if you're simply reading brief quotes from the Koran, which is what most non-Muslims do.

Most of the extracts from the Koran that you will encounter in this book, for instance, come in the form of short extracts of a few of its verses, like this one:

> Should you have any doubt about what We have revealed to Our servant, present one chapter comparable to it and call all your supporters, besides God, if your claim is true. If you do not produce such a chapter, and you never will, then guard yourselves against the fire whose fuel will be people and stones, and is prepared for those who hide the Truth. (2:23–24)

Straightforward enough!

Such short extracts can, of course, be extremely helpful in establishing guidance on narrow textual questions, particular points of law, or specific instructions on human conduct. As a result, one frequently encounters just such short bursts of the Koran in books, articles, research papers, and on World Wide Web.

What brief extracts cannot do, however, is offer someone who is unfamiliar with the Koran a sense of the unceasing (and river-like!) flow of the text, which is both utterly distinctive and impossible to imitate.

Points to Ponder

The Koran challenges all those who encounter it to produce equivalent text in Arabic capable of being mistaken for the Word of God. In earlier revelations, the Koran demanded a *group* of chapters that could be mistaken for a chapter from the actual text. In later revelations, it asked for smaller and smaller chunks; eventually, the challenge to skeptics was for them to provide a single convincing verse.

The "Flow" of the Koran

To get a sense of the extraordinary cascading quality that characterizes so much of the Koran, one should, ideally, read the text in the original Arabic. This is a difficult task—to say the least!—for a beginner.

The next best option is to read a translation, in order to get an approximation of the experience of reading the Koran in Arabic. A brief attempt at such an approximation follows; it is an extract from the second chapter of the Koran. This translated passage is offered to give you some limited sense of what it's like to navigate this remarkable river.

Notice that the following extract, titled "No Doubt," includes the short, seemingly self-contained passage you read a moment ago. Notice, too, that the names Allah applies to Himself (those beginning with capital letters, such as We, God, He, and so on)—shift constantly. Allah, in other words, refers to himself from different angles of perception—because he encompasses all possible angles of perception! This is a phenomenon that repeats itself again and again in the Koran.

The Second Sura: "No Doubt"

Verse	Passage
2:2	There is no doubt that this book is a guide for the pious;
2:3	the pious who believe in the unseen, attend to prayer, give in charity part of what We have granted them;
2:4	who have faith in what has been revealed to you and others before you and have strong faith in the life hereafter.

continues

The Second Sura: "No Doubt"   (continued)

Verse	Passage
2:5	It is the pious who follow the guidance of their Lord and gain lasting happiness.
2:6	Those who deny your message will not believe whether you warn them or not.
2:7	God has sealed their hearts and hearing and their vision is veiled; a great punishment awaits them.
2:8	Some people say, "We believe in God and the Day of Judgment," but they are not true believers.
2:9	They deceive God and the believers. However, they have deceived no one but themselves, a fact of which they are not aware.
2:10	A sickness exists in their hearts to which God adds more sickness. Besides this, they will suffer a painful punishment as a result of the lie which they speak.
2:11	When they are told not to commit corruption in the land, they reply, "We are only reformers."
2:12	They, certainly, are corrupt but do not realize it.
2:13	When they are told to believe as everyone else does, they say, "Should we believe as fools do?" In fact, they themselves are fools, but they do not know it.
2:14	To the believers they declare belief and, in secret to their own devils, they say, "We were only mocking."
2:15	God mocks them and gives them time to continue blindly in their transgressions,
2:16	They have traded guidance for error, but their bargain has had no profit and they have missed the true guidance.
2:17	(Their case) is like that of one who kindles a fire and when it grows bright God takes away its light leaving him in darkness (wherein) he cannot see (anything).
2:18	They are deaf, blind, and dumb and cannot regain their senses.
2:19	Or it is like that of a rain storm with darkness, thunder, and lightning approaching. They cover their ears for fear of thunder and death. God encompasses those who deny His words.
2:20	The lightning almost takes away their vision. When the lightning brightens their surroundings, they walk and when it is dark, they stand still. Had God wanted, He could have taken away their hearing and their vision. God has power over all things.

Verse	Passage
2:21	People, worship your Lord who created you and those who lived before you, so that you may become pious.
2:22	Worship God who has rendered the earth as a floor for you and the sky as a dome for you and has sent water down from the sky to produce fruits for your sustenance. Do not knowingly set up anything as an equal to God.
2:23	Should you have any doubt about what We have revealed to Our servant, present one chapter comparable to it and call all your supporters, besides God, if your claim is true.
2:24	If you do not produce such a chapter, and you never will, then guard yourselves against the fire whose fuel will be people and stones and is prepared for those who hide the Truth.
2:25	(Muhammad), tell the righteously striving believers of the happy news, that for them there are gardens wherein streams flow. Whenever they get any fruit from the gardens as food, they will say, "This is just what we had before (we came here). These fruits are produced very much like them (those we had before)." They will have purified spouses and it is they who will live forever.
2:26	God does not hesitate to set forth parables of anything even a gnat. The believers know that it is the truth from their Lord, but those who deny the truth say, "What does God mean by such parables?" In fact, by such parables God misleads and guides many. However, He only misleads the evil doers
2:27	who break their established covenant with Him and the relations He has commanded to be kept and who spread evil in the land. These are the ones who lose a great deal.
2:28	How dare you deny the existence of God Who gave you life when you initially had no life? He will cause you to die and bring you to life again. Then you will return to His Presence.
2:29	It is He who created everything on earth for you. Then, directing His order towards the realm above, He turned it into seven heavens. He has knowledge of all things.
2:30	When your Lord said to the angels, "I am appointing someone as my deputy on earth," they said (almost protesting), "Are you going to appoint one who will commit corruption and bloodshed therein, even though we (are the ones who) commemorate Your Name and glorify You?" The Lord said, "I know that which you do not know."

And Now—a Slow-Motion Replay

In the passage you just read, the Koran hurtles at great speed through a breathtaking sequence of governing pronouns, narrative points of view, and interlocking subjects.

Take a look at the verses once again. You will find:

- The (prominently placed) claim that the Koran is without any doubt, examined alongside the related notion of its serving to guide all those who are conscious of the Creator. (Verses 2–5; note that the Creator is here referred to by means of the "royal We."). This shifts to ...

- The observation that warnings are of no use to unbelievers. (Verses 6–7; note that here the Creator is referred to as "God," (or "Allah" in the Arabic.) This shifts to ...

- The beginning of an examination of the characteristics of hypocrites, and the discussion of the consequences of their actions. (Verses 8–16; note that in verse 15 the Creator is referred to as "He.") This shifts to ...

- The continuation of the discussion of hypocrites, offering specific examples and vivid parables illustrating their folly. (Verses 17–20; note that here the Creator is referred to as both "God" and "He.") This shifts to ...

- The pronouncement of a clear demand that humanity worship God. (Verses 21–22; note that here the Creator is referred to as "your Lord.") This shifts to ...

- The abrupt challenge to produce a "chapter comparable to" the Koran and to have both passages evaluated by judges—and the further challenge that, if one fails in this attempt to create a similar chapter, one remain on one's guard against "the fire whose fuel will be people and stones." (Verses 23–24; note that here God is once again referred to by means of the royal "We.") This shifts to ...

- The promise that there is a reward for believers. (Verse 25; note that here the Creator is not referred to at all by any name or pronoun, but is simply the unnamed entity offering the command to "convey good news.") This shifts to ...

- The assurances that the Creator is not limited in offering His parables, that believers and unbelievers will react to them differently, and that He is in control of this very process of differing reactions. (Verses 26–27; note that here the Creator is "God," " Lord," and "He.") This shifts to ...

- The powerful direct question, "How dare you deny the existence of God Who gave you life when you initially had no life?" (Verse 28; note that this passage is phrased in such a way as to remind the reader that the Creator, who is the only one who could possibly have knowledge of such matters, is posing the question ... but is here nevertheless choosing to speak of Himself in the third person, rather than as "I.") This shifts to ...

◆ The assurance that God created all, directed Himself to the heaven, made them complete seven heavens, and knows all things. (Verse 29; note that here we are still in the third person, with the Creator referred to as "He.") This shifts to …

◆ The sudden, and somewhat startling, dialogue between God and the angels, including the assurance that God knows what the angels do not. (Verse 30; notice that in this verse, the Creator is referred to as "the Lord"—and is also reported as using the pronoun "I.")

This sequence, suggesting the "river-like" cascade of interconnected divine messages, is only a small sampling of many such passages in the full text of the Koran.

If the small extract has piqued your interest, pick up a copy of the real thing and navigate the river yourself.

(Some of the) Reasons Muslims Believe the Koran Is the Literal Word of God

The river you've just "swum" in—briefly—is, Muslims would argue, the ultimate river.

There are many long and well-reasoned arguments in support of the belief that the Koran is the divine word of God. This book can't possibly relate them all, but here is a brief sampling of some of the most interesting points.

Its Own Testimony and Falsification Test

The Koran, as we have seen, challenges humanity to compose a sample of text in Arabic that could be confused with the genuine article. No such sample has surfaced.

Spotlight on Islam

Part of the reason for the difficulty in creating text that could be mistaken for the Koran is that the words used in the Arabic original very often can be translated in two, three, or more ways … rendering two, three, or more simultaneous meanings, all of which are consistent with one another! This extraordinary feature is one of the factors behind the constant emphasis on the point that any translation of the Koran is only a rendering of its "near meaning." Its actual meaning often points in multiple directions that cannot be translated in a single sentence.

Literary Quality

In its original Arabic form, the Koran is a literary masterpiece that has withstood all human competition for fourteen centuries. Such a text is not exactly what one would expect from an unlettered seventh-century merchant with no history of literary composition—great or otherwise—behind him.

Scientific Observations

The Koran discusses embryology, astronomy, cosmology, geology, and other scientific disciplines in a way that is simply impossible to explain given the state of scientific knowledge in Arabia in the seventh century C.E. Non-Muslims are often skeptical about this assertion ... but those who examine the facts closely and fairly are, more often than not, astounded by what the text has to say about scientific matters.

(For a fuller discussion of this remarkable subject, see Chapter 8.)

Distinctive Historical Factors

During the lifetime of the Prophet, one of his uncles, a man named Abu Lahab, opposed him relentlessly. A chapter of the Koran (111) is devoted to this man. It predicted without ambiguity that he would go to hell. For 10 years after this passage was shared with the world, Abu Lahab had the chance to prove the Prophet and the Koran wrong simply by announcing his conversion to Islam. Had he done so, he would have disproved the revelation of the Prophet, and thereby secured fame for himself and support from the followers of the Prophet!

Ten years passed—and there was no such attempt.

What human being, Muslims ask, would knowingly give his enemies such an opportunity? What force could predict accurately that an enemy would fail to take advantage of it?

Personal Faith

The ultimate reason to believe that the Koran comes from God is, of course, personal faith. Recently, the following message was posted to an Islamic online discussion group; the group had been debating, for over a month, the question of what factors demonstrated conclusively the divinity of the Koran:

> The "proof" of its divinity is simply that it takes over one's consciousness, as this thread indicates. Over what other volume is it likely intelligent and sane people could have such a debate?

Proof begins (perhaps) without one ever expecting anything out of the ordinary. One consults the text in a reserved, academic, even Hostile way ... but keeps reading. And one finds things to disagree with and things to agree with and ways to classify it and labels to put on it ... but one keeps reading. But that's not the "proof."

Later one encounters such elements as:

♦ Its accurate description of ocean storms (although Muhammad was a desert dweller).

♦ Its reference to worker-bees using a feminine verb form that indicates the author somehow knew that these insects were all female. (16:68)

♦ Its failure to attribute miraculous powers or doings to Muhammad— something that a forged document would surely have included.

♦ Its accurate description of human embryology.

♦ Its accurate contention that all life is water-based.

♦ Its accurate naming of the lost town of Iram.

♦ Its accurate identification of a subatomic realm of particles. And so on and so on. And the intellect reels. All of this in the seventh century?

But that's not the real "proof."

When ... finally ... one realizes that one's formerly diseased heart is in fact healing (as advertised) in direct relation to one's exposure to the Qur'an ... and when one returns to it ... and returns to it ... and returns to it ... and realizes one is becoming who one is really meant to be ... then one finds the ultimate proof. But it can only come, I think, to one person at a time. It cannot be demonstrated to another. This proof must be experienced.

One simply feels in reading the Qur'an that one is in the presence of something consistent and infinitely, utterly redemptive.

The yeast rises. The sapling sprouts. The mustard-seed grows to a great size and birds come to rest in its branches. (To quote another Prophet.)

The ultimate "test" of the Koran's authenticity, then, lies not with scholars or scientists or experts in Arabic literature ... but with you. Once you begin to navigate this river, it will be up to you to decide where it comes from, and where it is leading you.

The Least You Need to Know

♦ The Koran may be compared to a river.

♦ It is not what newcomers expect.

♦ It is impossible to imitate.

♦ Muslims believe it to be the word of God for a variety of reasons, including its own assertions, its literary quality, its scientific insights, distinctive historical factors, and—last but not least—the personal faith of the believer.

Chapter 7

The Koran and the Gospels

In This Chapter

- ◆ Jews and Christians in Islam
- ◆ Textual problems in the Gospels
- ◆ Similarities between a supposed early version of Jesus' message and the Koran

Islam regards the Koran as the culmination of the Judeo-Christian revelation, and refers to Jews and Christians as *People of the Book* or *Followers of the Book*. Islam also lays special emphasis on the importance of the role and ministry of Jesus—he is, for instance, named as the Prophet who will eventually do battle with, and defeat, the army of Satan. This means Muslims expect Jesus to return; this is a belief they share with Christians, although the details of Jesus' role in the final battle against evil are very differently portrayed in the hadith of the Prophet than they are in the Book of Reve-lation. Muslims, of course, hold that the Koran and the Sunna are authoritative sources to resolve these and all other issues, and that the New Testament is no longer an accurate representation of the Gospel of Jesus.

Because the ministry of Jesus is viewed with such deep reverence and respect by Muslims, and because that ministry is also at the center of the dominant Western religion—Christianity—it seems appropriate to examine that Jesus' work closely, and to explore its connections to the message of the Koran.

What the message of the Messiah might have been, then, is the focus of this chapter. We say "might have" because, in all that follows, Muslims would be quick to point out that the New Testament is not regarded in Islam as an authoritative revelation.

What Is the Earliest Gospel?

Muslims believe that the current texts of Christianity are not verbatim representations of the revelation they reflect, but documents that have been altered (or, to use an emotionally loaded term, "corrupted") by fallible human beings over time. In fact, they believe that, unlike the divinely authored and maintained text of the Koran, all the books related to the Prophets who came before Muhammad—including Jesus— have been either lost or changed.

Does what Western textual scholars now know about the original Christian Gospels actually support this idea?

What's It Mean?

In the Koran, the translated phrase *People of the Book* (or *Followers of the Book*) refers to those who have inherited a tradition of divine guidance. The phrases are generally understood to refer to Jews and Christians.

The Word

There are some among the People of the Book who believe in God and what is revealed to you and to them. They are humble before God and do not trade God's revelations for a small price. They will receive their reward from their Lord. God's reckoning is swift. (3:199)

A Textual Challenge

Not only Muslims, but the best non-Muslim scholars, hold that early Christians altered and revised the core materials of the Gospel texts to fit their own theological or evangelical purposes.

Those interested in exploring this possibility should closely examine scholarly works such as Robert J. Miller and Robert W. Funk's excellent *The Complete Gospels: Annotated Scholars' Version* (HarperCollins, 1994).

We should also, perhaps, bear in mind that scholars believe Jesus conducted his ministry in Aramaic, not in Greek. Greek, however, is the language of the traditional Gospels of Christianity. So, it would be remarkable if errors due to translation had not occurred at some point.

Points to Ponder _____

"The New Testament Gospels are complex works of literature that *draw on a variety of oral and written sources of tradition* ... These different formats for preserving and transmitting Jesus traditions *influenced the shape of the [later] New Testament narrative Gospels* ... No manuscripts from the hands of the original authors survive."

—From Miller and Funk's *The Complete Gospels* (emphasis added)

There are literally thousands of differences in wording among the surviving manuscripts of the Gospels. Consider the starkly different provenance of the Koran, which has been retained intact, in the original Arabic, for fourteen centuries, and about which Muslims have no textual disputes whatsoever.

The Koran itself using the divine "We" to reflect the viewpoint of the One God, has this to say on the subject of its authentic and protected status: We Ourselves have revealed the Koran and We are its Protectors. (15:9)

Four Different Versions

In the four traditional Gospels—Matthew, Mark, Luke, and John—we have inherited four differing—and, not infrequently, contradictory—versions of the Messiah's life, miracles, and sayings. They are, the best scholars agree, complicated assemblages of a variety of materials—documents that no doubt evolved as they were passed along from one community of believers to another.

The Source Problem

Even these difficult issues of composition are not the end of the challenges of finding the actual words of Jesus. There are equally frustrating questions of chronology to consider.

Most lay Christians without any scholarly background or interest, if asked when the Gospels were composed, would suggest that they were written in the five or so years immediately following the ministry of Jesus. Certainly this is what the canonical Gospels seem to suggest; all four have the feeling of eyewitness accounts to the events they describe, the feeling of roughly contemporary reports of the ministry of the Messiah.

And yet this feeling of "contemporary-ness" is a literary effect. All four Gospels, as we have seen, are complex compilations that date, in their current forms, from between 70 to 100 C.E. That is at least 40 years after the conclusion of the ministry of the Messiah.

A Present-Day Comparison

The Cuban Missile Crisis took place about 40 years ago. If someone today were to prepare an apparent "eyewitness account" of the events in the White House during the Cuban Missile Crisis, based on his or her own research into the subject and using a variety of sources ... and if that person were then to translate that account into French ... the resulting document might roughly parallel the documentary authority and linguistic reliability of the four canonical Gospels. In evaluating this "eyewitness" account of the decisions of the Kennedy administration in October of 1962, any reader would be justified in asking:

- ◆ What were your primary sources?

- ◆ How close were they in date to the actual events of the early 1960s?

- ◆ How authoritative were those sources?

- ◆ How closely did you adhere to them?

These are, not surprisingly, the same kinds of questions modern scholars of the Gospels ask.

While it's not the purpose of this chapter to answer these questions in any detail as they relate to the Gospels, we think it may be helpful to offer an overview of some of the relevant textual issues, and to suggest some conclusions that we may be able to draw about the Koran and the Gospel message. What we're trying to do is get as close as we can to the original Gospels—by penetrating to what is probably the earliest surviving layer of the Christian oral tradition, and then comparing what that layer says to what the Koran says.

And Now, A Word about Gospel Groups

The four Gospels can be divided into two groups: the synoptics (Mark, Matthew, and Luke, and John). The synoptics (the word is Greek for "same eye") are probably, on the whole, more reflective of the actual sayings of the Messiah than is John, which is heavily influenced by pre-existing Greek traditions and which assigns to Jesus many long monologues, or discourses. Many scholars doubt that these long speeches represent historical sayings.

Turning, then, to the synoptics, we find that Matthew and Luke derive much of their material directly from Mark, which appears to have been compiled before the other two works. This doesn't, however, mean that the earliest material about the Messiah appears in Mark. To learn why this is so, read on.

An Ancient Source

In addition to relying heavily on Mark, the Gospels of Matthew and Luke also relied heavily on at least one other common source: a controversial collection of sayings that some scholars believe predated all four of the now-familiar Gospels.

This early source of the teachings of Jesus, which no longer exists in its original form, is called Q. Some experts believe it can be partially and imperfectly reconstructed by deleting those portions of Luke and Matthew that are known to rely on Mark, and then identifying which passages in Matthew and Luke still agree with each other.

Miller and Funk's *The Complete Gospels* refer to this (now-hypothetical) text as "probably the first Gospel."

> ### Points to Ponder
>
> What matches up between Matthew and Luke (once Mark's influence is removed) is so often in exact verbatim or stylistic agreement that most modern scholars have concluded that the authors of Matthew and Luke copied and inserted large amounts from this original—but now lost—Gospel.
>
> This early Gospel, which may well provide our best perspective on the ministry of the historical Messiah, is today known as Q. The name is derived from the German word for "source," which is "Quelle."

The Koran and Q

Many people are unaware of how many direct parallels there are between this (imperfectly reconstructed) early Christian Gospel and the Koran.

Of interest to Christians is this fact: There is no new doctrine in what follows. There is only confirmation that the words that you are about to read, words that are and have for two millennia been attributed to Jesus, derive not from the end of the first century (when scholars believe the four Gospels were written), but, in all probability, from the *middle* of the first century. In other words, these words are drawn, unlike many other passages in the Gospels, from what is probably the most ancient source of the teachings of the Messiah, and are thus, arguably, closer to the words he actually spoke than many (or perhaps any) other passages in the received Gospels.

Given their remarkable parallels with the Koran, the following Q passages, extracted from the traditional Gospels, may be seen by some as evidence that God's message has indeed been consistent through the centuries on the most important issues: salvation, repentance, and the afterlife.

Muslims hold that the original Gospel—or *Injeel*, has been lost. But both Christians and Muslims are entitled to ask: Did the following themes from Q feature prominently in the actual, historical ministry of Jesus?

Theme #1: Monotheism

The Messiah of Q endorses a rigorous, uncompromising monotheism:

> Get thee behind me, Satan: for it is written, "Thou shalt worship the Lord thy God, and him only shalt thou serve." (Luke 4:8)

Compare those words with this passage from the Koran:

> Children of Adam, did We not command you not to worship Satan? He was your sworn enemy. Did We not command you to worship Me, and tell you that this is the straight path? (36:60–61)

Theme #2: The Right Path

Jesus identifies a path that is often difficult, a path that unbelievers will choose not to follow:

> Enter ye in through the narrow gate. For wide is the gate, and broad is the way that leadeth to destruction, and many there are that who go in there. Narrow is the gate, and narrow is the way, which leadeth unto life, and few there be that find it. (Matthew 7:13–14)

Compare those words with these passages from the Koran:

> The worldly life is made to seem attractive to the disbelievers who scoff at the faithful, but the pious, in the life hereafter, will have a position far above them. God grants sustenance to anyone He wants. (2:212)

> Would that you knew what the uphill path is! It is the setting free of a slave or, in a day of famine, the feeding of an orphaned relative and a downtrodden destitute person, (so that he would join) the believers who cooperate with others in patience, (steadfastness), and kindness. (90:12–17)

Theme #3: Uselessness of Earthly Advantages

Jesus warns any who stray from this straight path set out by God that their priorities are fatally misplaced ... and that what they enjoy in this life will be of little use to them in the next:

> Woe unto you that are rich! For you have received your consolation. Woe unto you who are full! You shall be hungry. Woe unto you who laugh now! You shall weep and mourn. (Luke 6:24)

Compare those words with this passage from the Koran:

> The desire to have increase of worldly gains has preoccupied you so much (that you have neglected the obligation of remembering God)—until you come to your graves! You shall know. You shall certainly know (about the consequences of your deeds). You will certainly have the knowledge of your deeds beyond all doubt. You will be shown hell, and you will see it with your own eyes. Then, on that day, you will be questioned about the bounties (of God). (102:1–8)

Theme #4: Generosity

Jesus preaches a way of life in which one must give generously from what one loves:

> Give to him that asketh thee—and from him that would borrow of thee turn not away. (Matthew 5:42)

Compare those words with this passage from the Koran:

> Spend for the cause of God out of what We have given you—before death approaches you, and say, "Lord, would that you would give me respite for a short time so that I could spend for Your cause and become one of those who do good!" (63:10)

Theme #5: Sound and Unsound Hearts

He reminds humanity that those who do not follow the way of God suffer from a disease of the heart—a disease of their own making.

> A good man out of the good treasure of his heart bringeth forth that which is good; and an evil man bringeth forth out of the evil treasure of his heart that which is evil: for of the abundance of his heart his mouth speaketh. (Luke 6:45)

Compare those words to this passage from the Koran:

> A sickness exists in their hearts to which God adds more sickness. Besides this, they will suffer a painful punishment as a result of the lie which they speak. (2:10)

Theme #6: Judgment by God

He assures his hearers that humans will be evaluated, after death, for their deeds ... and he assures us, at the same time, that the unrighteous will encounter a fate very different than that enjoyed by the righteous.

> Every tree that bringeth not forth good fruit is cut down and cast into the fire. And by their fruits ye shall know them. (Matthew 7:18–19)

Compare those words to this passage from the Koran:

> Consider (Muhammad) how God (in a parable) compares the blessed Word to that of a blessed tree which has firm roots and branches rising up into the sky and yields fruits in every season, by the permission of its Lord. God sets forth parables for people so that they may take heed. An evil word is compared to an evil tree with no firm roots in the land and thus has no stability. (14:24–26)

Theme #7: Carry Out the Will of God

Jesus informs us that reverence of the Messiah himself is not enough to secure salvation. To win that salvation, one must be careful to obey the will of God:

> Not everyone who saith unto me, "Master, Master," shall enter the kingdom of heaven—only he that doeth the will of my Father in heaven. (Matthew 7:21)

Compare those words to this passage from the Koran:

> (Muhammad), say to the People of the Book, "We must come to a common term. Let us worship no one except God, nor consider anything equal to Him, nor regard any of us as our Lord besides God." However, if they turn away from (the Truth), tell them, "Bear witness that we have submitted ourselves to the will of God." (3:64)

Theme #8: God Knows Everything

He assures all that the One God whose will humanity is to follow already knows everything that is in every human breast, and is in fact recording everything:

For there is nothing covered that shall not be revealed, nor hid that shall not be known. (Luke 12:2–3)

Compare those words to this passage from the Koran:

He knows very well whatever they conceal or reveal even when they cover themselves with their garments. God certainly knows the inner-most (secrets) of the hearts. (11:5)

Theme #9: Do Not Fear Earthly Enemies

He instructs humanity not to fear their enemies in this life, but to fear instead him who is Master over death and life and who has the power to cast the soul into hell:

And I say unto you, my friends, Be not afraid of them that kill the body, and after that have no more that they can do. But I will forewarn you whom ye shall fear. Fear Him, which after He hath killed, hath the power to cast into hell. Yea, I say unto you, fear Him! (Luke 12:4–5)

Compare those words to this passage from the Koran:

To Him belongs all that is in the heavens and the earth. God's retribution is severe. Should you then have fear of anyone other than God? (16:52)

Theme #10: Guard Against Evil

He warns humanity plainly to guard against evil, to strive internally for the good, and to prepare for the Last Day:

Now do ye Pharisees make clean the outside of the cup and the platter; but your inward part is full of greed and wickedness. Ye fools! Did not He who made that which is without make that which within also? (Luke 11:39–40)

and ...

Cleanse first that which is within the cup and platter, that the outside may be clean also. (Matthew 23:26)

and again ...

And I say unto you, that many shall come from the east and west, and shall sit down with Abraham, and Isaac, and Jacob, in the kingdom of heaven. But those who believe they own the kingdom of heaven cast out into the outer darkness. There shall be weeping and gnashing of teeth. (Matthew 8:11–12)

Compare those words to this passage from the Koran:

> By the heavens and that (Power) which established them, by the earth and that (Power) which spread it out and by the soul and that (Power) which designed it and inspired it with knowledge of evil and piety, those who purify their souls will certainly have everlasting happiness and those who corrupt their souls will certainly be deprived (of happiness). (91:5–10)

A Starting Point

Q is almost as interesting for what it doesn't contain as for what it does. It not only lacks a resurrection narrative, but it is also missing most of the miracles attributed to Jesus. It should, one can argue, be read closely by all who are interested in the ministry of the Messiah. It is certainly a good starting point for those interested in augmenting their understanding of the narratives presented in the four traditional Gospels.

There is, no doubt, a great deal more to be said about Q, but what has been said here is, perhaps, a responsible starting point for an interfaith discussion about Q and the Koran.

CAUTION

Caution! _____

Q is not identical to the Koran, nor does it represent the "uncorrupted" state of the teachings of Jesus. (Such an uncorrupted version of his revelation, alas, does not exist.)

The Least You Need to Know

- ◆ The Koran teaches that righteous Jews and Christians who submit to the will of Allah may attain salvation.

- ◆ Muslims believe the Koran to be divinely delivered and maintained. They believe that the revelations of Prophets who came before Muhammad, including Jesus, have been lost or corrupted.

- ◆ Q—a hypothetical lost text—may reflect the oldest Gospel of Jesus.

- ◆ A version of Q can be imperfectly reconstructed from the surviving Gospels.

- ◆ There are remarkable points of contact between the Koran and Q that may be of interest to both Christians and Muslims.

The Unique Koran

In This Chapter

- ◆ How the Koran makes God's voice heard
- ◆ The miracle of memorization
- ◆ Arabic as a clear language
- ◆ The Koran's knowledge of scientific facts
- ◆ The unique balance between the spiritual and the pedestrian

The word *unique* means singular—existing as the only one. If the adjective applies to any book on Earth, Muslims believe, it applies to the Koran.

The Koran is regarded by Muslims (as well as by those who know Arabic well and have studied the Koran solely from an academic perspective) not simply as a document, but as a wonder.

The true nature of that wonder is beyond human comprehension, but some of the unique elements associated with this unparalleled volume are worth exploring. In this chapter, you will find a brief discussions of some—but not, by any means, all—of the unique and fascinating things about the Koran that set it apart from the rest of the religious literature of the world.

From God to Muhammad

Muslims believe the Koran to be a word-for-word transcription of the revelation from God to the Prophet. Unlike other religious scriptures, the Koran doesn't take the form of discourse *about* interactions with or opinions concerning God. Islam's revelation takes the form of an extended address *from* God.

The Word

God exists. There is no God but He, the Everlasting and the Guardian of life. Drowsiness or sleep do not seize him. To Him belongs all that is in the heavens and the earth. No one can intercede with Him for others except by His permission. He knows about people's present and past.

No one can grasp anything from His knowledge besides what He has permitted them to grasp. The heavens and the earth are under His dominion. He does not experience fatigue in preserving them both. He is the Highest and the Greatest. (2:255)

The Koran is therefore a *first-person* revelation, and is regarded as the authentic expression of the divine voice of the Almighty. The Koran, Muslims believe, offers a revelation *from the point of view of God himself.* This is very different from most other religious texts. The New Testament, for instance, contains letters, accounts of the life of Jesus, and events from the early church … but it is not presented as a long monologue (or even a series of monologues) delivered by the Almighty. The Koran *does* present itself as the literal word of God. The difference in narrative perspective between the Koran and the scriptures of the other major monotheistic religions remains stark, and has been the cause of much scholarly analysis by non-Muslims.

Caution!

When reading the Koran, don't expect consistency of pronoun usage! As though to undercut any limited conception of the Infinite, the Koran uses a variety of pronouns—"I," "We," "They," and so on—as the point of view from which its message is delivered.

In short, Muslims believe that the Prophet was a transcriber, a spokesman, and that the source of what he transcribed was divine—the final answer to the question "Who is the true God?"

Remember This!

No other major religious text in the world has been memorized in its entirety by as many people as the Koran. The extraordinary tradition of committing the Koran to memory—by people of all ages, social ranks, and levels of intelligence—is regarded as an ongoing miracle by Muslims.

Spotlight on Islam

Despite the fact that it's roughly the length of the New Testament, the Koran is frequently (and with relative ease) memorized and recited by Muslims from all walks of life. While it is quite difficult to memorize the Torah or the Bible, memorization of the Koran is common in Muslim communities, even among children. Believers attribute this phenomenon to divine influence as well as to structural components of the text that make it easy to remember.

The Koran was revealed to Muhammad over a period covering more than two decades. Tradition (hadith) holds that the Prophet encouraged his followers to memorize each verse of the Koran as it was revealed to him, and to make regular recitations of it as a part of scheduled religious services. The Koran, in other words, was memorized in sections as it was revealed (as noted previously, its formal written form wasn't set down until some years after the Prophet's death).

Memorization and recitation of the Koran has been, and remains today, an important part of its role in Islamic life. If, for some strange reason, all existing written copies of the Koran were to be lost or destroyed, the community of believers would be able to reconstruct it quickly, with total accuracy, syllable for syllable.

It's Settled

Unlike the revered texts of Judaism and Christianity, which feature a seemingly endless number of scholarly debates over the proper sequence, authenticity, and authority of garbled or incomplete phrases (see Chapter 7), the Koran is virtually free of debates over its content. Its text is settled and has been regarded as definitive since the seventh century C.E.

One of the copies of the Koran circulated by the *Caliph* Uthman, who formed the committee that oversaw the Koran's transition to a single volume format following the death of the Prophet, is still in existence. This copy, which is currently preserved in the Museum of the City of Tashkent in Uzbekistan, offers

Points to Ponder

It seems reasonably well established that no material changes were introduced and that the original form of [the Prophet's] discourses were preserved with scrupulous precision.

—H.A.R. Gibb in his book *Mohammedism* (Oxford University Press, 1969)

What's It Mean?

A **Caliph** is a successor to the Prophet Muhammad (as leader of Islam). For many years the caliphate was a powerful institution; it was abolished in the 1920s, following the eclipse of the Ottoman Empire, which had co-opted it in the sixteenth century.

a text that is identical to modern editions of the Koran. There is an identical surviving copy of this edition of the Koran in Turkey, as well. (The committee formed by Caliph Uthman to formalize the Koran's written, rather than spoken, version, was headed by Zaid ibn Thabit, one of the Prophet's scribes.)

The extraordinary revelation received by Muhammad has been faithfully preserved. Its preservation stands in sharp contrast to the still-debated texts of the other major religions.

Holy Words, Holy Text

As noted previously, because it is regarded as the verbatim, word-for-word message of God Almighty, the Koran is, when translated into another language, no longer the Koran. Only the original Arabic text is regarded as divinely inspired. All translations are seen as commentaries, explanatory works undertaken from a single, limited point of view. Translations of the Koran may be helpful, and are often worthy of praise and admiration. But they are not to be confused with the divine revelation itself.

Spotlight on Islam

The Koran is the only holy text of a major religion that claims to consist entirely of the word of God as spoken by God. It is also the only received holy text that invites learned people to verify the authenticity of its contents.

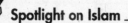

Caution!

All the English-language extracts from the Koran that appear in this book are, of course, translations—and not the actual revelation received in Arabic by the Prophet.

On a similar note, it is important to remember that Muslims regard the Arabic text itself as holy. A Christian may regard, say, the Gospel of Mark as a *record* of holy events and experiences critical to his or her faith, but he or she is unlikely to view the surviving Greek manuscripts of Mark as worthy of special religious reverence. A Muslim, however, is likely to think of the Koran in its Arabic form as a living force, as a dynamic expression of God's will—and not as a static "document." The words themselves are a mercy from the Lord:

> People, good advice has come to you from your Lord a (spiritual) cure for the disease of the hearts, a guide and a mercy for the believers. (10:57)

To gain a direct connection with the actual text of the Koran, it is necessary to read it in Arabic! For people who don't read Arabic, however, translations of the Koran allow them to begin to understand the distinctive ideas in the book.

Points to Ponder

If you decide you want to try reading the Koran in its original Arabic, you're in luck: There's a sampling of Internet resources for learning the Arabic of the Koran:

◆ Astrolabe Islamic Media
www.astrolabepictures.com/learnarabic.html

◆ Learn Quran
www.fortunecity.com/victorian/cloisters/384

◆ Quran Learning Tools
www.soundvision.com/info/quran/learningtools.asp

◆ Arab Academy (online Arabic courses)
www.arabacademy.com

For more Internet resources on the Koran and Islam, check out Chapter 21.

"Biblical" Passages (That Don't Appear in the Bible)

The Koran offers some intriguing details about figures and events related to the Old and New Testaments … information that doesn't appear in the scriptures of the Jewish or Christian religious traditions. The Koran offers, for instance, a pre-flood exchange between Noah and his son (11:42–43). This exchange doesn't appear in the book of Genesis.

For a fuller discussion of this fascinating material, see Chapter 5.

Scientific and Historical Information

The Koran features many passages that display a depth of understanding that simply cannot be explained as arising from the human store of knowledge in seventh-century Arabia.

For example, the Koran displays mastery of scientific principles that "shouldn't" have been available to anyone at the time of its delivery to the Prophet. Here are just a few examples of passages that have ignited fascinated discussion around the world by Muslims and non-Muslims alike:

◆ **The Big Bang:** The Koran parallels modern theories of the beginning of the universe in this passage:

Have the unbelievers not ever considered that the heavens and the earth were one piece and that We tore them apart from one another. From water We have created all living things. Will they then have no faith? (21:30)

The reference to the earth and the heavens—or "skies," as it is rendered in some translations—simply reflects the idea that the earth and all of its surroundings had a common origin. This is precisely the view of proponents of the Big Bang, who argue that there was a point in time when all forces in the universe occupied the same physical position—before the "symmetry breaking" between forces and particles that caused the explosion known as the Big Bang. This process may indeed be described as a great "tearing apart" (or "separating," as an alternate translation has it) of heaven and Earth.

The idea of multiple worlds arising from this opening, separation, or splitting-off is repeated dozens of times in the Koran.

A parallel has also been made to the Koran's frequent references to the Last Day and the phenomenon physicists describe as the Big Crunch, a scenario in which space-time, pockmarked with black holes, simply collapses.

Finally, notice that this extraordinary verse makes direct reference to the fact that life on Earth is water-based … a scientific discovery that lay centuries in the future at the time the Koran was first revealed.

◆ **Spherical planets traveling in orbits:** Predating the conclusions of scientists by centuries, the Koran speaks of spherical planets traveling in orbits:

> It is God who has created the night, the day, the Sun, and Moon and has made them swim in a certain orbit. (21:33)

Scientists now know that the sun travels a course through the universe, just as the planets do. At the time the Koran was delivered to the Prophet, the astronomical knowledge necessary to support theories of orbital motion was nonexistent.

◆ **Hydrology:** The idea that rainwater feeds underground lakes and springs may seem natural and obvious today, but only because we have been taught this from childhood. Prior to the sixteenth century, the prevailing belief was that the water of the oceans was somehow pushed within the physical borders of the continents, and flushed away again via a "great abyss" known as the Tartarus. And yet in the Koran we read:

> Have you not seen that God has sent down water from the sky and made it flow as springs out of the earth? He makes crops of different colors grow with this water and flourish, which then turn yellow and wither away. In this there is a reminder for the people of understanding. (39:21)

◆ **Geological structure:** A very recent addition to our geological knowledge has to do with the process known as "folding," which produced mountain ranges—and mountains with foundations far deeper than had been previously imagined.

This discovery has made famous a previously obscure passage in the Koran comparing mountains to the deeply imbedded pegs of tents, which corresponds to what we now know about the deep foundations of mountains:

> Have We not made the earth as a place to rest and the mountains as pegs (to anchor the earth)? (78:6–7)

♦ **The aquatic origin of life:** It is now accepted that life evolved originally from the seas, an idea that could hardly have originated among nomadic Arabian tribesmen of the seventh century. And yet the Koran explains the origin of life in this way:

> Have the unbelievers not ever considered that the heavens and the earth were one piece and that We tore them apart from one another. From water We have created all living things. Will they then have no faith? (21:30)

♦ **Principles of botany:** The science of botany was in no way advanced enough at the time of the Prophet to have concluded that plants have gender traits. But in the Koran we are told:

> He made a pair of every fruit and made the night cover the day ... (13:3)

♦ **Human embryology:** Most of us couldn't break down the sequence of development of the human fetus, but we are certainly aware that the fetus exists within the womb. This fact wasn't so clear to the people of the seventh century, who had developed a litany of superstitions and fables to explain the process of human development and birth. Yet the Koran speaks unmistakably of a human ovum attaching itself to the uterine wall, and of the processes of fetal development:

> He created man from a clot of blood. (96:2)

And ...

> The living germ, then, was turned into a shapeless lump of flesh from which bones were formed. The bones, then, were covered with flesh. At this stage, We caused it to become another creature. All blessings belong to God, the best Creator. (23:14)

The phrase "shapeless lump of flesh" is a strikingly accurate description of the embryo in its early stages of development. The phrase "covered with flesh" appears to refer to muscle development.

Points to Ponder

The Koran also provides historical details that weren't known to people during the time of Muhammad. For example, it mentions (89:7) a long-mysterious city known as Iram (or Aram). The passage seemed ambiguous for centuries, and some Muslims theorized that perhaps the passage referred to an individual, and not to a city—despite the fact that the text attributed to Iram "lofty buildings, the like of which were not created in (the other) cities."(89:7)

No historian was persuaded of the existence of the real-life city of Iram before tablets confirming its existence were excavated in present-day Syria in 1973. The story of the excavation of these records, which confirmed that the people of the ancient city of Ebla traded with those of Iram, is reported in detail in the December, 1978 issue of *National Geographic.*

This is just one of many fascinating examples of information appearing in the Koran that, logically, shouldn't appear in any document dating from the seventh century C.E.

By the Numbers

The Koran includes a number of mind-boggling statistical phenomena. Here's a condensed summary of a few of the simplest ones:

The Koran mentions (in Arabic, of course) …

- The word "month" exactly 12 times.

- The word "days" exactly 30 times.

- The word "prayer" exactly 5 times. (Muslims are required to pray five times a day.)

- The words "life" and "death" an equal number of times (145 and 145).

- The words "angels" and "devils" an equal number of times (88 and 88).

- The words "man" and "woman" an equal number of times (24 and 24).

Harmony Between the Divine and the Human

Finally, Muslims believe that the Koran's remarkable balance between the spiritual and material worlds sets it apart from any other book ever composed. It focuses on the Almighty's spiritual plan for humanity (by offering instructions related to prayer, pilgrimage, purification, and so on), without ever losing sight of the practical details necessary for human beings to live together peaceably here on earth, today. (For instance, the Koran offers guidance on the establishment of contracts, on the inheritance of property, on taxation to support the poor, and on many other matters of public law and administration.)

It is seen as the perfect plan for both personal spiritual growth and harmonious living among believers, and it is considered to be as relevant today as the day it was first spoken.

Muslims and others who have studied the Koran in Arabic believe that there has never been a book like the Koran, and there never can be.

The Least You Need to Know

◆ The Koran is set apart from other religious scriptures in many intriguing ways.

◆ The sequence and identity of the text itself has been settled since the seventh century.

◆ The Koran has a long tradition of being memorized by Muslims from all walks of life, despite its length.

◆ The Koran appears to possess scientific and historical information that doesn't correspond to the state of scholarship of seventh-century Arabia.

◆ The Koran offers a distinctive balance between the human and the divine.

Part  3

Allah and Humanity

The image of God in the Koran is that of a merciful Creator—and a Creator who is, at the same time, fair and just to humankind.

This part presents an overview of God's relationship to—and message for—humankind, as described in the Koran.

9

Your God Is One God: Islam's Monotheism

In This Chapter

- ♦ The Koran's distinctive emphasis on monotheism
- ♦ Why the Koran denies the Trinity of Christianity
- ♦ Belief in Allah is the first step in the faith
- ♦ Muhammad's status in the sight of Allah
- ♦ Submission before Allah, the One God

No core religious text in human history focuses as relentlessly and as eloquently on the notion of humanity's call to monotheism—a single True God—as does the Koran.

There are, scholars believe, threads of ancient polytheistic (many-god) traditions remaining in parts of the Judeo-Christian scriptures (such as the book of Genesis), even though both Judaism and Christianity embrace the notion of a single God. There are countless, vivid accounts of the many and varying expressions of the Divine within the staggeringly diverse Hindu tradition. And there are many (often logically confounding) hints that Buddhism rejects the notion of a (separate) God altogether.

A Distinctive Emphasis on Monotheism

Among the major faiths—or any faith, for that matter—Islam stands alone in its consistent, unambiguous, and purposeful setting-out of the principle that a single God exists, a God who can have no associates, and who calls upon humanity to acknowledge him.

This principle is one of the foundations of the faith, and is one half of Islam's famous profession: "There is no God but God, and Muhammad is His Messenger."

The Koran in many places urges its readers and hearers to use their powers of reason. In doing so, they are led to the inevitable conclusion that God, the Creator, can only be One, almighty, ever-living and Omniscient. The Koran states this all-important core idea hundreds of times and in hundreds of different ways. In this chapter, you'll get a brief sampling of the Koran's rigorous and unapologetic teachings on monotheism, its rejection of polytheistic practices, and the eloquence of its insistence on belief in a single God as an article of faith.

> **Points to Ponder**
>
> In Genesis 3:22, we read that God reacts to the disobedience of Adam and Eve with these words: "Behold, the man is become as one of us, to know good and evil." Scholars believe that this line may reflect an ancient polytheistic (many-god) tradition that remains within the creation story. The Koran, too, uses "we" language for the Almighty—but its Arabic form is closer to that of the "royal we" in English. (Think of Queen Victoria's "We are not amused.")

No Associates

The idea of making an "associate" with Allah—and thereby committing the sin of shirk—can be thought of in three ways:

- **Assigning one of Allah's creations the status of a partner in Allah's being.** In other words, saying that someone or something is a co-equal with Allah—which Muslims regard as an absurd idea on the face of it. How could a limited creation control and sustain the universe?

- **Assigning one of Allah's creations status as a partner in worship.** Only Allah deserves to be worshipped.

- **Assigning one of Allah's creation status as a partner in his deeds.** None of Allah's creations engage in his deeds, such as providing sustenance to any part of creation; this is Allah's action alone.

No Trinity

Conventional Christianity promotes Jesus as the Son of God, thereby violating the believer's duty not to associate anything with Allah. The Messiah is portrayed in the Koran, however, as a Prophet who submits utterly to Allah—without having any such association. (The Koran includes a dialogue between Allah and Jesus in which Jesus explicitly rejects ever having instructed people to worship him or his mother.)

In the Koran, the classical Trinity of Christianity—recognizing God as Father, Son, and Holy Ghost—is considered a form of polytheism:

> Those who say that God is the third of the Three, have, in fact, turned to disbelief. There is no Lord but God, the only One Lord. If they will not give-up such belief, the disbelievers among them will suffer a painful torment. (5:73)

The starkly differing views of Jesus offered by the Koran and by Christians have, of course, been the subject of much discussion over the years.

Spotlight on Islam

The Koran's message regarding the central figure of Christianity is clear: There is no god but Allah, and those who consider humans to be associates of Allah have made a serious mistake. We must recall, however, that Jesus is remembered and hailed as a great Prophet within the Islamic tradition, a Prophet who received special favor from Allah. Consider the following passage from the second Sura of the Koran:

> We gave the Book to Moses and made the Messengers follow in his path. To Jesus, the son of Mary, We gave the miracles and supported him by the Holy Spirit. Why do you arrogantly belie some Messengers and murder others whenever they have brought you messages that you dislike? (2:87)

To learn more about the Islamic view of Jesus, see Chapter 7.

No False Gods

Those who have associated false gods with Allah, we read in the Koran, will find them of little help on the Last Day. In the tenth Sura, *Yunus*, we read of the fatal error of those who promote other gods beside Allah, and of the bitter disappointment they will receive at the final reckoning:

The Word

False gods, the Koran reminds us repeatedly, will be of little aid on the Last Day.

They will be told to call their idols. They will call them but will receive no answer. They will see the torment approaching and wish that they had sought guidance. (28:64)

We will tell the pagans on the day when every one is resurrected, "Stand with your idols wherever you are." Then We will separate them (from their idols) and their idols will protest against them saying, "You did not worship us. God is Sufficient Witness for us that we were not aware of your worship." (10:28–29)

The practice of associating partners with Allah in worship is, as we have seen, known as shirk in Islam. It is portrayed over and over again within the Koran as a grievous sin. Humans who commit shirk do so at the peril of their own souls.

Allah's Unchallengeable Oneness

The Koran offers a wealth of instruction on a vast number of topics in human relations—but the guiding principle behind all of these teachings is that of obedience to the One God, Allah, and to no one or nothing else.

Many passages speak of the importance of acknowledging Allah's unique role once a believer has encountered it. Other passages—and there are many of these—speak of the fact that it is due to Allah's Oneness that he is kind and merciful toward humanity. An excellent example of this kind of passage comes from the well-known (and lengthy!) second Sura, *The Cow:*

> Our Lord is the only Lord. There is no God but He, the Beneficent and Merciful. (2:163)

The Word

The pronouns may shift, but Allah's message—that there is One God—remains clear in the following passage:

(Muhammad), say, "This is (the Quran) which tells us about the (beliefs of the people) in my time and those who lived before me." Most of them do not know. Moreover, the truth is that they neglect (the question of belief altogether).

To all the Messengers that were sent before you We revealed that I am the only God to be worshipped. (21:24–25)

In the same Sura, we find instruction on how to respond to the efforts of those who attempt to convert followers of Islam to other faiths. Here, as elsewhere in the Koran, explicit instruction is offered on what to say in response to outsiders; in this case, the emphasis is on the submission to the One God pursued by Abraham. At the same time, the Koran makes clear the importance of believers' rejecting of Judaism and Christianity (whose original message of salvation is considered to be corrupted):

> The Jews and the Christians have asked the Muslims to accept their faith to have the right guidance. (Muhammad) tell them, "We would rather follow the upright religion of Abraham, who was not a pagan." (2:135)

Non-Muslims often ask: How can Islam claim to be a tolerant religion when it explicitly rejects the option of following Judaism and Christianity? The answer is pretty simple. The Koran is held to outline a final and uncorrupted revelation; it holds its followers accountable to obedience to that revelation. At the same time, the faith does not permit its followers to engage in any form of religious compulsion or persecution. (A famous passage from the Sura 109, entitled *The Unbelievers*, reads, "To you be your religion, and to me mine.")

What's It Mean?

Hanif means "true in faith."

Allah, the Only God, as All-Seeing Sustainer of Creation

The Koran presents its reader with a picture of a single, eternal God who supports the entire structure of Creation:

> God exists. He is the only Lord, the Everlasting and the Guardian of life. (3:2)

Nothing is hidden from, or obscure to, this all-seeing, all-creating God:

> Nothing in the heavens or the earth is hidden from God.

> It is God who shapes you in the wombs as He wills. He is the only Lord, the Majestic, and All-wise. (3:5–6)

These are only two of the Koran's many, many references to Allah's infinite knowledge and the sustaining role due to his power. He plays in Creation seen and unseen. The two themes recur frequently throughout the book, as does the revelation that Allah is, in the end, utterly beyond the comprehension of human beings.

Allah, the Only God, as King of the Last Day

With an eloquence and passion that defy translation, the Koran warns humanity to avoid serving false gods, and to reject them in favor of Allah, the One True God, who will judge them on the Day of Judgment. This is a day whose consequences (for unbelievers) will be both horrifying and unending.

God has sent a message about the consequences of disbelief to all of his Prophets, including Noah, as the following passages indicate:

> We sent Noah to his people. He told them, "Worship God for He is your only Lord. I am afraid of the punishment that you might suffer on the great Day (of Judgment)" (7:59)

> Everyone in the heavens and earth will be terrified on the day when the trumpet will be sounded except those whom God will save. Everyone will humbly come into the presence of God. (27:87)

For a more in-depth discussion of the consequences of unbelief, see Chapter 12.

Allah, the Only God, as Selector of the Final Prophet

Allah's status as One True God, the Koran tells us, is announced unambiguously through the Prophet Muhammad, to whom God's exact words were delivered. In the following passage, he instructs Muhammad on how to deliver his message:

> (Muhammad), tell them, "People, I have come to you all as the Messenger of God, to whom the Kingdom of the heavens and the earth belongs. There is no God but He. In His hands are life and death. Have faith in God and His Messenger, the unlettered Prophet who believes in God and His words. Follow him so that you will perhaps have guidance." (7:158)

There are many passages in which Allah instructs Muhammad in the nature of his role in relaying his message of monotheism. These passages often suggest that the Prophet was deeply grieved at the fate of those who rejected his message. A good example appears in the eleventh Sura, *Hud*:

> Perhaps you, (Muhammad), may by chance leave (untold) a part of that which is revealed to you and feel grieved because they say, "Why has some treasure not been sent to him or an angel sent down with him?" Say, "I have come only to warn you." God is the Guardian of all things. (11:12)

Allah, the Only God, as Deliverer of the Believers

The Koran reminds us repeatedly that troubles in this world are transitory, while the rewards of the world to come reserved for believers in the One True God are eternal. The Koran instructs each believer to pay attention unceasingly to the One God in order to attain salvation:

> (Muhammad), say, "My prayer, sacrifice, life, and death are all for God, the Lord of the Universe.
>
> Nothing is equal to Him. Thus are the commandments which I have received and he is the first Muslim (submitted to the will of God)." (Muhammad), tell them, "Should I take a lord besides God when He is the Lord of all things?" All one's evil deeds are against one's own soul. No one will be considered responsible for another's sins. You will all be returned to your Lord who will tell you what is right and wrong in disputed matters among you. (6:162–164)

Allah, the Only Being Worthy of Worship

The One God's inscrutable, pervasive, and all-illuminating nature is the subject of a particularly famous passage, one that has set the hearts of believers glowing for thirteen centuries:

> God is the light of the heavens and the earth. A metaphor for His light is a niche in which there is a lamp placed in a glass. The glass is like a shining star which is lit from a blessed olive tree that is neither eastern nor western. Its oil almost lights up even though it has not been touched by the fire. It is light upon light. God guides to His light whomever He wants. God uses various metaphors. He has the knowledge of all things. (24:35)

A similar sense of wonder pervades the brief Sura 112, which is reproduced below in its entirety:

> (Muhammad), say, "He is the only God. God is Absolute. He neither begets nor was He begotten. There is no one equal to Him." (112:1–4)

At one time, the Prophet Muhammad once described this famous Sura as "one-third of the Koran." On another occasion, he held that it supported the heavens and the earth. This much-quoted Sura is perhaps the most direct and powerful expression of the Islamic belief in *Tawhid*.

What's It Mean?

Tawhid means the oneness or singularity of God. To reject it is to reject Islam.

The Least You Need to Know

- ◆ The Koran teaches that Allah is the only God, and that there is no god besides him.

- ◆ Islam features a distinctive, rigorous emphasis on monotheism that sets it apart from the other faiths of the world.

- ◆ The Koran's emphasis on Allah's singularity takes many forms.

- ◆ The Koran instructs believers to pay attention constantly to Allah, to reject associates or partners with him, and to submit to him.

- ◆ Allah, who is beyond human comprehension, is frequently presented as the only being deserving to be worshipped in the Koran.

10

Glory Be to Thee: Submission to Allah

In This Chapter

◆ Remembering Allah often

◆ The power of belief

◆ Repentance and forgiveness

◆ The necessity of good works

In the last chapter, you encountered some of the Koran's teachings concerning acceptance of Allah as the One and only God. The act of submission to the One God, Allah, gives Islam its primary focus (and its name—which, as we have seen, means "submission").

In this chapter, you will learn what the Koran has to say about four important principles very closely related to this submission to Allah and the Islamic faith.

Four Principles

Four principles related to the submission to Allah are ...

◆ Remembering Allah often.

◆ Belief in and adherence to the teachings of Allah's prophets.

◆ Repentance in order to receive Allah's forgiveness.

◆ Performing good works, as instructed by Allah.

Let's examine each in turn.

Remembering Allah Often

The Koran reminds believers to remember or speak of Allah very often, and under all conditions. This is necessary for the survival of one's belief in him. Without it one's belief in Allah will recede.

The Koran emphasizes that remembrance of Allah must be a constant feature of one's daily life:

> To God belongs all that is in the heavens and the earth and He has power over all things. The creation of the heavens and the earth and the alternation of the day and the night are evidence (of the existence of God) for people of reason. It is these who commemorate God while standing, sitting, or resting on their sides and who think about the creation of the heavens and the earth and say, "Lord, you have not created all this without reason. Glory be to you. Lord, save us from the torment of the fire." (3:189–191)

Required patterns of prayer and observance are clearly laid out within the Islamic tradition (see Chapter 13 for more on these). At the same time, however, believers are instructed in the Koran that remembering Allah very often in one's everyday life, and not merely the performance of external rituals of worship, is what matters most.

Notice how, in the following passage, the practice of remembering Allah often is *not* restricted to the weekly communal gathering:

> Believers, on Friday when the call for prayer is made, try to attend prayer (remembering God) and leave off all business. This would be better for you if only you knew it. When the prayer ends, disperse through the land and seek the favor of God. Remember Him often so that perhaps you will have everlasting happiness. (62:9–10)

Remembrance of Allah is clearly linked to Allah's remembrance of the individual believer. The following passage from the second Sura, *The Cow*, offers an example:

> ... (R)emember Me and I shall remember you. Thank Me and do not hide the truth about Me. (2:152)

The Gift of Dhikr

The Arabic word for remembrance of Allah is *dhikr*. This remembrance can take a number of forms; the most common is the repetition of phrases praising Allah (such as "alhamdulillah," which means "All praise is due to Allah").

Islamic teaching holds that dhikr carries great spiritual benefits, and that it may be performed during everyday activities (such as driving an automobile or sewing a piece of clothing). No special preparation is necessary.

Muslims believe that one who keeps dhikr in his heart, and transcends the attachments of worldly life, is one who has followed the example and instruction of the Prophet.

And while we're on the subject of Muhammad, the Final Prophet, it's appropriate to recall the importance of …

Belief in the Teachings of Allah's Prophets

The Koran instructs that belief in Allah entails belief in the teachings of his Prophets, a series of messengers extending through most of human history from Adam to Muhammad. These teachings, Muslims believe, are founded on three basic ideas that have remained consistent down through the centuries:

◆ God's authority is unchallengeable.

◆ Each human being is personally accountable for his or her deeds.

◆ Earthly life is transient. It will pass, and in the afterlife we will be judged on how we dealt with the tests we encountered during this life.

This, the Koran tells us, is Islam. It is not new. It did not originate with Muhammad. Failure to submit to the will of Allah by accepting this three-part message of his Prophets, the Koran warns, will carry dire consequences:

> Every soul will be recompensed for its deeds. God knows best whatever they have done. The disbelievers will be driven to hell in hordes. Its gates will be opened when they are brought nearby and the keepers will ask them, "Did Messengers from your own people not come to you to recite your Lord's revelations and to warn you about this day?" They will reply, "Yes, the Messengers did come to us, but the unbelievers were doomed to face the torment." (39:70–71)

Waverers who know better but opt to turn their backs on Allah's Prophets are to be denied salvation.

> Believers, have faith in God and His Messenger, the Book which is revealed to him, and the Bible which has been revealed before. Whoever refuses to believe in God, His angels, Books, Messengers and the Day of Judgment, has gone far away from the right path. God will not forgive or guide to the right path those who first believe, then disbelieve, again believe and disbelieve, and then increase their disbelief. (4:136–137)

The Word

In the Koran, Allah promises deliverance to believers, and urges them all to accept those to whom he has imparted his message:

> Allah left the believers in their existing state for no other reason than to distinguish the evil-doers from the virtuous ones. Allah does not inform you of the unseen. He chooses for such information anyone of His Messengers that He wants. Have faith in Allah and in His Messengers. If you have faith and are pious, there will be a great reward for you. (3:179)

Repentance in Order to Receive the Forgiveness of Allah

Allah, the Koran teaches, demands repentance from those who submit to him. Believers must turn away from sin, and earnestly seek forgiveness.

One's thoughts and feelings, not merely one's outward actions, are subject to scrutiny:

> God will call you to account for all that you may reveal from your souls and all that you may conceal. God will forgive or punish whomever He wants. God has power over all things. (2:284)

True repentance, the Koran tells us, is followed by divine mercy of a kind that surpasses human comprehension.

Indeed, to repent (that is, to become regretful, to sincerely resolve not to commit the sinful act and to ask Allah for forgiveness) is an essential expression of one's faith, or iman. And yet repentance does not free one from obligations arising from one's actions. If one steals, one has an obligation to reimburse those from whom one stolen, even though one may be sincerely remorseful for ones actions.

What's more, repentance is never to be used as some kind of legalistic defense against Allah's justice. It must follow immediately after one realizes one has sinned, it must be sincere, and it must result in positive change in one's life. God will only accept the repentance of those who commit evil in ignorance, if they repent immediately:

> ![CAUTION] **Caution!**
>
> The Koran insists on a variety of repentance that rejects all sins (2:284). Believers must be ever watchful!

God is All-knowing and All-wise. There is no forgiveness for those who commit sin and do not repent until the last moment of their lives nor for those who die as unbelievers. For these people We have prepared a painful torment. (4:17–18)

Spotlight on Islam

One of the most fascinating aspects of the Koran is its reference to the existence of angels and jinn.

Angels are creatures who do not commit any sins. Like human beings, they receive sustenance and life from Allah, but their bodies are very different from those of human beings. (For one thing, they have wings; for another, they are almost always invisible to humans.) The most important angel is Gabriel, or Jibril, whose appearance before Muhammad is of central importance to the Islamic faith.

Angels, Muslims believe, are created by Allah. They serve as messengers between the realms of heaven and Earth; they also carry out many other tasks by the command of Allah.

On Earth, Islam holds, there are human beings, demons (shaitans), and the jinn—invisible beings created from fire who, like humans, have the capacity to choose between good and evil. And like human beings, the jinn will be held accountable for their actions on the Day of Judgment.

Performance of Good Works

Submission to Allah is an inherently generous thing. The Koran warns that eternal punishment will be meted out to those who encourage uncharitable ways of living, as well as to those whose generosity is not genuine, but merely for show.

Belief in Allah, in other words, must not merely be a matter of spoken words, or vain display, but must take the form of actions that spread mercy and kindness. Belief must be accompanied by selfless generosity; to fail in this is not only to disbelieve, but to become an associate of Satan!

Consider, as just one of many possible examples, the following passage:

God does not love the proud and boastful ones, the stingy ones who try to make others stingy, or those who hide the favors that God has bestowed on them. We have prepared a humiliating torment for the disbelievers, those who spend their property out of a desire to show off and not because of their belief in God and the Day of Judgment, and (lastly) those who choose Satan for a friend; what an evil friend! How could it have harmed them if they had believed in God and the Last Day and spent their property for the cause of God? God knows them very well. (4:36–39)

Those who perform acts of generosity shall, the Koran promises, find themselves surrounded by far greater gifts in return. The performance of good works is clearly defined as a duty to the Lord—and, above and beyond that duty, there are optional activities for attaining "extra credit" with Allah.

Those who seek after righteousness are given a clear formula for obtaining it—the distribution of that which is dearest to them:

> You can never have extended virtue and righteousness unless you spend part of what you dearly love for the cause of God. God knows very well whatever you spend for His cause. (3:92)

The Koran's specific instructions about charity are discussed in Chapter 15.

In Search of the True Way of Submission to Allah

There are many, many other examples of the ways in which the Koran instructs humanity to submit to Allah.

A good starting point, however, may be found in the Koran's stirring teachings on four critical points.

- The first is remembering him very often and in all things.

- The second is believing in him and his Prophets.

- The third is repenting with a true repentance in order to receive his forgiveness.

- And the fourth is performing good works as he has instructed, and giving generously from what we love.

The Least You Need to Know

- The Koran teaches that Allah must be often and in all things.

- The Koran teaches the necessity of believing in Allah and his Prophets.

- The Koran teaches that believers must repent to receive Allah's forgiveness.

- The Koran insists that believers perform good works, giving generously from what they love.

Therefore Serve Him: Hallmarks of Belief

In This Chapter

◆ Believers are the recipients of Allah's love

◆ They are grateful to him

◆ They are patient

◆ They are righteous

How can you spot a believer?

Certain hallmarks of Islamic belief distinguish believers from unbelievers. The Koran offers hundreds of such distinctions. In this chapter you'll learn some of what the Koran has to say about how to recognize someone who submits to Allah.

Fear, Generosity, and Faith

A famous passage in the eighth Sura offers a memorable portrait that captures some of the most essential characteristics of believers:

When God is mentioned, the true believers begin to feel fear of Him in their hearts and when His revelations are recited to them their faith strengthens. In God alone do they trust. They are steadfast in prayer and spend part of what We have given them for the cause of God. Such are the true believers. Their reward from their Lord will be high ranks, forgiveness, and a generous provision. (8:2–4)

As this passage suggests, fear of Allah, generosity, and faith are among the most important hallmarks of believers in the faith system that is Islam.

By the way, don't be misled by the use of the word "fear" in the Koran in reference to Allah. This is not, in any way, the fear one might feels before an abusive boss, or a power-hungry public official, or a tyrant. This kind of fear is a deep concern for the status of one's own relationship to Allah, a concern that arises from what one knows about one's own weaknesses and shortcomings.

There are many other characteristics of believers to consider, as well. One of the most important has to do with Allah's love.

Believers Know They're Loved

The Koran tells us repeatedly, and without any ambiguity, that Allah *loves* those who believe in him and follow his instructions. And those who read the Koran and follow its guidance consider it to be ample proof of Allah's love for those who do as he wishes. Allah's love is of paramount importance in Islam.

This hallmark of belief is often overlooked by those who are not familiar with the faith, or by those who have been led to believe that Muslims worship a God who is hostile, uncaring, and harsh. Nothing, the Koran insists, could be further from the truth. (For more on this topic, see Chapter 17.)

The Word

Allah instructs his Prophet: (Muhammad), tell them, "If you love God, follow me. God will love you and forgive your sins. God is All-forgiving and All-merciful." (3:31)

Allah also brings his unfathomable love into the lives of all who follow him devoutly and follow his command to perform good works:

To the righteously striving believers God will grant love. (19:96)

He shines his love upon all those who choose righteousness and turn away from sin:

Give money for the cause of God but do not push yourselves into perdition. Do good; God loves the people who do good deeds. (2:195)

Allah's love is bountiful to those believers who maintain their word and root out all tendencies toward disbelief:

> Those who keep their promise and observe piety should know that God certainly loves the pious ones. (3:76)

He loves those who labor tirelessly on his behalf and show resiliency of spirit:

> Many godly people fought to help the Prophets in the cause of God. They did not lose courage, show weakness, or give in when facing hardships in their fight for the cause of God. God loves those who have patience. (3:146)

The Koran also teaches that Allah's love is extended amply to those who spend their wealth in charitable causes, and to those who both receive forgiveness and grant it freely. In this simultaneous emphasis on obtaining forgiveness and forgiving others, the Koran presages the famous prayer of St. Francis of Assisi: "It is in forgiving that we are forgiven."

Believers Give Thanks

Those who believe in Allah and follow his instructions show gratitude for the Creation he has brought into existence. They are humbled to show thankfulness for Allah's Creation in all situations:

> Blessed is He who has established constellations in the sky and made therein a lamp and a shining moon. It is He who has made the night and the day, one proceeding the other, for whoever wants to take heed or give thanks. (Among) the servants of the Beneficent God are those who walk gently on the earth and when addressed by the ignorant ones, their only response is, "Peace be with you." They are those who spend the night worshipping their Lord, prostrating, and standing. (25:61–64)

Believers, we read, are those who follow the example of the Prophet Solomon—a man who, the Koran tells us, prayed with deep gratitude in the following words:

> Lord, inspire me to thank you for Your favors to me and my parents and to act righteously so as to please you. Admit me, by your mercy into the company of Your righteous servants. (27:19)

Believers set themselves apart from those who are ungrateful, and they know that Allah sees whether or not there is gratitude in their hearts:

If you disbelieve, know that God is certainly independent of you. He does not want disbelief for His servants. If you give thanks, He will accept it from you. No one will be responsible for the sins of others. To your Lord you will all return and He will tell you about what you have done. He knows best what the hearts contain. (39:7)

Believers, the Koran instructs, go out of their way to extend the greatest glory and honor to him whom they consider to have brought about their world, their sustenance, and their very existence, all of which are signs of Allah's guiding hand and abundant gifts. And that's not all. Believers accept with thankfulness his signs and his guiding role in all events:

Further evidence (of His existence) are the ships which stand as mountains in the sea. Had He wanted, He could have stopped the wind and let the ships remain motionless on the surface of the sea, in this there is evidence (of the Truth) for all those who are patient and grateful. (42:32–33)

Exactly what kind of evidence, you may ask, do ships on the sea constitute? What about that phenomenon makes one grateful? Here, the Koran challenges you to figure out exactly what it's getting at.

The Koran contains many such passages, in which believers are asked to study evidence, such as the transition of day to night and back to day again, or the fact that species propagate themselves in pairs, or the fact that ships on the sea move only when wind blows them. These, the Koran tells us, are the signs of Allah: the order and processes of the natural world he has created. In the passage about ships you just read, for instance, Koran asks its readers and hearers to consider that all human progress or attainment is dependent up Allah's mercy and grace … just as a ship navigating the sea is dependent upon the wind.

Believers Walk the Straight Path

The very first Sura of the Koran, as we have seen, features the voice of the believers appealing to Allah to show them the way to salvation:

(Lord), You alone We do worship and from You alone we do seek assistance. (Lord), guide us to the right path. The path of those to whom You have granted blessings, those who are neither subject to Your anger nor have gone astray. (1:5–7)

This image of believers pursuing the right path, the straight path, the direct way to liberation and salvation, is consistent throughout the Koran. Believers seek with earnestness the straight path the Lord has set out for them, and in so doing, they are usually contrasted with those who have no concern for identifying such a path.

Believers are brought safely from the errors of the unbelievers to walk the straight path by the will of Allah:

> God, through His will, sent guidance to the believers. God guides to the right path whomever He wants. (2:213)

Seeking out the right path, of course, is a lifetime's work. The message transmitted by the Prophet is essential in helping believers to identify and stay fixed upon this straight path:

> How could you turn back to disbelief when the words of God are recited to you and you have in your midst His Messenger? Those who seek the protection of God will certainly be guided to the right path. (3:101)

By means of an unforgettable image, the Koran reminds humanity that all those who pursue Allah's way are like people who have learned to walk tall:

> Can one who walks with his head hanging down be better guided that one who walks with his head upright? (67:22)

The contrast of the blindly meandering unbeliever, who rejects the very notion of eternal life, against the purposeful, directed journey of the believer, who moves toward salvation, is set out powerfully in the Koran again and again. At several points, Allah reminds the Prophet that his job is only to warn humanity, and that he should not be surprised if many of those with whom he shares his message continue to "blindly persist in their rebellion." (23:75)

The path set out by Allah is not an easy path, the Koran tells us but it leads to salvation. In a famous passage in the ninetieth Sura, the Koran assures believers that God has pointed out to believers an "uphill path," and laments that it has gone untraveled. The same Sura explains what, precisely, constitutes the "uphill path": setting free those in bondage, helping those in need, and seeing to those who are poor and without resources. (The teachings in this Sura are strikingly similar to

> **Caution!**
> The Koran urges humanity to listen carefully to the word of Allah, to serve him, and to walk the path he has set out. Failing to walk the right path may lead to worldly gains but not in the eyes of Allah!

> **What's It Mean?**
> **Inordinacy** means "exceeding the limits." This is the English rendering of an Arabic word that shows up (among other places) at Sura 23, verse 75 of the Koran, and is also sometimes translated "rebellion." The basic idea is that of willfully moving past the guidelines set by the Almighty.

those of Jesus, who told his followers that the road to hell is wide and traveled by many, but the road to salvation is narrow, and traveled by few.)

The Koran asks its readers, in literally thousands of ways, whether they are persisting in their *inordinacy*, blindly wandering on, and ignoring their God—or faithfully following the path set out for them by their Lord. This, Muslims believe, is a question worth examining very closely indeed. And the act of examining the question closely is itself a hallmark of belief within Islam.

Believers Are Patient

The virtue of patience—especially patience during times of chaos or trial—is promoted many times in the Koran. We read over and over again that believers should build up the reservoirs of faith and strength necessary to pass the tests that may come their way.

Sometimes the Koran reminds believers to develop patience as part of a cultivation of the kind of humility that must replace religious hypocrisy, as in the following passage:

> Would you order people to do good deeds and forget to do them yourselves even though you read the Book? Why do you not think? (2:44).

Sometimes believers are instructed to show patience in order to deepen their trust in the promises of the Lord:

> (Muhammad), exercise patience. The promise of God is true. Seek forgiveness for your sins and glorify your Lord with His praise in the evenings and in the early mornings. (40:55)

Sometimes believers are counseled to be patient in dealing with the verbal attacks of unbelievers, or in addressing the seeming inequalities of earthly life:

> (Muhammad), have patience with what they say, glorify your Lord, and always praise Him before sunrise, sunset, in some hours of the night and at both the beginning and end of the day, so that perhaps you will please your Lord. Do not be envious of what We have given to some people as means of enjoyment and worldly delight. Such means are a trial for them, but the reward that you will receive from your Lord will be far better and everlasting. (20:130–131).

Believers are instructed to show patience when their faith in Allah is ridiculed:

> We have told people various parables in this Koran. Even if you had shown them a miracle, the unbelievers would have said, "You are only the followers of falsehood." Thus does God seal the hearts of those who do not know. Be patient. The promise of God is certainly true. Let not the faithless make you despair of the promise of God. (30:58–60)

Those who are patient know that the inner strength necessary to be so comes from the Almighty:

> Exercise patience and let it be only for the cause of God. (16:127)

In the Koran, believers learn, too, that they have an obligation to encourage patience, steadfastness, and openheartedness in their interactions fellow believers. They are reminded that cultivating this kind of patience will ensure that each believer remains among the "people of the right hand."

Believers know that patience is required in the service of the Lord:

> He is the Lord of the heavens and the earth and all that is between them. Worship Him and be steadfast in your worship of Him; none is equal to Him. (19:65)

Believers know, too, that patience in human affairs means acknowledging the final authority of Allah:

> Follow what is revealed to you and have patience until God issues His Judgment; He is the best Judge. (10:109)

> **Points to Ponder**
>
> The Koran frequently makes reference to the "people of the right hand" and the "people of the left hand." The first group is that of the believers in the communications of Allah, those who submit to his will. The second group is that of the disbelievers, who are condemned to everlasting torment.

Perhaps most important of all, they know that their patience in the service of Allah is the same as obedience to him. Believers accept that obedience to Allah means obedience to a force that surpasses both human understanding and the ravages of time. They know from the Koran that such obedience will secure his favor in this life and in the afterlife:

> Whatever you possess is transient and whatever is with God is everlasting. We will recompense those who exercise patience with their due reward and even more. All righteously believing (ones), male or female, will be granted a blessed happy life and will receive their due reward and more. (16:96–97)

Believers Are Righteous

Righteousness, the Koran teaches, is to be sought after constantly. It is an endless commitment to the process of acting in accordance with the will of Allah.

Strength during trial, a sense of justice and fair dealing, an enduring commitment to follow the instructions of the Lord, generosity toward the poor, an unrelenting strength in guarding against evil, careful fulfillment of one's duty—these, the Koran tells us, are some of the characteristics of the righteous believer.

Spotlight on Islam

Righteousness within Islam means following the guidance of Allah. This means obedience to the Koran and to the Sunna, and to Islamic law (Shari'a) derived from both sources. The need for an understanding of the specifics of humankind's obligations to Allah has given rise to a number of important scholarly works, among them tafsir (this means an explanation of the Koran) and hadith (this means a statement considered to have come from the Prophet).

Righteousness and scholarship have a long history of interaction within Islam. This is not at all surprising, given the emphasis on wisdom, scholarship, and teaching that appears in the Koran itself:

> We have revealed the Koran to you so that you could tell the people what has been revealed to them and so that perhaps they will think. (16:44)

The righteous, we learn in the Koran, are not distracted by the pleasures of this world:

> Worldly desires, wives, children, accumulated treasures of gold and silver, horses of noble breed, cattle, and farms are all made to seem attractive to men. All these are the bounties of the worldly life but in the life to come God has the best place for people to dwell. (Muhammad), ask them, "Shall I tell you what is far superior to worldly pleasures? Those who have fear of God will have (as their reward) gardens wherein streams flow and wherein they will live forever with their purified spouses and with the consent of God. God knows all about His servants." (Such will be the reward of) those who say, "Lord, we have believed in you. Forgive us our sins and save us from the torment of fire," who exercise patience, speak the truth, who are devoted in prayer, spend their property for the cause of God and seek forgiveness from God during the last part of the night. (3:14–17)

The righteous, we read in the Koran, guard constantly against evil, tell the truth, give generously from that which they love, and seek always and everywhere to please Allah—and are thus spared the torments of hell. The righteous are, on the Day of Judgment, assured of an eternal reward:

> The pious ones will rest amid the shade, springs, and fruits of the kind which they desire. (They will be told), "Eat and drink in good health as a reward for what you have done." Thus do We reward the righteous ones. (77:41–4)

Only the Beginning!

Many other hallmarks of belief are addressed in the Koran, but the few examined in this chapter can serve as an introduction to the subject.

Those who are truly interested in identifying all the qualities that mark out believers will find the answers laid out with great beauty and authority in the full text of the Koran itself.

The Least You Need to Know

- There are several hallmarks of belief within Islam.
- Being loved by Allah is one of these hallmarks.
- Following the path set out by him is another.
- Patience is another.
- Righteousness is a fourth hallmark.

12

The Greatest Losers: Hallmarks of Unbelief

In This Chapter

- ◆ The disaster of unbelief
- ◆ The follies of those who neglect their duty to Allah
- ◆ The chance for salvation

In the previous chapter, we saw what the Koran has to say about some of the distinguishing characteristics of believers. In this chapter, you'll learn of its warnings for those who choose *not* to believe once the truth has been revealed to them.

There are many such warnings, but they can all be condensed into a single message of caution: While the believers will be the winners in the life that follows this one, the disbelievers will be the losers.

"I would rather be a loser anywhere," one believer mentioned recently, "than a loser in the hereafter."

Inmates of the Fire

The system laid out in the Koran is, first and foremost, one of fairness and justice.

We will all be held accountable in the next life for our actions in this life. To those who would protest that any form of punishment in the afterlife is unfair, the Koran asks: Should those who raped, killed, cheated, and abused others during their earthly lives be treated the same as those who cared for the sick, looked after widows and orphans, spent from their own wealth to help the poor, and did everything they possibly could to follow the instructions of the Lord?

Those who disbelieve in Allah and ignore his communications once they are revealed to them, says the Koran, must deal with a terrible consequence of those choices. They will find themselves denied Allah's forgiveness because of their own actions. By means of their conscious disbelief, in other words, they wound their own souls and set disease into their own hearts.

Those who choose to reject the guidance of Allah, the Koran tells us time and time again, will be consigned to the flames:

> But those who would deny the Truth and reject Our revelations would be the companions of the Fire in which they would live forever. (2:39)

Not all disbelievers will suffer eternal damnation; those who have even a tiny amount of faith in Allah will eventually be allowed to enter Paradise. People whose lives featured enough good actions to avoid hell, but who are not yet ready to enter Paradise, may spend time in a place known as the Heights. Others will descend into the pit of hell-fire to suffer unimaginable torments. Some will be released after they serve their term. Some, however—such as those who publicly claim faith in Allah but choose to disregard his commands—will be consigned to hell forever. The final decision on all these matters, of course, is Allah's.

Everyone, the Koran tells us, has to see hell after death. The truly righteous will simply pass over it on the way to Paradise. Others, however, will be separated from Allah's mercy, either forever or for a limited period of time.

And by the way: The Koran's description of the torments of hell are so vivid and so terrifying that they serve as powerful motivators to believers not to spend *any time whatsoever* there! (See the discussion of the afterlife that appears in Chapter 19.)

Make no mistake. Unbelievers, the Koran assures us, will repent—but their repentance will come too late to save their own souls:

> They will also say, "Had We listened or used our minds, we would not have become the dwellers of hell." They will confess to their sins, but the dwellers of hell will be far away from God's (mercy). (67:10–11)

None of the advantages that unbelievers may have accumulated to themselves during their life on Earth will be of any use to them when their life-records are consulted:

> The wealth and children of the unbelievers will never serve them as a substitute for their belief in God. Such people will be the fuel for the fire. They do as the people of Pharaoh and those who lived before them did. They called Our revelations mere lies. God punished them for their sins. God is stern in His retribution. (3:10–11)

The Word

The very eyes, ears, and skins of the unbelievers bear witness against them on the Last Day:

> They will be spurred on until (on the brink of it) their eyes, ears and skin will testify to their deeds on the Day when the enemies of God are driven to the fire. They will ask their own skin, "Why did you testify against us?" They will reply, "God, who has made everything speak, made us also speak. It was He Who created you in the first place and to Him you have returned. You did not (think) to hide your deeds from your ears, eyes and skin and you felt that God would not know all that you had been doing. This was how you considered your Lord, but He knows you better than you know yourselves. Thus, you are now lost." (41:19–23)

The Condemned Shall Long in Vain to Serve God

The inability to submit to Allah is itself one of the torments of hell. Once they are dead and have been condemned to hell, unbelievers will be utterly unable to follow their (deep) desire to serve Allah:

> On the day when the terrible torment approaches, they will be told (in a mocking way) to prostrate themselves, but they will not be able to do it. Their eyes will be lowered and disgrace will cover them. They had certainly been told to prostrate themselves before God when they were safe and sound. Leave those who reject the Koran to Me, and I shall lead them step by step to destruction, without their being aware of it. I shall give them respite (and bear with them); however, My plan is so strong that they will never be able to escape from it. (68:42–45)

According to the Koran, the unbelievers will find that memories of their pleasures during earthly life will be of no use to them in their torment, and they will wish with all their hearts that they had served the Lord while they lived. Surrounded by the flames of hell, they will bitterly regret having wasted their lives.

They Bring Trouble Upon Themselves

Unbelievers, the Koran teaches, are those who have chosen not to obey Allah. They are, as a result, the architects of their own loss. They bring punishments down upon themselves, and they are the losers of their own souls.

According to the Koran, the ultimate destination of one's own soul is the responsibility of each individual. Those who believe know the truth when they hear it. As for the rest, they have shut themselves off from Allah and his mercy:

> Those whom We have given the Book recognize him as they recognize their sons; (as for) those who have lost their souls, they will not believe. (6:20)

Those who reject the path of Allah, present their own lies as the word of Allah, and construct ways of living based on sin and injustice, are, we learn in the Koran, sure to be repaid for their actions:

> Who are more unjust than those who ascribe falsehood to God? When such people are brought into the presence of their Lord, the witness will say, "These are the ones who told lies about their Lord. Certainly God will condemn the unjust who prevent others from the way of God, seek to make it appear crooked, and who have no faith in the life hereafter. Such people will never weaken God's (power) on earth nor will they find any guardian besides God. Their punishment will be doubled and they will not be able to hear or see. They have lost their souls and their false deities will turn away from them. In the life to come they will certainly lose a great deal. (11:18–22)

They Seek to Delude Themselves and Others

We read in the Koran that some disbelievers will encourage others to stray from the truth, as well. To such a person, death that takes place before sincere repentance is truly the beginning of a supreme misfortune:

> God will never forgive the disbelievers who prevent others from the way of God and who die as disbelievers. (47:34)

Points to Ponder _____

Believers—those who submit to the will of the Lord—are set apart from unbelievers on the Last Day: Believers go to Paradise, and unbelievers to hell. Not surprisingly, Muslims believe that one's true friends are those who are concerned for the long-term residence of one's soul, not with the entertainments or distractions of earthly life.

They Doubt the True Revelation

Doubt about the legitimacy of the Koran is one of the chief characteristics of unbelievers.

Unbelievers who lived during the Prophet's time cast doubt on the authenticity of his message. Contemporary Muslims face similar challenges from those who attack the Koran and its message. Such challenges, we learn, are to be expected:

> (Muhammad), had We sent you a Book on paper (instead of revealing the Koran orally through the Angel Gabriel), the unbelievers would have touched it with their hands but would still have said, "It is no more than plain sorcery." (6:7)

Concerning the status of the Koran, believers are challenged today with a very similar attitude of skepticism about the work's origin. More than one Christian has declared the Koran to be not only the work of other worldly forces, but to have originated with Satan!

Muslims ask: Would Satan spend so much of his book cataloguing the various torments of hell, and to be so eloquent in urging people to avoid it?

Islam regards the factuality of Allah's final disposition of all human souls as Reality, with a capital R. Nevertheless, during earthly life, unbelievers may be counted upon to dispute with believers and to dismiss their beliefs as fantasy:

> Some of them listen to you, but We have veiled their hearts so that they cannot understand and made them deaf. They disbelieve all the evidence (of Our existence) that they may have seen. They only come to you for the sake of argument and the disbelievers say that (whatever Muhammad says) is no more than ancient legends. (6:25)

They will attack the Koran itself, and claim that it is a human creation, or some kind of forgery, or a collection of ancient traditions:

> The unbelievers say, "This (Koran) is no more than a slanderous statement which he (Muhammad), with the help of some other people, has falsely invented." Certainly, this statement is unjust and sinful. They have also said, "It (the Koran), is only ancient legends, which were written down while they were dictated to him in the mornings and the evenings." (Muhammad), tell them, "The One who knows all the secrets of the heavens and the earth has revealed it; He is All-forgiving and All-merciful." They say, "Why does this Messenger eat food, and walk in the streets? Why has not an angel been sent to him so that they could preach the message together? Why has a treasure not been laid out for him or a garden from which he could eat been given to him." The unjust ones say, "You are merely following a bewitched person." Look at their various views about you! They have gone astray and are not able to find the right path. (25:4–9)

Not even exposure to the divine message, it seems, can penetrate the hearts of those committed to unbelief.

Allah, however, who has opened his revelation to them, knows their hearts, and knows even what they imagine to be their secrets.

They Are Seduced During Earthly Life by the Pleasure of Their Deeds

Those who reject Allah but appear to embrace him publicly, like those who openly promote sinful ways of living, sometimes appear to enjoy an advantage over believers. But the end of such people, the Koran teaches, will be shameful agony.

Points to Ponder

The Koran frequently depicts unbelievers as having hearts that are diseased. Allah provides a remedy for that disease—submission to the will of Allah—but unbelievers consciously reject it.

Some of them are entranced by the transient appeal of their own evil deeds:

> Can one whose evil deeds seem attractive and virtuous to him (be compared to a truly righteous person)? God guides or causes to go astray whomever He wants. (Muhammad), do not be grieved because of their disbelief. God knows well whatever they do. (35:8)

They Worship Their Own Desires

Those who reject Allah so that they may worship their own baseness choose not to consider the grave damage that they wreak on their own souls. They reject all guidance and all warning:

> Have you seen the one who has chosen his desires as his lord? God has knowingly caused him to go astray, sealed his ears and heart and veiled his vision. Who besides God can guide him? Will they, then, not take heed? (45:23)

They Deny the Coming Day of Judgment

The Koran teaches that by trusting in possessions, money, and rank, the unbelievers attempt in vain to deny the inevitable reckoning. People who consider themselves, rather than Allah, to be the source of their wealth, it advises, are in for a disappointment. And anyone who doubts that Allah can bring human beings back to life for the Day of Judgment, the Koran warns, hasn't thought the matter through carefully enough:

> The pagans say, "When we become mere bones and dust, shall we then be brought back to life again?" (Muhammad), say "Yes, even if you become rocks, iron, or anything that you think is harder to be brought to life." They will soon ask, "Who will bring us back to life?" Say, "The One who created you in the first place." They will shake their heads and say, "When will He bring us back to life?" Say, "Perhaps very soon. On the day when He will call you, you will answer Him with praise and think that you have tarried for only a little while." (17:49–52)

Other unbelievers, we learn, consider instances of the Lord's mercy to be proof of their own power, and assume that they will enter Paradise easily:

> When We grant him mercy after his suffering, he (boldly) says, "This is what I deserved. I do not think that there will ever be a Day of Judgment. Even if I will be returned to my Lord, I shall still deserve to receive better rewards from Him." We shall certainly tell the unbelievers about their deeds and cause them to suffer a severe punishment. (41:50)

On the Day itself, those who relied on themselves, rather than Allah, will find themselves confronted with their own words of disbelief, and set apart from the presence of God:

> Woe, on that day, to those who have rejected God's revelations and those who have rejected the Day of Judgment. No one rejects it except the sinful transgressors

who, when listening to Our revelations, say, "These are only ancient legends." They will never have faith. In fact, their hearts are stained from their deeds. On the Day of Judgment, they will certainly be barred from the mercy of their Lord. They will suffer the heat of fire. (83:10–16)

CAUTION

Caution! _____

Those who believe the Lord does not conduct a final reckoning, the Koran warns, are in for an unpleasant surprise:

The disbelievers have said, "There will be no Hour of Doom." Say, "By my Lord, it certainly will come. My Lord knows the unseen. Not even an atom's weight in the heavens or the earth remains hidden from Him. Nothing exists greater or smaller than this without its record in the illustrious Book." (34:3)

And Finally ...

Consider the following extract, the conclusion of the extraordinary ninth Sura, *Repentance*, which spends a good deal of time discussing the fate of unbelievers. The passage begins by addressing the situation faced by the Prophet whenever he would share a new Sura (chapter) of the Koran. To some, the momentous event is a powerful, faith-strengthening experience:

When a chapter (of the Koran) is revealed, some people ask others, "Whose faith among you people has received strength from this (revelation)?" It (the revelation) certainly strengthens the faith of the believers and they consider it to be a glad news. (9:124)

To others, however, exposure to the newly revealed word of God only adds to their spiritual illness:

But to those whose hearts are sick, it adds more filth to their hearts and they die as disbelievers. (9:125)

They fail to understand that the revelation they have encountered is in fact a test from God to determine whether they will repent and avoid damnation:

Do they not realize that God tests them once or twice a year but, nevertheless, they do not repent and give it proper thought? (9:126)

They furtively seek the silent support of other unbelievers, and try to maintain a low profile. But they cannot keep a low profile before God:

> They look at one another and their eyes silently ask this question, "Has any one noticed the disappointment on our faces?" Then they walk away. In fact, God has turned their hearts away (from the truth); they are a people who have no understanding. (9:127)

This act of hardening one's heart, of willful disbelief is, we learn, a source of personal sorrow to Muhammad:

> A Messenger from your own people has come to you. Your destruction and suffering is extremely grievous to him. He really cares about you and is very compassionate and merciful to the believers. (9:128)

Yet the Koran offers instructions that even such unbelievers may attain salvation, if only they choose correctly before they die. To those who abandon not Allah, but their unbelief—to those who make the right choice and make that choice part of their identities—the Koran offers one of its most beautiful, enduring, and inspiring verses:

> (Muhammad), if they turn away from you, say, "God is Sufficient (support) for me. There is no God but He. In Him do I trust, and He is the Owner of the Great Throne." (9:129)

The Least You Need to Know

- Allah does not forgive those who disbelieve in him.

- They are separated from Allah's mercy on the Day of Judgment.

- Any advantages they may have accumulated during their earthly lives will be of no use to them then.

- Those who submit to Allah's will before they die, however, are assured salvation.

Part 4

Obligations of the Faith

Man is a social being, and the Koran addresses this fact directly and at some length. Our relationships to other people—and to God—often take the form of obligations.

In this part of the book, you'll explore the Koran's conceptions of virtue, justice, family, and duty as they are expressed as obligations in the lives of believers.

Chapter 13

Putting Faith into Practice

♦ Prayer in Islam

♦ Fasting during Ramadan

♦ Making the pilgrimage

♦ Ideological obligations

Prayer is one of the most visible hallmarks of Islam. Five times each day, Muslims must stop what they are doing, turn toward Mecca, and prostrate themselves before Allah. Like most other actions devout Muslims take, a daily pattern of prayer is prescribed in the Koran. (The specifics of the prayers themselves are derived from the Sunna.)

Prayers, then, are an example of conduct mandated in the Koran—conduct that distinguishes believers from unbelievers. In addition to instructing believers on more abstract matters of faith (such as the belief that Allah is the creator of the universe), the Koran tells Muslims how to put that faith into practice through their actions.

On the following pages you'll learn about some of these obligatory activities: prayer, fasting, and pilgrimage. You'll also find a brief explanation of Shari'a law and how it governs Muslim actions.

Prayer: The Greatest Act of Worship

The Koran tells us:

> (Muhammad), recite to them what has been revealed to you in the Book and be steadfast in prayer; prayer keeps one away from indecency and evil. Speaking of Allah is the greatest act of worship. Allah knows what you do. (29:45)

For simplicity's sake, we'll look at two groups of prayers that connect to the Koran's instructions for pious living. The first kind of prayer is known as salat, a word that describes a set of words and actions Muslims must perform at least five times a day. (There are special situations that can reduce the daily prayer obligations somewhat.) The second group of prayer we'll look at is—you guessed it—everything else addressed to Allah besides salat. Some of the prayers in the "everything else" category are obligatory, and some are optional ... but all are in keeping with the Koran's instructions to worship Allah.

Spotlight on Islam

Sunni and Shi'a Muslims differ in everyday religious practice in certain respects, but both groups accept the divine authorship of the Koran and the importance of submitting to its guidance, and both groups view the Sunna as binding. This chapter focuses on obligatory actions accepted by both groups.

In the United States, as in the world at large, Sunni Muslims form the larger body of believers. It has been estimated that Sunni Muslims make up 80 to 85 percent of all Muslims worldwide; a similar ratio appears to prevail in North America.

Prayers: Salat

When people talk about "praying" within Islam, they are usually talking about salat, an Arabic word that is sometimes translated as "contact prayer," and that literally means "red-hot connection." This kind of prayer, in other words, involves the establishment of directly speaking to God. It is the cornerstone of the faith.

Making *salat* involves the performance of a set of actions, known as *rak'ats*, which we'll get to in a moment. Praying also involves certain important preparations on the part of the believer—notably wudu', a manner of personal cleansing mandated in the Koran and the Sunna. Performing wudu' is obligatory when water is available. Wudu' has five components:

1. Intention: This means making a decision for performing wudu' in obedience to the command of Allah.

2. Washing one's face, hands, rinsing out one's mouth, cleansing one's nostrils (a step considered optional by Shi'a Muslims), and washing one's face.

3. Washing one's forearms (from the elbows to the fingertips).

4. Wiping one's head.

5. Wiping or washing one's feet.

In addition, one's clothes must be clean, lawfully useable, and one must be dressed properly; standards differ slightly between men and women on proper dress for prayer, but the basic idea is that modesty should be maintained even during the bowings and standings of the rak'ats. One must also select a clean and lawfully useable place to pray (in other words, no breaking and entering), and one must be sure that the time for prayer is correct.

Assuming that all of the above is taken care of, believers may make salat in groups (ideally, at a mosque) or by themselves. A congregational prayer at noontime on Fridays is similar to the Jewish Saturday sabbath or the Christian Sunday sabbath. When it is held at a mosque it usually marks the largest weekly gathering of the community of believers.

Here's how it works. If men and women join their prayers in congregation, men may form lines in front of the women, or may pray in an adjacent section, or may pray on a lower or upper floor. This is not because men have some kind of superior status, but because men looking at women is seen as more distracting to worship than women looking at men. Group prayers are led by a single member of the group; the congregation follows along behind him or her. (In Shi'a practice, this person must be well qualified for the task of leading prayers.); the congregation follows along behind him or her. Yes, women can, and routinely do, lead prayers; the only requirement is that the congregation be composed of women. One faces toward Mecca. One makes a silent or spoken intention (as mentioned in the discussion on wudu') about the prayer to be delivered, and the first rak'at begins.

So much for the prerequisites. Now then, what is a rak'at? Basically, it's a set of actions and sayings that is repeated (and varied slightly) depending on the number of repetitions required; this in turn depends on the time of day at which one is praying. Here is a simplified summary:

What's It Mean?

Islamic Dictionary

Allahu Akbar means "God is greater than …"; it suggests that Allah is greater than any noun with which one might choose to complete the sentence. The phrase is said at various points of the **rak'ats**, which form the individual units of the larger act of worship known as **salat**.

♦ **Takbir:** One lifts both hands up to the ears and says, *Allahu Akbar*.

♦ **Qawam:** Standing. (At this point, selected portions of the Koran are recited.)

♦ **Takbir:** As before, both hands are lifted to the ears, and one says "Allahu Akbar."

♦ **Ruku:** One leans forward with palms over the knees and repeats a phrase that translates as "Glory Belongs to Allah."

♦ **Qawam:** Standing, one says a phrase that translates as "Good hears those who praise him."

♦ **Takbir:** As before, both hands are lifted to the ears, and one says "Allahu Akbar."

♦ **Sajdah:** Palms, forehead, tip of nose, knees, and toes touch the ground, and one repeats a phrase that praises Allah. While sitting up, one repeats "Allahu Akbar." Then back again to down to ….

♦ **Sajdah:** Palms, forehead, tip of nose, knees, and toes touch the ground, and again one repeats a phrase that praises Allah. While sitting up, one repeats "Allahu Akbar."

♦ **Qawam:** Standing. (At this point, selected portions of the Koran are recited, and the process begins again.)

What you've just read is an oversimplified explanation of the basic movements and sayings; some minor variations and additions on the basic sequence must be memorized when one actually performs the rak'ats in units of two, three, or four over the course of a day. This is the manner in which the prayers are performed by millions of Muslims each and every day of the year.

The breakdown is as follows:

♦ Two rak'ats after dawn before sunrise.

♦ Four rak'ats shortly after noon.

♦ Four rak'ats in the late afternoon.

♦ Three rak'ats after sunset.

♦ Four rak'ats before midnight.

Caution!

Mastering salat means understanding—and memorizing—a certain amount of Arabic, which can be challenging for an English speaker, and coordinating the Arabic words with certain movements. The process takes time and practice. Seek out a colleague or teacher who can help with pronunciation and the proper movements.

Prayers: Other Kinds

The five daily prayers of salat are obligatory; to overlook them is considered a sin. Other situations in which prayer is obligatory include the following:

◆ After an unusual natural happening, such as earthquake

◆ Following Tawaf, which is the act of walking around the Ka'ba seven times during a visit to Mecca (see the section on pilgrimmage later in this chapter)

◆ After the death of a member of the community

◆ Prayers resulting from some vow, or covenant, with Allah (for instance, a commitment made by the individual to Allah to complete six, rather than five, daily prayers for a period of 40 days)

Believers may, and often do, pray in addition to these situations. The salat prayers just described are not to be confused with a believer's appeal to God for help with a specific situation or problem. That kind of appeal is not salat, but supplication.

The distinction is an important one. The purpose of salat is to establish humble, submissive obedience to Allah. When we ask Allah for forgiveness for sins, or for help in dealing with a challenging family situation, or to guide our actions during an anticipated challenge at work, or to aid us any of a thousand other possible settings, we appeal to Allah to listen to our supplications. The Koran promises that Allah will listen to each believer's heartfelt supplication, or du'a (meaning to call for help). Any personal request of the Lord is a du'a.

The Word

Say your prayer when the sun declines until the darkness of night and also at dawn. Dawn is certainly witnessed (by the angels of the night and day). Say your special (tahajjud) prayer during some part of the night as an additional (obligatory) prayer for you alone so that perhaps your Lord will raise you to a highly praiseworthy position. (17:78–79)

The Word

(Muhammad), if any of My servants ask you about Me, tell them that the Lord says, "I am near; I accept the prayers of those who pray." Let My servants answer My call and believe in Me so that perhaps they may know the right direction." (2:186)

Common du'as taken from the text of the Koran, and that are repeated in many everyday situations by believers, include the following:

♦ Our Lord! Grant us good in this world and good in the life to come and keep us safe from the torment of the Fire. (2:201)

♦ Our Lord! Bestow on us endurance and make our foothold sure and give us help against those who reject faith. (2:250)

♦ Our Lord! Take us not to task if we forget or fall into error. (2:286)

There is a third category of observance that corresponds roughly with the Western notion of "prayer"—dhikr. This is remembrance of God, pure and simple. Dhikr often involves the use of rosary beads, and it usually incorporates the repetition of a short phrase from the Koran (such as "alhamdullilah," or "All praise is due to Allah).

Fasting

With just a few exceptions, believers can fast at any time during the year in order to purify themselves. Eating, drinking, and inhaling things besides air invalidate a fast. Fast begins from dawn and ends at sunset. Certain sexual acts and immersing one's head in water also invalidate one's fast. When the sun sets, the time of fasting for the day ends, and one may eat, drink, and enjoy sexual relations with one's spouse in the normal way until dawn.

The Koran tells believers:

The month of Ramadan is the month in which the Koran was revealed; a guide for the people, the most authoritative of all guidance and a criteria to discern right from wrong. Anyone of you who knows that the month of Ramadan has begun, he must start to fast. Those who are sick or on a journey have to fast the same number of days at another time. Allah does not impose any hardship upon you. He wants you to have comfort so that you may complete the fast, glorify Allah for His having given you guidance, and that, perhaps, you would give Him thanks. (2:185)

Fasting is therefore obeying Allah and simultaneously disciplining one's manners; it helps to provide the most favorable condition and state of mind in which one can speak to Allah more sincerely and attentively.

Believers hold that Allah will not accept the fast of a person who indulges in sinful or misguided activity (such as spreading rumors or provoking conflict with others) during Ramadan. They also believe that the good deeds one performs during Ramadan are multiplied in their effect on the spiritual state of the one performing them.

Pilgrimage

Hajj means pilgrimage to Mecca. This important duty is mentioned in the following passage of the Koran:

> The first house (of worship) that Allah assigned to men was in Bakka (another name of Mecca). It is a blessed one and a guide for all people. In (Bakka), there are many clear signs (evidence of the existence of Allah). Among them is the spot where Abraham stood. Whoever seeks refuge therein will be protected by the laws of amnesty. Those who have the means and ability have a duty to Allah to visit the House and perform the hajj (pilgrimage) rituals. The unbelievers should know that Allah is Independent of all creatures. (3:96–97)

The pilgrimage comes in two forms: the greater pilgrimage, known as Hajj, takes place in the twelfth lunar month. Once one completes the Hajj, one has the right to use the title "Hajji." The lesser pilgrimage, known as 'Umrah, can take place during the other 11 months of the year. This is regarded as a pious undertaking, but does not fulfill the individual believer's requirement to make the pilgrimage, as outlined in the Koran.

Male pilgrims must wear a special white garment; all pilgrims must refrain from sexual activity, from shaving the body or cutting the nails, from the use of cologne or perfume, and from killing any living being, among other prohibitions. There are a number of important rituals associated exclusively with the pilgrimage.

Spotlight on Islam

It is obligatory to make the pilgrimage to [Mecca] at least once in a lifetime if one qualifies. Muslims from all walks of life, from every corner of the globe assemble in Mecca in response to the call of Allah. It is to commemorate the Divine rituals observed by the Prophet Abraham and his son Ishmael, who were the first pilgrims to the house of Allah on earth: the Ka'bah. It is also to remember the great assembly of the Day of Judgment when people will stand equal before Allah. Muslims go to Mecca to glorify Allah, not to worship a man. The visit to the tomb of Prophet Muhammad at [Medina] is highly recommended but not essential in making the Hajj valid and complete.

—from www.themodernreligion.com

Millions upon millions of believers travel to Mecca during the sacred month of the Hajj. Explaining exactly what they experience during this time can be a difficult undertaking. Many Muslims believe that the benefit of Hajj can only be properly understood through pure intent and personal experience.

Shari'a Law

The established body of Islamic law is known as Shari'a. The word means "the path," and this is an apt way to describe this body of law, which seeks to illuminate the divinely appointed path for humanity. Its primary sources are the Koran and the Sunna. Shari'a law places human activities under five categories:

- ◆ Obligatory acts (must be performed)
- ◆ Prohibited acts (may never be performed)
- ◆ Recommended acts (ought to be performed)
- ◆ Undesirable acts (ought not to be performed)
- ◆ Permissible acts (to perform or not to perform)

Any action undertaken or abstained from in accordance with Shari'a law, and with the sincere effort to draw closer to Allah, is considered 'ibadah, or worship. Thus it is important for Muslims to know what their faith prohibits, and what it requires as well. If a believing Muslim neglects to perform divinely appointed obligations or commits forbidden acts, that person becomes a sinner. Sins, if not forgiven, will make the person subject to punishment according to Allah's system. Asking forgiveness and pardon from Allah may remove one's sins.

The Word

Allah addresses the condemned on Judgment Day:

O assembly of jinn and men! did there not come to you apostles from among you, relating to you My communications and warning you of the meeting of this day of yours? They shall say: We bear witness against ourselves; and this world's life deceived them, and they shall bear witness against their own souls that they were unbelievers. (6:130)

Obtaining forgiveness is always contingent upon the grace and mercy of God. According to the Prophet Muhammad, mercy for past wrongdoing is obtained in one of three ways:

The Prophet (sallallaahu 'alayhi wa sallam) said, "Indeed Allah is pleased with three things: That you worship Allah alone without associating any partner along with Him; that you hold fast altogether to the Rope of Allah and not to become split-up; and that you give sincere advice to whomever Allah puts in charge of your affairs." (Hadith—Sahih Muslim [3/1340] and Ahmad [2/367])

("The Rope of Allah" refers to the means by which people can become closer to Allah, one of which is the Koran.)

Caution!

Prohibited actions include ...

♦ Helping others to commit sins or injustice
♦ Being unconcerned about the wrath of Allah
♦ Denying miracles
♦ Denying the life to come or one of the principles of religion
♦ Denying such religious matters that are unanimously accepted
♦ Refusing to commemorate the holy names of Allah
♦ Ridiculing believers
♦ Being extravagant
♦ Persisting in committing smaller sins

Apostasy

If a Muslim rejects in disbelief any of the basic principles or any matter that all Muslims unanimously accept and practice, he will be considered an apostate and non-Muslim. Apostasy is a crime comparable to high treason in contemporary law. An apostate is subject to capital punishment; in certain cases, repentance is acceptable.

Points to Ponder

Islam holds that all things truly belong to Allah, not to human beings, and that people are only granted temporary trusts over certain amounts of wealth.

Apostasy is not simple carelessness or inattentiveness. It involves the conscious rejection of core principles of the faith. It is an extremely serious offense.

The Last Word

The Prophet effectively summarized the various obligations of Islam in a single unforgettable sentence. It is a sentence that believers recall often:

You should worship Allah as though He is watching you: If you do not see Him, He sees you.

The Least You Need to Know

♦ The Koran tells Muslims to worship Allah five times a day.

♦ Pilgrimage to Mecca is an obligation of the faith.

♦ If a believing Muslim fails to perform certain obligations or commits forbidden acts, that person becomes a sinner.

♦ Believers who sincerely turn to Allah in repentance will be granted forgiveness.

♦ A Muslim who rejects any of the fundamental beliefs or any unanimously accepted practice is regarded an apostate.

14

Women and the Family

In This Chapter

- How Islam views the role of women
- A remarkable woman from the early history of Islam
- Why Muslims believe Allah liberated women fourteen centuries ago

This chapter is entitled "Women and the Family"—not "Women" and not "The Family," but both linked together. This is because the Koran mandates a distinctive role for women—just as it mandates a distinctive role for men.

The Koran's divinely mandated role for women, the mothers of humankind, centers around the family. This role has been the subject of much misinterpretation by non-Muslims. In this chapter, you'll get an overview of what the Koran has to say about the role of women in society.

Check Your Preconceptions at the Door

A word of advice: Be prepared to be surprised.

Many non-Muslims expect to find passages in the Koran identifying women as subhuman entities, or as beings intellectually or spiritually inferior to men. No such passages exist.

As we shall see, the Koran is a uniquely egalitarian spiritual document. It stands in sharp contrast to the pagan Arab rituals of the time—and, truth be told, to the teachings of the early Christian fathers, who placed female members of the congregation on a distinctly *unequal* spiritual footing. (Early Christians argued that women had no souls, and held that Christian women would enter heaven as sexless entities; many other religions feature similarly discriminatory teachings regarding female spirituality.)

Nevertheless, non-Muslims sometimes assume that women in Islam occupy an inferior position before God. Or they may assume that women are "forced" by the Koran to avoid developing their intellects, to put up with mistreatment from their husbands, to agree with their husbands on all issues, and so on. Many Westerners also assume that there is a single accepted standard of dress for women within Islam, and that this standard is outlined in the Koran (see Chapter 1 for more on this issue).

It comes as something of a surprise, then, to learn that these are all misconceptions—or, for that matter, to hear devout Islamic women, when asked about "women's liberation," respond by saying that "Allah already liberated women in the seventh century!"

In order to better understand what is meant by such a statement, let's examine the remarkable—and influential—life of the very first *Muslimah*—Khadija, the first wife of the Prophet.

> **What's It Mean?**
>
> A **Muslimah** is a female who submits to the will of Allah. The term can be used to describe individuals or groups of female believers. Within the Koran, the term "Muslim" is applied to the entire body of believers, male and female.

Khadija's Story

Khadija ul-Kubra, the first wife of the Prophet, was born in 555 C.E. She was, at the end of the sixth century C.E., a wealthy, intelligent, and widely respected business woman. Having heard about her cousin Muhammad's reputation for integrity and hard work, she enlisted him to help her carry out her business dealings. He proved to be a superb employee. She eventually fell in love with him, and despite a decade-and-a-half difference in their ages, used an intermediary to broach the idea of marriage. The two were in fact wed; Khadija was to remain Muhammad's only wife until her death in 620 at the age of 65. (A side note: Khadija's age and number of children are disputed.)

After receiving his first instruction from God to preach his religion through the angel Gabriel, he returned home to his wife and told her of his remarkable experience. He was uneasy when he considered the size of the task before him; when he explained what had happened to his wife Khadija, she comforted him and said: "O son of my uncle, be of good cheer. Allah has chosen you to be His messenger. You are always kind to your neighbors, helpful to your kinsfolk, generous to the orphans, the widows and the poor, and friendly to the strangers. Allah will never forsake you."

It was Khadija who encouraged him to follow the path of God as it was laid out for him. Over the next decade, she was his chief ally and source of personal support—and often his *only* ally in carrying out his remarkable mission.

Khadija's Remarkable Role

Khadija was a loving wife, a caring mother, a wise counselor, and an unfailing supporter of the Prophet's difficult and dangerous undertaking.

She supported her family financially when Muhammad turned his full attention to teaching and establishing an Islamic community. She was the first woman to embrace Islam, and the first human being other than her husband to accept the divinity of his revelation. She is one of the most important figures in the history of the faith, and certainly one of the most important figures, male or female, in human history. Her life and influence upon Islam is worthy of close study by anyone who is under the misconception that the history of Islam is devoid of strong, resilient, creative, intellectually powerful women.

It is clear that she served as a pillar of strength to the tiny initial community of Muslims who made the hijrah with her husband. She thus played a critical role in the divinely ordained perpetuation of the communications received by her husband, and in the establishment of the first Islamic society. The Prophet mourned her loss for years.

> **Points to Ponder**
>
> It is more than a little odd that this extraordinary woman, so influential to the initiation of one of the great religious and social movements in human history, has not received more attention from Western historians. To learn more about her, you may wish to read *Khadija tul Kubra*, by Syed A. A. Razawi, published by Tahrike Tarsile Qur'an, Elmhurst NY. The text is also available through the Al-Islam website, at www.al-islam.org/khadija.

A Revolutionary Message

The Koran was delivered to humanity at a time when civilizations in not only Arabia, but also Greece, China, India, and Rome held that women not only had no legal rights—falling below the status of children or slaves—but were somehow imperfect spiritually. Women were, not infrequently, treated more abominably than animals in this period.

And yet the Koran states without reservation or ambiguity that men and woman stand as equals before God, and sets out a vision of society in which men and women play different social roles ... but share an equal obligation to grow in wisdom:

> All righteously believing male or female will be granted a blessed happy life and will receive their due reward and more. (16:97)

Spiritual Equality

Let's look more closely at what may well be the Koran's most important message regarding men and women: that of their spiritual equality. The Koran frequently speaks to the community of believers as "believing men and women," as in this famous passage:

> God has promised forgiveness and great rewards to the Muslim men and the Muslim women, the believing men and the believing women, the obedient men and the obedient women, the truthful men and the truthful women, the forbearing men and the forbearing women, the humble men and the humble women, the alms-giving men and the alms-giving women, the fasting men and the fasting women, the chaste men and the chaste women, and the men and women who remember God very often. (33:35)

It explicitly states that men and women derive from a single soul:

> People, have fear of your Lord who has created you from a single soul. From it He created your spouse and through them He populated the land with many men and women. Have fear of the One by whose Name you swear to settle your differences and have respect for your relatives. God certainly keeps watch over you. (4:1)

And, as we have seen, it states clearly that men and women who submit to the will of the Lord shall earn a place in Paradise. This divine teaching is delivered without any ambiguity, and is regarded as a divine truth by all Muslims.

The Word _____

Allah will not waste the work of a single believer, male or female!

Their Lord answered their prayers saying, "I do not neglect anyone's labor whether the laborer be male or female. You are all related to one another. Those who migrated from Mecca, those who were expelled from their homes, those who were tortured for My cause, and those who fought and were killed for My cause will find their sins expiated by Me and I will admit them into the gardens wherein streams flow. It will be their reward from God Who grants the best rewards." (3:195)

These supposedly "modern" notions of spiritual equality are, believers insist, ancient and enduring eternal principles ordained from the beginning of time, and set out clearly in the Koran by God himself.

The Koran's pronouncements on spiritual equality regardless of gender, and its insistence on chaste behavior from both men and women, were revolutionary in the seventh century. They represented direct challenges to the social and religious practices of contemporary Arabia.

> **Points to Ponder**
>
> In the seventh century, when the Prophet began to receive the Koran, pagan Arab peoples were in the habit of burying female infants alive, forcing women to strip naked and dance in the general area of the Ka'ba during festivals, and denying any and all rights to women. Islam rejects such practices just as emphatically as it rejects the idea that women are, unlike men, inherently responsible for human sinfulness. The biblical account of the temptation of Adam and Eve places the blame for the event on Eve, who listens to the serpent and is cursed with the pains of childbirth for doing so. In the Koran, by contrast, God holds both parties equally responsible, and grants forgiveness to both.

Mutual Obligations in Marriage

In dealing with the subject of marriage and human sexuality, the Koran uses a particularly beautiful turn of phrase to describe the mutual guardianship of man and wife:

> It is made lawful for you, during the nights of fasting, to have carnal relations with your wives. They are your garments and you are their garments. (2:187)

It continues by suggesting that men and women are meant to clothe each other— to protect each other from hardship and the possibility of sinful misconduct.

A fundamental notion of partnership between husbands and wives is expressed in the Koran's descriptions of the ideal marriage. Husbands and wives are to live together in peace:

> **Points to Ponder**
>
> The Koran offers a realistic approach to human limitations. It does not require that spouses stay away from lawful carnal desires for the entire month of Ramadan.

Some evidence of His existence are His creating you from clay and from that you became human beings scattered all around; His creating spouses for you out of yourselves so that you might take comfort in them and His creating love and mercy among you. In this there is evidence (of the truth) for the people who (carefully) think. (30:20–21)

The Koran views the relationship between a married couple as sacred; it places no requirements upon a wife to perform housework, avoid work outside the home, breast-feed children, or perform other such tasks. There may well be cultural or family traditions that encourage decisions in one direction or another on these activities, but the Koran is silent on them.

The Koran teaches that married partners are to embrace the institution of marriage as God-given and as worthy of reverence. This is because embarking upon marriage, and raising a Muslim family, is an act that is pleasing to God. Mothers, specifically, are due special reverence and respect. (The relevant passage, 46:15, orders the believer to do good to his or her parents, and acknowledges the troubles of pregnancy and labor.)

The Koran, in short, envisions a marriage bond that is strong and enduring, respected by both men and women, and supportive of the family structure. Divorce is permitted, but it is seen as a last resort (as when a husband habitually mistreats his wife). Indeed, Islam views with deep misgiving any Muslim who rejects the institution of marriage.

Significantly, marriage requires the free consent of both the man and the woman within Islam. It also requires that each partner accept certain responsibilities.

Caution!

Unlike Christianity, Judaism, Buddhism, or other faiths, Islam doesn't accept life-long abstention from carnal desires as a worthy religious goal. Muhammad explicitly rejected the idea of monastic devotion, and the Koran makes it clear that marriage is to be promoted as a vitally important part of the lives of believers. The Prophet is quoted as saying, "Whoever keeps away from it (marriage) is not from me."

A husband has the primary responsibility to provide financial support for his family. Again, a wife is not *required* under Islamic law to perform housework and provide emotional support and moral instruction to children, but as a practical matter wives usually take on these roles in Islamic families. These responsibilities and undertakings, Muslims believe, are not artificially imposed "gender roles" imposed by a man-made social system to benefit one or another gender, but rather part of a system of mutual support.

Men and women, in other words, have different responsibilities and roles on Earth, but they are equals before God, who makes distinctions based only upon personal obedience to his will:

The believers, both male and female, are each other's guardians. They try to make others do good, prevent them from committing sins, perform their prayers, pay the religious tax, and obey God and His Messenger. God will have mercy on them; He is Majestic and All-wise. (9:71)

Mutual Obligations in Religious Practice

All the well-known obligations—or pillars—of Islam (including belief, prayer, fasting, almsgiving, and pilgrimage) are placed upon men and women equally in the Koran. There is no discrimination along gender lines in these fundamental duties, except for some very minor differences in observance related to the physiology of women (notably the menstrual cycle, which is regarded in Islam, as in other religious systems, as requiring a time of purification).

Legal Parity

The Koran mandates equality of property and contract rights for men and women, a fact that usually comes as something of a surprise to non-Muslims. It also clearly endorses the concept of freedom of expression for women as well as men:

God has certainly heard the words of the woman who disputed with you about her husband and who (after not having received a favorable response from you) complained to God. God was listening to your argument. He is All-hearing and All-aware. (58:1)

In some situations, the Koran acknowledges a man's obligation to provide for his family by granting him a larger share of an inheritance than a woman would receive in the same situation. This fact is often misinterpreted by non-Muslims who try to suggest that the Koran is "anti-woman." These commentators, however, have forgotten that the Koran doesn't demand any financial obligations whatsoever of women, but does place significant financial burdens upon men to support their families.

Similar apparent "inequalities" exist in the Koran's guidance for the resolution of certain legal disputes. For instance, in certain civil cases, the Koran requires the testimony of either two men, or one man and two women. One must remember, however, that these requirements are to be met within the larger context of a dynamic social system—one in which men and women play different but complementary roles in society. Those who object to the entire system, while knowing only of one or two of its guiding verses, may be surprised to learn how well the system as a whole functions in practice, especially in comparison with other legal systems.

Is the system fair? Perhaps the best answer to this question is not to be found by reading a book like this, but by talking to Muslimahs themselves, most of whom don't consider the notion of differing roles for men and women to be hypocritical or reflective of prejudice.

What Was That About Wife-Beating?

A much-examined passage in the Koran offers a series of progressively more impossible-to-ignore options to the man who fears that his wife may be committing adultery (or be preparing to do so). A careful reading reveals that the emphasis throughout this passage is on maintaining some kind of contact in a strained marriage, repairing the fractured relationship between man and wife, and securing a supportive family relationship for the couple's past and future children.

I've included one translation of this frequently-debated passage here. It should, despite its having been the cause of much stereotyping and anti-Islamic propaganda, be understood within the overall context of maintaining familial and social harmony in the face of a crisis that could shatter a marriage.

> Men are the maintainers of women because Allah has made some of them to excel others and because they spend out of their property; the good women are therefore obedient, guarding the unseen as Allah has guarded; and (as to) those on whose part you fear desertion [note: the Arabic word here can also be translated as "disloyalty" or "rebellion,"] admonish them, and leave them alone in the sleeping-places and beat them; then if they obey you, do not seek a way against them; surely Allah is High, Great. (4:34)

What is usually forgotten in discussions of this passage is that in the seventh century many Arab men would *kill* women whom they merely suspected of harboring adulterous plans, so the Koranic instructions are actually moderate by the standards of the time. In discussing this verse, it is worth remembering, too, that the Prophet placed special emphasis on the obligation of husbands to show kindness to their wives, and spoke out passionately against the practice of wife-beating. Near the end of his life, after the verse in question had been revealed, the Prophet said of it, "I wanted one thing, but God has willed another thing—and what God has willed must be best." He also stipulated that the instruction could only be applied in situations where the wife "has become guilty, in an obvious manner, of immoral conduct."

> **Caution!**
>
> Don't forget that any Islamic woman who is mistreated by an over-suspicious husband has the right to obtain a divorce.

By the way, the "beating" mentioned in this verse is a judicial matter that requires proper supporting evidence. Only a qualified judge, through proper legal procedures, may sanction such a correctional measure, and the judge must do so within the limits of the authentic sources of law.

Make No Mistake ...

The Koran *does not* advocate the physical or emotional abuse of women. Whatever "beating" is administered by the jealous husband guided by chapter 4, verse 34 must conform to commands set out elsewhere in the Koran, commands that clearly forbid the perpetuation of a cycle of abuse:

> Do not force them (your wives) to live with you in suffering to satisfy your hostility. Whoever commits such transgressions, he has only harmed himself. (2:231)

> Always treat them (your wives) reasonably. If you dislike them, you could be disliking that which God has filled with abundant good. (4:19)

Spotlight on Islam

Here are a few websites that may be helpful in determining how contemporary Muslimahs celebrate the gender equality set out clearly in the Koran.

- The Muslim Women's Homepage
  www.jannah.org/sisters
- Karamah: Muslim Women Lawyers for Human Rights
  www.karamah.org
- Women's Islamic Study Circle
  http://hometown.aol.com/yasmin3579/family/index.htm
- Women in Islam
  www.usc.edu/dept/MSA/humanrelations/womeninislam
- Islam Today: Women in Islam
  www.islamfortoday.com/women.htm

A History of Strong Women

A chorus of powerful female voices have always existed in Islam. These voices embrace the notions of motherhood and family set out in the Koran, and thus frustrate some non-Muslims for whom the word "egalitarian" can only be defined as "identical to prevailing American or European values."

It must be noted here that many modern Western notions of "women's liberation" are viewed by Muslims—millions upon millions of them, both male and female—as misguided (or cynical) attempts to exploit woman's beauty, degrade her sense of self-worth, or even destabilize her family or pollute her soul. Countless Muslims and Muslimahs also cite with concern the weakening of the institution of marriage in the West that has accompanied the acceptance of various feminist schools of thought.

Non-Muslims may disagree with these assessments, but they should not make the mistake of believing that only male Muslims express such concerns. Islam has a history of strong women believers, and they are quite capable of speaking for themselves. The truth is that most Westerners who accuse Islam or the Koran of unfairness to women have never spoken to a Muslimah about her faith.

The Least You Need to Know

- Misconceptions abound about the status of women in Islam.

- The Koran sets out a fundamentally egalitarian vision of spirituality.

- Men and women have different social responsibilities within Islam.

- There is a long tradition of strong women within Islam, including (notably) Khadija.

- Many Westerners who argue that Islam or the Koran is inherently "oppressive" or "demeaning" to women have never spoken to a Muslimah (Muslim woman) about the matter.

Chapter 15

The Importance of Charity

In This Chapter

♦ The importance of giving

♦ Spiritual benefits of charity

♦ Good news for servants who obey

The Koran's relentless insistence on charitable giving is unique in the world's religious scriptures.

The command to give money to support those in need and to worthy charitable causes is not only explicit—it is restated and elaborated throughout the text of the Koran, and it is reviewed and discussed from many angles. In other words, it is a central component of the faith.

In this chapter, you learn about some of the Koran's most compelling injunctions regarding charitable giving.

Spend Charitably ... While You Can!

Islam distinguishes between two types of charity:

♦ *Zakat:* Charity equaling 2.5 percent of gold or silver currency or their cash equivalents; all Muslims must give zakat each year. Believers can

What's It Mean?

Zakat, the charity required of all Muslims, means "purification;" when one gives of one's wealth, that money is purified. Zakat is a devotional act of worship comparable to the five daily prayers; it is not optional. *Sadagah,* on the other hand, is voluntary charity.

pay zakat at their mosque. (There is also a 20 percent tax on profits and found wealth known as Khums, as well as taxes on farm goods or cattle; interpretations on the proper levying of these taxes can vary.)

♦ *Sadagah:* Voluntary charity above and beyond the amount required as zakat.

Both types of giving are discussed in the Koran and the Sunna.

Wealth, in Islam, is regarded not as man's possession, but as God's. The Koran repeatedly makes reference to the proper distribution of "what We have given you":

> Spend for the cause of God out of what We have given you before death approaches you, and say, "Lord, would that you would give me respite for a short time so that I could spend for Your cause and become one of those who do good." (10)

The Koran teaches that every form of support—financial, material, spiritual, intellectual—is to be regarded by believers as a gift from Allah. Each and every believer is, in turn, obligated to use some of that support in the service of Allah, to help and support other human beings. This duty must be carried out while there is time; our life can end at any moment, and we will be judged in the afterlife by how well we carry out the instructions of Allah.

The Koran tells us that riches may be a spiritually disastrous distraction from one's duties to God:

> Believers, do not let your wealth and children divert you from remembering God. Whoever is diverted will suffer a great loss. (9)

The necessity of giving financially before the onset of death is emphasized, not once, but many times in the Koran. (Particularly urgent teachings in the Koran—about repentance, charity, and many other issues—and appear again and again.) In the fourteenth Sura, humanity is warned about a time that will come when good works will no longer be possible, when wealth may no longer be accumulated and dispersed in the name of the lord, and when humans will no longer be able to support each other in friendship:

> Tell My believing servants to be steadfast in prayer and to spend for the cause of their Lord, both in private and in public, out of what We have given them. Let them do this before the coming of the day when there will be no merchandising or friendship. (14:31)

Be Steadfast in Giving!

Believers are called again and again to fulfill their charitable obligations. In the following verse, the Koran assures believers that spiritual benefits will come to the person who gives. They are warned that God is fully aware of all their actions—with the clear implication that any attempt to avoid giving charitably will meet with his disfavor:

> Be steadfast in your prayer and pay the religious tax. You will receive a good reward from God for all your good works. God is Well-aware of what you do. (2:110)

Use Collected Money for the Right Purpose!

Those who collect mandatory charitable donations from believers may not simply apply them to whatever cause they see fit. The Koran sets out specific purposes for which zakat donations may be used. The ninth Sura sets out a detailed list of appropriate recipients for the funds that includes the poor, the heavily indebted, and needy travelers.

Misappropriation of zakat funds constitutes a major sin with serious legal and spiritual consequences.

Points to Ponder

Charity in Islam is not merely a practical matter related to maintaining the poor and ensuring the performance of socially constructive deeds. It is a spiritual discipline that encourages reverence to God and restores divinely revealed priorities.

Only those who are, out of fear of Him, humble before their Lord, who believe in the revelations of their Lord, who consider nothing equal to their Lord, who spend their property for the cause of God, and whose hearts are afraid of their return to God, these are the ones who really compete with each other in virtuous deeds and are the foremost ones in the task. (23:57–61)

Giving Is More Important Than Ritual

The specifics of religious ritual, believers are warned, are not what determine whether one is a pious believer. Rather, this is determined by charitable acts, patience, and faith:

> Righteousness consists of the belief in God, the Day of Judgment, the angels, the Books of God, His Prophets; to give money for the love of God to relatives, orphans, the destitute, and those who are on a journey and in urgent need of

money, beggars; to set free slaves and to be steadfast in prayer, to pay the religious tax (zakat) to fulfill one's promises, and to exercise patience in poverty, in distress, and in times of war. Such people who do these are truly righteous and pious. (2:177)

Anonymous Donors

While believers are commanded to give of their wealth, calling attention to one's charitable activities is specifically forbidden:

Points to Ponder

Announcing one's charitable giving to others is not the point. Improving one's relationship with God, who already knows all, is the point!

Believers, do not make your charities fruitless by reproachfully reminding the recipient of your favor or making them feel insulted, like the one who spends his property to show off and who has no faith in God or belief in the Day of Judgment. The example of his deed is as though some soil has gathered on a rock and after a rain fall it turns hard and barren. Such people can not benefit from what they have earned. God does not guide the unbelievers. (2:264)

Elsewhere, the Koran suggests that the most spiritual benefit is gained when a charitable gift is made anonymously:

It is not bad to give alms in public. However if you give them privately to the poor, it would be better for you and an expiation for some of your sins. God is Well-Aware of what you do. (2:271)

It is not surprising, then, that a long-standing tradition of anonymous giving to charitable causes exists in the Islamic world.

Aiding Those Who Strive for the Cause of God

A Muslim's obligation is to give to those in need—whether the needy are believers or non-believers. At several points, however, the Koran emphasizes the special importance of helping people whose charity is the direct result of a commitment to carry out the will of Allah. Those who strive in the cause of the Lord are set apart for special notice in the Koran, which warns its readers that identifying and helping such people is particularly important.

(If the recipients of charity are) the poor whose poverty, because of their striving for the cause of God, has become an obstacle for them, and who do not have the ability to travel in the land, they seem rich compared to the ignorant, because of their modest behavior. You would know them by their faces. They would never earnestly ask people for help. God knows well whatever wealth you spend for the cause of God. (2:273)

Giving that furthers religious undertakings is specifically encouraged:

> Those who spend their property for the cause of God, any time during the day or night, in public or in private, will receive their reward from their Lord. There will be no fear for them nor will they grieve. (2:274)

Spotlight on Islam

All those who maintain faith in the One God, perform righteous acts, keep up their daily prayers, and pay the poor-rate are told clearly that they will have no reason to fear or mourn when they are brought before the Lord. While we're on the subject of financial matters, we should note that the Koran regards charging interest as a major sin. The two subjects are addressed almost simultaneously in the thirtieth Sura:

God will not allow to increase whatever illegal interest you try to receive in order to increase your wealth at the expense of people's property. Whatever amount of zakat you give to please God will be doubled (for you). (30:39)

Harshness in Collecting Debts Forbidden

Charity can take other forms than giving money to the poor. It can also involve forgiving debts or extending payment deadlines. If someone who owes money is facing a crisis of some kind, the Koran insists that this person be allowed more time to pay. Overlooking such a loan entirely, and regarding it as a charitable gift, is clearly described as a spiritual benefit for the creditor:

> One who faces hardship in paying his debts must be given time until his financial condition improves. Would that you knew that waiving such a loan as charity would be better for you! (2:280)

Beware Mocking the Givers!

The Koran warns us that those who mock the believers who give freely to charitable causes will find themselves in turn mocked by God:

> God mocks those (hypocrites) who blame and mock the rich or poor believers who donate to the welfare funds, and He has prepared a painful torment for them. (9:79)

The Word

Do they not know that it is God who accepts the repentance of His servants and receives the welfare funds and that it is God who is All-forgiving and All-merciful? (9:104)

Give to the Near of Kin First!

At several points, the Koran instructs that voluntary charity should to blood relatives first, and then to other members of society. Notice who comes at the head of the list in the following passage:

> Give the relatives, the destitute, and the needy travelers their share (of charity). (30:38)

Good News for the Servants Who Obey

Those who give freely, we read in the Koran, are those who receive freely of God's blessing:

> He has blessed me no matter where I dwell, commanded me to worship Him and pay the religious tax for as long as I live. (19:31)

And in the twelfth Sura we read this:

> God will give the reward to those who give charity. (12:88)

The connection of receiving blessing to one's fulfillment of divine instructions of charity and devotion echoes many Christian teachings. God's pleasure descends, we are told repeatedly, on those who give without hesitation and submit to the will of God:

> He would order his people to worship God and pay the religious tax. His Lord was pleased with him. (19:55)

The Koran's message concerning charity is, finally, a message of great joy and deliverance. It is a message of union with the Almighty and mercy received from him:

> Your God is One God and you must submit yourselves to His will. (Muhammad), give the glad news (of God's mercy) to the devoted servants of God: Those whose hearts are filled with awe on hearing about God, who exercise patience in hardships, who are steadfast in prayer, and who spend their property for the cause of God. (22:34–35)

The Least You Need to Know

- The Koran's relentless insistence on the importance of charitable giving is distinctive.

- Believers regard all wealth in all forms as God's, and see humans as trustees of that wealth.

- Charity in Islam falls into two categories—required and voluntary.

- Giving designed to call attention to oneself is discouraged in the Koran.

- Financial giving is regarded as a means of spiritual growth in Islam.

- God's pleasure descends, the Koran teaches, on those who give without hesitation and submit to the will of God.

16

The Truth About Jihad

In This Chapter

- ♦ How the misinterpretation of *jihad* arose
- ♦ What *jihad* really means
- ♦ Distinguishing between greater and lesser jihads

The average Westerner knows very few real Arabic words—but there is one that he or she is likely to feel fairly certain about, and that is the word *jihad*.

Many in the West have concluded with certainty that this word means "holy war" in Arabic. In fact, it means "striving" or "struggling," and a good deal of confusion has arisen over the misuse of this term.

Let's look first at how the misinterpretation seems to have arisen—and then let's examine what "jihad" really means to Muslims.

What Gets Lost in the Translation

How is it that so many Westerners who know nothing else of Islam "know" that "jihad" means "holy war?" How is it that they "know" that the Koran counsels a military aggressiveness toward unbelievers that is sanctioned by scripture? (It does not, but this is the misperception.)

What's It Mean?

Jihad doesn't mean "holy war," at least not in the Koran. It means "striving." The Arabic words for "war" used in the Koran are *harb* or *qital*.

Usage After the Early Islamic Period

Part of the answer to these important "why" questions involves mistranslations of the word "jihad" by Muslim writers during and after the period of the Crusades—a long and bloody series of military adventures that were initiated by Christians against Muslims.

Simple Laziness

Another, and probably more important, factor in the modern usage of the term "jihad" has to do with the unwillingness of Western reporters and analysts to do the work necessary to explore the principles and history of Islam first hand. This is, in many ways, a puzzling state of affairs.

In passing along to their readers and viewers the details of, say, a local scandal involving misappropriation of funds, most Western journalists would be sure to check and recheck their sources before filing a final report on the subject. The reason for this caution is simple: Reporters want to avoid passing along an error or a preconceived opinion that cannot be verified by the facts. We have yet to reach a point in the United States, however, where the same journalists will check and recheck their sources to ensure the same level of accuracy in reports on Islam, and in particular with regard to the use of the word "jihad."

Caution!

It is important to bear in mind that changes in human language are irrelevant to the question of the teachings of the Koran. These divine teachings, Muslims believe, do not change over time, because the word of God is permanent and definitive.

As a result, many errors, misconceptions, preconceived notions, and unfortunate stereotypes persist in Western reportage on Islam, and particularly with regard to the Koran's use of the term "jihad."

Complexity of the Term as It Is Actually Used in the Koran

A third reason for the confusion in the West over the proper use of this term has to do with the complexity of "jihad's" actual meaning.

As you will learn shortly, there are quite a few different ways to "strive" in behalf of Islam, and summarizing them all in a single, memorable catch-phrase is impossible.

The term "holy war," however, is impossible to forget and by no means is the primary use of the term.

So in combination with the first two factors—Muslim usage of the word "jihad" centuries after the death of the Prophet and a general unwillingness among Western commentators to expend effort to learn about Islam—the many applications of the word "jihad" have helped to solidify misunderstanding about the word.

> **Spotlight on Islam**
>
> The term "jihad," meaning striving, struggling, or exerting oneself, doesn't necessarily refer to armed struggle—although it certainly can carry that meaning in certain situations. However, "jihad" may also refer to personal, ideological, or any number of other kinds of struggles.

> **Points to Ponder**
>
> Many Western writers and broadcasters thoughtlessly use the word "jihad" as a synonym for "holy war" because (a) they have never bothered to look up the earliest uses of the word "jihad" and (b) the mistranslations of later centuries correspond with negative stereotypes habitually connected with Islamic practice and belief. Such observers actually overlook the Koran's emphasis on the practice of humane warfare—a systematic, codified approach to armed conflict that has no parallel in Judeo-Christian scriptures, and that has behind it a long history religious tolerance ... not its opposite.

The Many Varieties of "Striving"

Literally, "jihad" means striving or struggling; it applies to any type of concerted, sustained human endeavor, especially an endeavor undertaken against opposition or in difficulty. It would be appropriate to use "jihad" in any of the following situations:

- A third grader struggling to improve her grade after a poor performance on a spelling test.

- A husband striving to make amends with his wife by reforming his character after mistreating her.

- An employee struggling to win the favorable attention of his boss so as to secure a raise.

- A mayor striving to win enough positive recognition from the public to ensure his re-election.

Jihad Isn't Just for Muslims

The Koran uses the Arabic verb form of "jihad" (translated in the following passage as "try to force") to refer to the activities of both Muslims and non-Muslims. Consider the following verse:

> If they try to force (struggle with, strive with) you to consider things equal to Me, which you cannot justify, equal to Me, do not obey them. Maintain lawful relations with them in this world and follow the path of those who turn in repentance to Me. To Me you will all return and I shall tell you all that you have done. (31:15)

Notice that in the passage you just read, those who are jihad-ing—striving, contending, struggling—are non-Muslims who are eager to get Muslims to commit the sin of association, or shirk.

Two Kinds of Jihad

Broadly speaking, there are two varieties of jihad within Islam.

The Prophet's term "Greater Jihad" refers to the personal struggle against evil that each individual Muslim must undertake during the course of his of her life. This variety of "jihad" is by far the most prominent in the Islamic tradition. This kind of struggle has a great deal to do with the state of one's direct relationship to God—and one's relationship to God is, of course, of paramount importance within Islam.

There is also, according to Muhammad, the "Lesser Jihad." This variety of struggling, striving, or contending involves group activity in the context of what should, in this narrow context, properly be called "legal war" (rather than "holy war").

At this point, it must be understood that Islam condones fighting only when the conflict involves self-defense, defense of one's religion from the assaults of unbelievers, and in response to the forcible displacement of people from their living quarters. Even in situations where military conflict is seen as "legal," Islam mandates that one deal mercifully with one's enemies. Civilians, in particular, are to be dealt with humanely, and no violence is to be extended to women, the aged, or children.

Such requirements are apparently beyond the understanding of extremist groups that target civilians, and call such violations of law "jihad."

> **CAUTION!**
>
> **Caution!**
>
> Western notions of "holy war" often overlook the Islamic obligation of observing civilized codes of conduct during times of war. Jihad—struggle— is never to be employed as a means of forcing religious conversion, and Islamic combatants are reminded in the Koran to "Fight for the cause of God, those who fight you, but do not transgress, for God does not love the transgressors." (2:190)

It is worth noting here, too, though, that the Koran explicitly forbids the forced conversion of unbelievers by military or any other means. ("There is no compulsion in religion" is one of the Koran's clear teachings on this subject.)

Again and again, the Koran urges tolerance and kindness toward unbelievers who do not physically assault or otherwise disrupt the Muslim community. This guidance, it must be emphasized, rules out warfare for the purpose of religious dominance!

The Word

We shall certainly guide those who strive for Our cause to Our path. God is certainly with the righteous ones. (29:69)

Indeed, on several occasions the Koran informs its readers that devout, submitting *non-Muslims* will share in salvation on the Day of Judgment:

> The believers, Jews, Sabaeans, and the Christians who believe in God and the Day of Judgment and who do what is right will have nothing to fear, nor will they be grieved. (5:69)

Having reminded ourselves of these important points, let's look for a moment at the forms that each of the kinds of jihad—greater and lesser—may take in Islamic life.

The Greater Jihad: Personal Struggle

Personal struggles, or the greater jihad, can take many forms. The following sections detail various kinds of greater struggles or strivings.

Loving the Creator Above All Things

It's easier to love something you can see than something you can't.

Allah is, as the Koran reminds us frequently, all too easily ignored and overlooked by humanity. It is not surprising, then, that it is often a struggle to love God more than the material attractions of the world or the regard of other human beings:

> Believers, do not accept your fathers and brothers as your guardians if they prefer disbelief to faith, lest you be unjust. (Muhammad), tell them, "If your fathers, children, brothers, spouses, relatives, the property that you possess, the trade you fear may have no profit and the homely life are more beloved to you than God, His Messenger and fighting for His cause, wait until God fulfills His decree (of making the right distinct from the wrong). God does not guide the evil-doers." (9:23–24)

Disregarding Those Who Reject the Faith

Withstanding the pressures of unbelievers is another constant opportunity for striving among Muslims. The pressures of living in a land where unbelievers are the majority can be strong indeed, and the Koran counsels believers to struggle against this pressure:

> Do not yield to the unbelievers but launch a great campaign against them with the help of the Koran. (25:52)

Following the Straight Path Without Hesitation

Pursuing with full commitment the religious path laid out by Allah is another form of striving for the individual believer.

This kind of jihad is indeed warfare—but it is warfare waged within the individual, a perpetual striving to follow the path laid out by God:

> Strive steadfastly for the Cause of God. He has chosen you but has not imposed on you hardship in your religion, the noble religion of your father, Abraham. God named you Muslims before and in this Book, so that the Messenger will witness (your actions) and will be the witness over mankind. Be steadfast in your prayer, pay the religious tax, and seek protection from God; He is your Guardian, a gracious Guardian and Helper. (22:78)

Bravery to Speak of the Message of Allah to Unbelievers

The Koran offers many stories of Prophets who struggled against unbelief in their community. Individual Muslims are not Prophets, of course—Muhammad was the Final Prophet—but they are instructed to call all of humanity to the true religion, submission to the will of God, and to lead lives of righteousness that may serve as an example to the world:

Spotlight on Islam

In dealing with the personal struggle (jihad) to maintain one's faith in a hostile environment, the Koran counsels believers not to assault their persecutors, but to emigrate to lands where no religious persecution is likely.

Who speaks better than one who invites human beings to God, acts righteously and says, "I am a Muslim." (41:33)

Or again:

The believers are those who believe in God and His Messenger, who do not change their belief into doubt and who strive hard for the cause of God with their property and persons. They are the truthful ones. (49:15)

The Lesser Jihad: Military Conflict

Islamic teachings hold that it is unholy to initiate armed conflict, but that some such conflicts cannot be avoided. When an opponent requests an end to hostilities and makes a sincere request for peace, the request must be respected.

The Word

The Koran renounces all acts of hatred and injustice:

Virtue and evil are not equal. If you replace evil (response) by virtuous ones, you will certainly find that your enemies will become your intimate friends. Only those who exercise patience and who have been granted a great share of Allah's favor can find such an opportunity. (41:34–35)

Remember God's favors to you and the firm covenant that He has made with you. You said because of this covenant, "We have heard (the words of the Lord) and have obeyed Him." Have fear of God; He knows well all that the hearts contain. (5:7)

Believers, be steadfast for the cause of God and just in bearing witness. Let not a group's hostility to you cause you to deviate from justice. Be just, for it is closer to piety. Have fear of God; God is Well Aware of what you do. (5:8)

God has promised forgiveness and a great reward to the righteously striving believers. (5:9)

The Koran acknowledges as legitimate causes for military action a number of specific situations, including those described in the following sections.

Defense When the Community of Believers Is Attacked

The Koran permits armed resistance when believers are under direct attack:

Permission to take up arms is hereby granted to those who are attacked; they have suffered injustice. God has all the power to give victory. (22:39)

Freeing Oppressed Peoples

We read that Allah also grants permission to liberate weak groups that are clearly the victims of oppression:

Why do you not fight for the cause of God or save the helpless men, women, and children who cry out, "Lord, set us free from this town of wrong doers and send us a guardian and a helper?" (4:75)

The Word _____

> To those who were unjustly expelled from their homes only because they said, "God is our Lord." Had it not been for God's repelling some people through the might of the others, the monasteries, churches, synagogues, and mosques in which God is very often worshipped would have been utterly destroyed. God shall certainly help those who help Him. He is All-powerful and Majestic.
>
> He will certainly help those who, if given power in the land, will worship God through prayer, pay the religious tax, enjoin others do good, and prevent them from committing evil. The consequence of all things is in the hands of God. (22:40–41)

There is, no doubt, a great deal more that could be said about Islam's instructions in military matters. There is a long tradition within the faith of following the Prophet's remarkable adherence to standards mandating humane warfare. Combatants are forbidden, for instance, to destroy the crops of the enemy, or to target the clergy, or to engage in suicide attacks. These are established interpretations of Islamic law dating back to the time of Muhammad.

Non-Muslims should know that those who issue dubious "rulings" sanctifying attacks on civilians (such as Osama Bin Laden) face two significant obstacles to their interpretations. First, these individuals lack authority to issue such rulings. And second, in doing so, they show an utter disregard for the legal precedents of roughly fourteen centuries.

Think of it this way: If Osama Bin Laden should declare himself to be a member of the Supreme Court of the United States, and were to issue a "ruling" declaring the First Amendment to be null and void, would that prove anything at all about the U.S. Constitution? Or would it instead prove that a madman had taken it upon himself to make pronouncements he had no right to make?

The Least You Need to Know

- ◆ "Jihad" does not mean "holy war," but rather "struggle" or "striving."

- ◆ This struggling, striving, or contending may take place in a variety of settings.

- ◆ Western observers routinely mistranslate the word "jihad."

- ◆ "Greater Jihad" refers to personal struggles with a spiritual dimension.

- ◆ "Lesser Jihad" refers to group struggle and armed conflict.

- ◆ Islam enforces strict codes of conduct on those believers who wage war.

Part 5

Life on Earth and the Afterlife

What are we doing here? Where are we going next?

These are timeless questions, and the Koran addresses them directly. This part of *The Complete Idiot's Guide to the Koran* shows you what Islam teaches believers concerning the purpose of life on Earth, how Muslims should treat unbelievers, and what awaits us all after death.

17

God's Plan for Us

In This Chapter

- ◆ The purpose of life on Earth
- ◆ Questions about God's justice
- ◆ The right path

What is the meaning of life? Why must we die? And if there is a God, then why does he let bad things happen to good people?

These are some of life's *big* questions—the kinds of questions that college students stay up all night debating and that philosophers and theologians spend their careers trying to answer. Fortunately for Muslims, the Koran addresses these and other of life's biggies.

Everything Is from God

The Koran tells us that life on Earth is not all there is to existence.

It reminds us that our familiar daily life on Earth is part of a much larger, divinely mandated plan—a plan that tests each person, a plan that is perfect. This is a plan that encompasses both life and death, both joy and misfortune, both pleasure and pain. And it is a plan, the Koran teaches, that we are all part of. God, we read, has given us a series of tests—and in fact all occurrences, whether they appear to relate to us individually or not, are part of this test.

The Word

"There's going to be a quiz"—A reminder from the Koran about God's tests:

God does not impose on any soul a responsibility beyond its ability. Every soul receives whatever it gains and is liable for whatever it does. Lord, do not hold us responsible for our forgetfulness and mistakes. Lord, do not lay upon us the burden that You laid on those who lived before us. Lord, do not lay on us what we cannot afford. Ignore and forgive our sins. Have mercy on us. You are our Lord. Help us against the unbelievers. (2:286)

The thought of being tested constantly can be a difficult idea for the human mind to grasp. All the same, these teachings are, believers insist, important and worthy of the attention of each of us who must make the journey between birth and death.

Life, people often tell themselves, is something we must prolong at all costs; death, we often like to assume, is something to be considered later, not unlike a disease that may someday be conquered or an unpleasant task that can be postponed. Like soldiers contemplating the battlefield, most people are uneasy about the prospect of facing death. We often consider it the ultimate misfortune, something to be avoided, something we can evade. Certainly, we are inclined to consider it to be the opposite of life.

The Koran insists, however, that life and death each operate together as part of the divine plan. What's more, the Koran challenges us not to avoid that fact, but rather to accept it as a precondition of human existence. Death is, we are assured, part of our "contract"—as is the life to come:

Have you not seen those who were told to stop fighting, to say their prayers, and pay the religious tax? When they were ordered to fight, some of them feared other men as much as or more than they feared God and so they said, "Lord, why have you ordered us to fight? If only you would give us a little time." (Muhammad), tell them, "The pleasures of the worldly life are trivial. The life hereafter is best for the pious ones. You will not be treated the slightest bit unjustly.

Wherever you are, death will find you even if you hide yourselves in firmly constructed towers. Whenever people experience good fortune, they say that it is from God but whenever they experience misfortune, they say it is because of you," (Muhammad).

Tell them, "Everything is from God." What is wrong with these people that they do not even try to understand? (4:77–78)

"Good luck" (someone gives us a high-paying job) "bad luck" (we are diagnosed with cancer)—all of it is from our Creator, the Koran insists, and all of it is part of our Creator's plan. In both "good luck" and "bad luck" situations, the Koran teaches, we must ask ourselves: How can I best submit to Allah's will? (Does our new job help us to set a humble, good example to others in the area of charitable giving? Does our terminal illness help us show others what a peaceful, faithful return to the Creator looks like?)

Why Are We Here?

The Koran offers a direct answer to the common philosophical question, "What is the purpose of our existence?"

We are here so that we may make a good return to God and attain salvation on *al-Hisab*. We came from Allah; we will die, and then we will return to Allah. When we die, we will be judged on the merits of our life. If we misuse the time we have been given to spend on Earth (by failing to worship Allah, disobeying Allah's commands, or persisting in sin), then we will fail our test and be cast into hell. The purpose of human existence, the Koran teaches, is nothing more or less than to pass our coming test on the Day of Judgment.

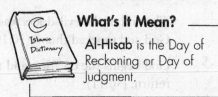

What's It Mean?

Al-Hisab is the Day of Reckoning or Day of Judgment.

There are many verses in the Koran that illustrate this tenet of Islamic belief. In the eleventh Sura, the Creator tells Muhammad to share the following words with the people:

> Seek forgiveness from your Lord and turn to Him in repentance for your sins. He will provide you good sustenance for an appointed time and will reward everyone according to his merits. I am afraid that you will suffer torment on the great Day (of Judgment) if you turn away (from God).

> To God you will all return. God has power over all things. (11:3–4)

The Creator does not tell the Prophet to share these words with *some* of the people, but with everyone! All of us are limited, the Koran teaches; all of us have engaged in misconduct, although we are not always aware of the true dimensions of our deeds.

Is the Koran Bleak?

There are some people who come away from the teachings of the Koran believing that it portrays a God who is somehow misguided, cruel, or unjust.

They conclude that the Islamic holy book shows us an entity who has somehow neglected the possibility of the rehabilitation of sinners and gone on to endorse a bleak and hopeless vision of human existence. They may also cite the vivid descriptions of the punishments awaiting sinners and the fact that God allows for bad things to happen to good people. The Koran is prepared for such attacks, however, and has responses to all such criticisms.

The "Harshness" Factor

It is a common question among those examining Islam to ask whether Allah is too harsh. The harshness, we learn from the Koran, does not originate with Allah, but with humanity. Allah does not do injury to our souls—we do that injury ourselves.

> The end of the evil-doers was terrible, for they had rejected the revelations of God and mocked them. (30:10)

> God begins the creation and then causes it to turn back, and to Him you will all return. (30:11)

We are tested again and again by Allah for his purposes, not ours. We may not learn, during our lives on Earth, the true nature or purpose of the tests that have been sent to us. To be sure, the Koran tells us, the plans of Allah may often appear to be illogical to us. The Koran goes on to assure us that we may still be confident that we are being tested by God, and that all is unfolding according to his plan, which is sound and fair and well beyond human comprehension. What is also clear enough in the Koran's teaching is that both "good fortune" and "bad fortune" may be trials from Allah—and that death and a return to God are inevitable:

> Every soul has to experience the taste of death. We test you with both hardships and blessings. In the end you will all return to Us. (21:35)

It was quite common, when the Prophet delivered his message of salvation, for him to be questioned by skeptical people who heard his recitations. Often, they would ask about whether a just Creator could or would really bring people back to life after their death, when exactly this judgment he kept talking about would take place, and why God would select him in the first place to pass along communications about such matters. No doubt a number of them wondered whether God's benevolence could permit even the existence of such a place as hell. The Koran tells us that God offered Muhammad clear instructions for dealing with those who expressed such doubts:

> If they turn away, tell them, "I have warned every one of you equally. I do not know when the torment which you have to suffer will take place. God knows well all that is spoken aloud and all that you hide. I do not know (why God has commanded me to warn you of the torment). Perhaps it is a trial for you, and a respite for an appointed time." (21:109–111)

Points to Ponder

The Koran teaches that those who try to resist the guidance of Allah are the authors of deep injury to their own souls. It repeatedly warns its readers and hearers that such resistance will be detrimental to one's eventual happiness, even if it results in temporary pleasures here on Earth. Such pleasures may well be a trial from Allah—a test to see whether we will express appropriate gratitude to Allah … or even, perhaps, a test of what we are willing to give up in order to obey God's will.

Is the Creator Unjust?

Allah, the Koran teaches, is *not* unjust or cruel to humanity … but he did give humanity freedom to choose their actions, and humans often choose to take actions that do damage to their own souls. The consequences of this choice are laid out clearly throughout the Koran.

There's a story from the American Civil War about the great Confederate General Robert E. Lee, who was to preside over a court-martial proceeding, during which the guilt or innocence of a young private was to be determined. Lee noticed that the young man was trembling, so he walked over to him, touched him on the shoulder, and said, "Don't worry, son—you'll be tried fairly here."

The private gulped and said, "That's what I'm afraid of, general."

In a similar vein, but with a much more important issue at stake (namely, where we will each spend eternity), the Koran warns us that Allah will judge us all fairly. If we have spent our lives rebelling against divine guidance, we may well have reason to tremble at that justice—regardless of how many sensual pleasures, possessions, or temporary advantages our rebellion against Allah's guidance has secured for us in the short term. The long term, we are advised, is what we should be concerned about:

> When We saved you, you started to rebel unjustly in the land. People, your rebellion will only harm yourselves. You may enjoy the worldly life but to Us you will all return and We will let you know all that you had done. (10:23)

Spotlight on Islam _____

A verse in the Koran about human misfortune has been open to a great deal of misinterpretation. In the forty-second Sura, the Koran reads:

> Whatever hardship befalls you is the result of your own deeds. God pardons many of your sins. (42:30)

This has been interpreted by some to mean that any misfortune that befalls *any human being* is exclusively the result of his or her own actions. This interpretation, however, ignores the fact that the words are addressed by Allah exclusively to unbelievers—that is, to people who maintain willful rejection of the message of the Koran, despite its having been revealed to them with great clarity and in a manner that no rational person would reject. What the verse is actually saying, in other words, is that God may bring earthly hardships to those who knowingly reject the divine truth and harden themselves against its guidance. This kind of misfortune can, of course, take many forms, some of it obvious, some of it less so. On the larger question of (apparent) "good luck" or "bad luck," the Koran's message is clear: We may expect to be tested during both good times and bad.

God the Guider

If one examines the Koran carefully, one finds that the emphasis throughout is on Allah's care and love for humanity, and on his concern that his message of salvation and repentance be circulated as widely as possible. We find a Creator who is deeply concerned about humanity, and we learn that it is all too often humanity, and not God, who has strayed from the true path.

It is worth noting briefly here, once again, the respect and high regard in which the Koran holds the prophetic mission of Jesus. In reading the New Testament sayings attributed to the Messiah, it's hard for a Muslim not to be struck by the number of times that he shares his message by referring to God Almighty as the Father of all humanity: "Your heavenly Father." "Your father who knows what you need and what you lack." In the Lord's Prayer, for instance, he says: "*Our* Father, who art in heaven …"

This is an extraordinary Christian metaphor, one whose actual application is easy to overlook. A good father guides, corrects, and supports his children as they grow and develop. A good father does not, however, offer blind acceptance of anything and everything a child might choose to do. That would be dangerous! If he did that, he would certainly be a bad father. A good father, by contrast, says something when he sees a child about to make a serious mistake.

When a good earthly father notices that his child has chosen a path that is likely to lead to pain or injury, he speaks up. He consistently speaks up and issues warnings when he notices the child taking the wrong path. He patiently reminds the child, in other words, of the right purpose and the right action.

It is in this sense, perhaps, that we should understand the metaphor of God being not an earthly father, but humanity's patient guide—the one who sets us on the right path and reminds us of the right purpose and the right action when we lose sight of them. Certainly, this kind of guidance pervades the Koran.

In the Koran, Allah patiently reminds believers of the truth when they might otherwise ignore it or imagine themselves superior to it:

> Do they say that he, (Muhammad), has invented falsehood against God? Had God wanted, He could have sealed up your heart. God causes falsehood to vanish and, by His words, firmly establishes the truth. He has full knowledge of what the hearts contain. He knows their actions and their inclinations, and forgoes punishment when they admit their errors to Him:
>
> It is He who accepts the repentance of His servants, forgives their evil deeds and knows all about what you do. (42:24–25)

He listens to their entreaties to him that he set them on the right path:

> (Lord), You alone We do worship and from You alone we do seek assistance. (Lord), guide us to the right path. The path of those to whom You have granted blessings, those who are neither subject to Your anger nor have gone astray. (1:5–7)

And he reminds them constantly about exactly what their purpose on Earth is—attaining success in the afterlife:

> God will reform your deeds and forgive your sins. One who obeys God and His Messenger will certainly achieve a great success. (33:71)

The Least You Need to Know

- The Koran teaches that the purpose of our earthly life is to prepare us to make a good return to God and attain salvation.
- It teaches that God has plans that surpass human comprehension.
- It teaches that God tests people with both good times and bad times.
- It teaches that humans are the authors of injuries to their own souls.
- It teaches that God is just.
- It teaches that God directs us constantly to the right path.

18

Muslims and Non-Muslims: How to Get Along

In This Chapter

◆ Advice for believers

◆ Advice for unbelievers

◆ The role of the Ummah

Many who are unfamiliar with Islam are surprised to learn how lenient its pronouncements are to believers concerning relationships with unbelievers. Short of a situation involving military occupation, believers are told not to attempt to set themselves apart from the obligation to show kindness and mercy to those who reject Allah's communications.

The Koran requires the Islamic community to permit non-Muslims to exercise their beliefs within its boundaries ... but it also sets out clear guidelines for interactions between believers and non-believers.

In this chapter, you will learn how the Koran regulates relationships between believers and unbelievers.

Different Perspectives

For someone who accepts the Koran as the literal word of God, the act of reading or reciting the Koran has a specific purpose: to determine what course God Almighty has laid out for the believer, what the "straight path" actually is. (Muslims believe that the Sunna explains in detail the guidance set down in general terms in the Koran on determining the "straight path.")

To someone who is *not* seeking the moral guidance of the Koran as a believer seeks it, the situation is very different.

For this person, the act of evaluating the content of the Koran may well be a purely academic or intellectual pursuit. This person is usually quite skeptical of the claim that God delivered a book to a human being on the Arabian plain fourteen centuries ago—or perhaps even hostile to that claim. Either way, this person is unlikely to be approaching the Koran to determine what is right and what is wrong.

These, then, are two very different mindsets—and two very different groups of people. As it happens, the Koran offers advice to both groups.

The Word

The Koran tells believers what to say to unbelievers:

You follow your religion and I follow mine. (109:6)

An update from the "gee-this-sounds-familiar" department: You'll probably notice, as you make your way through this chapter of the book, that advice on how to deal with unbelievers shows up *throughout* the Koran, rather than in a single Sura. If you were to read the entire Koran from beginning to end, you might also notice that the advice in one part of the Koran on this subject does not conflict with advice appearing on the same subject elsewhere in the Koran.

This is one of the remarkable features of the Koran. Although the Suras appeared over a span of more than two decades, they offer utterly consistent teachings on a staggering variety of topics. Dealings with unbelievers is only one of those topics. But as you review what the Koran has to say about this issue, bear in mind that, as the Prophet Muhammad addressed it, he faced a dizzying array of groups and individuals, some of whom were hostile to his message, some of whom were indifferent, and some of whom were receptive to it. During part of the time when the advice you're about to read was first circulated, the Muslim community was literally fighting for its life; during another part of the time when these instructions were given, Muhammad was the emperor of a mighty kingdom. Yet the message clicks together into a single powerful set of ideas.

The Koran's Advice to Believers About Unbelievers

Although the Koran distinguishes some unbelievers from others by designating Christians and Jews as "People of the Book," it is quite clear in rejecting the idea that a believing Muslim can or should take unbelievers as close friends. The relevant Arabic word here is *waliy*.

Taking a nonbeliever as one's waliy rather than establishing such a relationship with a believer is hazardous to one's spiritual health, according to the Koran. Doing so, we are told, endangers one's relationship with Allah—the very last thing a believer should consciously choose to do.

What's It Mean?

Waliy is an Arabic word with a broad range of meaning that encompasses the ideas of "guardian" and "trusted ally or close personal friend."

> The believers must not establish (close) friendship with the unbelievers in preference to the faithful. Whoever does so has nothing to hope for from God unless he does it out of fear or for protection. God warns you about Himself. To God do all things return. (3:28)

It is worth noting, however, that here and elsewhere the Koran does not preclude any contact whatsoever with unbelievers, or even acquaintanceship with unbelievers, as it might very easily have done. Instead, it urges believers to be on their guard, and not to take unbelievers as allies or close friends.

It is tempting to conclude that the Almighty wished the example of upright living provided by believers to "rub off" on unbelievers, but at the same time didn't want the example of unbelievers to "rub off" on believers.

Points to Ponder

The Koran frequently restates and repeats its instructions to humanity.

The message is elaborately restated and reformulated in the fourth Sura:

> Believers, do not make unbelievers your intimate friends and supporters rather than believers. Do you want to establish clear evidence against yourselves before God? (4:144)

Here again, the Koran explicitly instructs that believers should be the allies and close friends of fellow believers—an instruction with obvious positive effects for the believing community as a whole. Mutual support in the *deen*—or way of life—established by Allah is much easier when one has Muslim friends. (In fact, trying to follow that way of life without Muslim friends is probably impossible.)

Notice, though, that the second half of the verse moves from the level of the community to the level of the individual. The Koran pointedly asks the reader (or hearer) how much evidence he or she really wishes to submit to the "prosecution" on Judgment Day! Forming close alliances with nonbelievers when one could form the same alliance with believers, the Koran tells us, is "proof against" one's own faith.

The message is elaborated still further in the thirty-third Sura:

> Do not yield to the disbelievers or the hypocrites. Ignore their annoying you. Trust in God. God is your all Sufficient Protector. (33:48)

Spotlight on Islam _____

The Koran specifically instructs Muslims to show kindness and forbearance in their dealings with unbelievers who are not engaged in military occupation:

It may be that Allah will bring about friendship between you and those whom you hold to be your enemies among them ... Allah does not forbid you respecting those who have not made war against you on account of (your) religion, and have not driven you forth from your homes, that you show them kindness and deal with them justly; surely Allah loves the doers of justice. (60:7–8)

On Relations with Jews and Christians

The Koran warns Muslims of the dangers of growing weak in faith because of relationships with even monotheistic unbelievers such as Jews and Christians:

> And the Jews will not be pleased with you, nor the Christians until you follow their religion. Say: Surely Allah's guidance, that is the (true) guidance. And if you follow their desires after the knowledge that has come to you, you shall have no guardian from Allah, nor any helper. (2:120)

What Gives?

Anyone eager to limit contact between Muslims and non-Muslims might be tempted conclude, at this point, that the Koran takes a negative or hostile attitude toward any kind of sustained interaction between believers and unbelievers.

And yet this is not what actually appears in the text. Having warned believers to be on their guard against the hypocrisy of unbelievers, and having instructed believers not to take unbelievers as close allies, the Koran also offers some fascinating counsel on interactions with Jews and Christians. These are, as we have seen, the "People of the Book," groups who share a common spiritual heritage with the believers.

Muslims and Christians

Christians, Muslims are told, will sometimes be sympathetic to the cause of God, and may actually be deeply moved on its behalf:

Caution!

Do not assume that the Koran places monotheistic (one-God) unbelievers and polytheistic (many-God) unbelievers on the same footing. Islam specifically acknowledges that pious Jews and Christians who do as Allah commands will gain entrance to Paradise (2:62). All those who persist in worshipping associate gods after hearing the message of the One God, however, will go to hell.

> When they hear what is revealed to the Messenger, you can see their eyes flood with tears, as they learn about the Truth. They say, "Lord, we believe (in this faith). Write our names down as bearing witness to it. Why should we not believe in God and the Truth that has come to us and hope that the Lord will admit us into the company of the righteous people?" (5:82–4)

Clearly, interactions with Christians that expose them to God's word are permitted. In fact, such interactions, the Koran implies, are to be encouraged.

Muslims and Jews

The Koran also tells us that there are many followers of the Jewish faith who will attain salvation:

> However, the learned among them (the Jews) and the faithful believe in what God has revealed to you (Muhammad) and to the others before you and those who are steadfast in prayer, pay their religious tax, and believe in God and the Day of Judgment. They all will receive a great reward from Us. (4:162)

The Koran also tells us, however, that Muslims should expect to encounter intense opposition in many of their dealings with Jewish people. Near the very same passage that painted a picture of the Christian who weeps in gratitude when he hears the word of Islam, we find this warning:

> You will find Jews and pagans among the worst of the enemies of the believers. (5:81)

And this opposition has in fact been part of the history of Islam. Muslims are not at all surprised when it is pointed out that, from the seventh century to today, there have been far more Christian converts to Islam than Jewish converts. Here, as in so many other places in the Koran, the author knew exactly what he was talking about.

Advice for Unbelievers About Believers

The Koran's advice to unbelievers concerning believers is simple—and it is repeated and elaborated hundreds of times within the text. Unbelievers are urged to join the community of believers while there is still time to do so, and to acknowledge that all of us must eventually return to God to be judged by our Creator.

Here is just one example:

> Can one who walks with his head hanging down be better guided that one who walks with his head upright? (Muhammad), say, "It is God who has brought you into being and made ears, eyes, and hearts for you, but you give very little thanks." Say, "It is God who has settled you on the earth and to Him you will be resurrected." (67:22–24)

The Koran also explains quite clearly, however, that many will ignore this call, will continue to worship their own low desires, and will in this way become the authors of their own doom.

God's Plan

In the end, we must remember that it is Allah himself who regulates the two groups and guides them toward their very different destinies:

> Those who deny your message will not believe whether you warn them or not. God has sealed their hearts and hearing and their vision is veiled; a great punishment awaits them. (2:6–7)

Just a few lines later, unbelievers are warned in no uncertain terms about the consequences of mere superficial adherence to the rules set out for the community of believers. Pretense of belief (in order to win social status, say) may be possible among human beings, but it will not, we are told, fool God:

> (The hypocrites) have deceived no one but themselves, a fact of which they are not aware. A sickness exists in their hearts to which God adds more sickness. Besides this, they will suffer a painful punishment as a result of the lie which they speak. (2:9–10)

To the *Ummah*, as the global community of believers is called, the Koran gives the responsibility of spiritual role model to the entire world—a role that takes as its inspiration the mission of the Prophet himself.

The Koran also promises the nation of believers that they are guided by God himself and that their faith will, in the end, bring forth a great harvest:

> We have made you (true Muslims) a moderate nation so that you could be an example for all people and the Prophet an example for you. (2:143)

What's It Mean?

The **Ummah** is the worldwide community of Muslim believers. Aspiring to the **deen,** or way of life, of the Prophet Muhammad, is one of the goals of the Ummah.

The Least You Need to Know

◆ The Koran advises believers to tell unbelievers, "You shall have your religion and I shall have my religion."

◆ Believers and unbelievers approach the Koran in very different ways.

◆ The Koran urges caution in dealings with unbelievers, but does not prohibit contact with them.

◆ The Ummah—the global community of believers—is envisioned as a spiritual role model for the entire world.

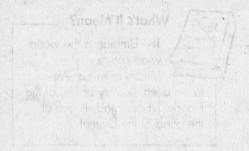

What's It Mean?

The Ummah is the world wide community of Muslim believers. As any ... dean ... any of ... the Prophet Mohammed is a part of the Ummah.

19

Where Are We Going?

In This Chapter

◆ Two reliable factors about human nature

◆ The afterlife

◆ The certainty of the believers

There are, one can argue, two utterly predictable things about human nature.

The first is that we are inclined to seek out enjoyable experiences and avoid traumatic or distressing ones; and the second is that we are deeply uncomfortable with the unknown. These factors are well known to contemporary trainers, therapeutic professionals, and experts in human behavior. We process information about our surroundings according to these principles. Apparently, though, these modern-sounding principles are not exactly modern discoveries, because a book composed fourteen centuries ago displays an intimate knowledge of their workings.

The Koran's message to humanity is, it will come as no surprise, one of glad news and warning—but it is also, amazingly, a message that takes into account the way human beings process information about their environment and learn to interact effectively with it. Many centuries before the work of such people as Sigmund Freud and B.F. Skinner, the Koran delivered important teachings about the afterlife regarding the ultimate enjoyable experience—namely that of being *sa'id*—and the ultimate ordeal of suffering, that of being *haqiy*. What's more, the messages of the Koran resolve (for believers) any possible uncertainty about the ultimate unknown: death.

> **What's It Mean?**
>
> **Sa'id** means blessed or fortunate; **haqiy** means condemned or unfortunate. In the Koran, those who are sa'id earn entrance to Paradise; those who are haqiy earn the torments of hell.

The author of the Koran, in other words, made abundantly clear the extraordinary trauma and suffering associated with disobeying divine instructions. The same author also conveyed the joy associated with the only experience Muslims regard as true success: the reward received after death for following the instructions of Allah. The Koran also brings to believers a unique clarity and certainty to the most vexing questions related to human mortality.

The Afterlife

The beauty, complexity, and intricacy of the Koranic teachings about the afterlife are frequently underestimated by non-Muslims. Many people unfamiliar with the Islamic faith believe that its followers hold a "simplistic" view of the afterlife. Believers hold a view of the afterlife that accepts the Koran's extraordinary guidance on the subject (some samples of which appear in this chapter). They also acknowledge that a final human understanding of God's purposes is utterly impossible, because human beings are limited and Allah is not. Such an approach, Muslims argue, is anything but simplistic.

Accepting the limitations of our own intellects, let's examine some of what the Koran has to say about where we are all going and what we are likely to find when we get there. There is no better place to start than with a sobering excerpt from the powerful seventieth Sura of the Koran. It tells us of haqiy, and demonstrates how severe the torments are that await those who reject Allah's communications:

> (On the Day of Judgment,) even intimate friends will not inquire about their friends, though they may see each other. A sinner will wish that he could save himself from the torment of that day by sacrificing his children, his wife, his brother, his kinsmen who gave him refuge (from hardship) and all those on earth. By no means! For the raging flames of the fire will strip off the flesh and drag into it anyone who has turned away (from obeying God), and who accumulated wealth without spending it for a good purpose. (70:10–18)

Muslims file this whole vivid passage under "that which is to be avoided at all costs." Is a more compelling portrait of the predicament of the damned necessary—or even possible?

In the lines following the chilling scene you just read, the Koran tells us of those who *avoid* the punishments of Allah—those who are sa'id. They are, we read, those who are generous with the property that has been entrusted to them by their Lord; those who are constant in their prayers; those who acknowledge the reality of the Day of Judgment; those who are truthful; those who closely monitor their own thoughts and actions in accordance with the will of their Creator. Such people will "receive due honor in Paradise." (70:35)

Muslims file *this* outcome under "that which is to be obtained at all costs."

> **Caution!**
>
> After the 9/11 attacks, an urban legend arose that the Koran promised 72 female virgins to men who die in suicide missions. The Koran contains no such verse. The myth appears to have derived from a reported saying of the Prophet that had nothing whatsoever to do with suicide missions, and that applied to male and female believers alike. The saying's authenticity is dubious.

Death Is Unavoidable

Death, mankind is told in the Koran, is part of the deal. We cannot negotiate our way around it or talk our way through it. It comes to all men and all women. Death, believers maintain, is the means by which all of us are returned to God and evaluated for our responses to the tests and trials God has sent our way:

> Every soul has to experience the taste of death. We test you with both hardships and blessings. In the end you will all return to Us. (21:35)

Human beings, believers note, are often very eager to consider themselves beyond the reach or influence of the Almighty. The Koran, however, challenges people to reconsider this attitude. One of the most unsettling questions it poses concerning this imagined independence from God—an attitude that is, we must acknowledge, fairly common in modern secular society—appears in the fifty-sixth Sura:

> Why can you not help a soul dying right before your very eyes? We are closer to him than you, but you cannot see. If you are true to your claim that there is no Day of Judgment, why can you not bring it (the soul) back (to life)? (56:83–87)

Spotlight on Islam

The Holy Koran envisions death, not as a payment for the first woman's sin, but as part of a divinely ordained process:

> It is God who makes all kinds of seeds grow, brings forth the living from the dead, and the dead from the living. It is God who does such things, so how can you turn away from Him? (6:95)

That process is an unavoidable part of the human experience:

> Every soul has to experience the taste of death. We test you with both hardships and blessings. In the end you will all return to Us. (21:35)

The point is not to overcome any obstacle of "original sin," but to make the journey between birth and death in submission to the will of Allah, as revealed by his Prophets:

> Abraham left this legacy to his sons and, in turn, so did Jacob saying, "God has chosen this religion for you. You must not leave this world unless you are a Muslim (submitted to the will of the Lord of the Universe)." (2:132)

There Will Be a Judgment

In the face of skepticism from unbelievers, the Koran teaches that a Day of Judgment is imminent for humanity. It devotes many of its verses to instructing Muhammad—and, by extension, all believers—in what, precisely, they should say to unbelievers who doubt the inevitability of the judgment of each human soul by God. (This, by the way, is one of the Koran's recurrent themes; it addresses over and over again the subject of how to respond to those who doubt the Resurrection.)

Here is just one of the many passages the Koran offers concerning the Resurrection and the Day of Judgment:

Points to Ponder

Some of the Koran's instructions on the Final Judgment—as well as other passages—suggest that time is relative, rather than fixed. This is certainly a remarkable insight for a document of the seventh century C.E.!

The pagans say, "When we become mere bones and dust, shall we then be brought back to life again?" (Muhammad), say "Yes, even if you become rocks, iron, or anything that you think is harder to be brought to life." They will soon ask, "Who will bring us back to life?" Say, "The One who created you in the first place." They will shake their heads and say, "When will He bring us back to life?" Say, "Perhaps very soon. On the day when He will call you, you will answer Him with praise and think that you have tarried for only a little while." (17:49–52)

There Will Be an Accounting

The Koran teaches that all human beings will be held accountable on the Day of Judgment for their actions. All of one's deeds will be inquired into, and God himself will evaluate the events of one's life.

If the tendency to avoid suffering and pursue enjoyable things is a motivator for human behavior, then surely the prospect of having each and every one of one's earthly actions evaluated by the Almighty is a sobering prospect. The possibility of this accounting, most of us would admit, is quite capable of attracting one's attention and interest.

The Koran describes the accounting in this way in the seventeenth Sura:

> We have made every person's actions cling to his neck. On the Day of Judgment, We will bring forth the record of his actions in the form of a wide open book. We will tell him, "Read it and judge for yourself." One who follows guidance does so for himself and one who goes astray does so against his soul. No one will suffer for the sins of others. We have never punished anyone without sending them Our Messenger first. (17:13–15)

Those who have earned the favor of the Lord, the Koran tells us repeatedly, will enter Paradise. Those who have not will enter hell. The message is restated often, because of its extraordinary importance:

> There is no doubt that evil doers who are engulfed in sins are the companions of hell fire wherein they will live forever. As for the righteously striving believers, they will be among the people of Paradise wherein they will live forever. (2:81–82)

The preceding passage tells believers that those who are "engulfed in sins" will be consigned to hell forever. At the other end of the continuum are those immediately transported over hell directly to Paradise, the "righteously striving" believers.

Not all human beings will fall into these two groups, however. Some people will be delivered to hell for a period of (agonizing) purification; others, with better records in their books, will be transported to a place called the Heights until they are ready to enter Paradise.

The Word

The Koran reminds us that earthly life is our only opportunity to come to terms with God:

From those who have rejected the truth and died in disbelief, no ransom will be accepted even though they may pay a whole earth of gold. They will suffer a painful torment and no one will help them. (3:91)

The torments of hell are described in the Koran in such a way as to encourage believers to make every possible attempt to avoid it. The joys of Paradise, similarly, are given the kind of vivid description likely to encourage believers to do all they possibly can to win God's favor.

The Word

The Koran teaches that some, but not all, will earn hell's punishment eternally. Atheists, for instance, will earn membership in the group that earns eternal punishment:

Those who deny My existence and die with such attitude will be subject to the condemnation of God, the angels, and all people. They will live condemned forever, will have no relief from the torment, and no attention will be paid to them. (2:161–162)

For those who are concerned about the status of their souls, the Koran counsels good deeds, repentance for sins, obedience to the instructions of Allah and his Final Prophet, and remembrance of Allah in the from of prayer (dhikr). The best short prayer, according to Islamic tradition, is one of the simplest: "Ash hadu anla illaha illa Allah, Muhammadun Rasulu Allah." (I testify that no one is deserving of worship except Allah, Muhammad is the Messenger of Allah.)

The Mission of Iblis

The Koran tells believers that the proud Iblis, also known as Satan, refused to bow down before Adam as Allah had ordered, and was cast out of Paradise as a result:

... Allah asked, "What made you disobey Me?" Satan replied, "I am better than Adam, for You have created me out of fire and Adam out of clay." (7:12)

Those who enter hell, the Koran tells us, will do so because of the work of Iblis; thanks to him, they will be deprived of the presence of Allah. At one point in the Koran, Allah says the following to Iblis:

God said, "The path which leads to Me is an straight one and you have no authority over My servants except the erring ones who follow you. Hell is the promised place for them all. (15:41–43)

Iblis is known as the "slinking whisperer," the one who seeks to enter the hearts of human beings, mislead humanity and place as many souls as possible on the path to hell. He has a clear mission: to ensnare humanity. The Koran, however, teaches that Iblis *must* (and does) abandon his efforts to tempt someone to sin once that person calls upon Allah for help. The final Sura of the Koran, *Mankind*, is an appeal to Allah for refuge from the influence of Iblis.

The Punishments of Hell

A series of horrific punishments awaits those who have chosen not to follow God. Those permitted by God to believe and follow him are warned to avoid these punishments, and certainly their specifics, believers hold, are ample motivation for that. (Those upon whose hearts he has set a seal, the Koran tells us, will regard even these warnings with indifference.)

Unbelievers, we are told, had better be fond of fire:

> But those who would deny the Truth and reject Our revelations would be the companions of the Fire in which they would live forever. (2:39)

Their skins, once burned off, will be replaced:

> We will make the rejectors of Our revelations suffer in hell fire. As soon as the fire destroys their skins, We will give them new skins so that they may suffer more of the torment. God is Majestic and All-wise. (4:56)

In one particularly memorable passage (7:41), the Koran informs its readers that people who reject the revelations of Allah as a result of their own pride will not be permitted to enter Paradise "until a camel passes through the eye of a sewing needle." The Koran tells us that for such disdainful people—people who turned away from the guidance of Allah and used their earthly lives only to repeat Iblis's sin of pride—hell will be both their cradle and their blanket.

Spotlight on Islam

The Koran's reference to certain residents of hell being unable to enter heaven "until a camel passes through the eye of a sewing needle" forms a direct parallel with an important Gospel saying of Jesus. In Matthew 16:23 we read that "it will be easier for a camel to pass through the eye of a needle than for a rich man to enter the Kingdom of Heaven." The parallel is all the more interesting in the light of modern criticism of the Koran complaining that the Koran does not—and could not have—incorporated the recorded sayings of Jesus, since the New Testament was not translated into Arabic until well after the time of Muhammad.

Torment, we read, will be placed upon torment for those who turned away from the commands of the Lord during their earthly lives. There will be no conclusion to this suffering, because during their years on earth those who hardened their hearts against God already secured a (very limited) pleasure. The picture after their judgment, however, will be very different:

> Thereafter they will face hell fire wherein they will drink boiling water. As they sip the unpleasant water, death will approach them from all sides, but they will never die. In addition to this, they will experience the most intense torment. (14:16–17)

Those who enter hell, the Koran warns, will ask for relief from those who have been granted entry to Paradise. They will be bitterly disappointed.

The dwellers of the fire will ask the people of Paradise to give them some water or other things that God has granted to them. They will reply, "God has deprived the unbelievers of the blessings of Paradise." (7:50)

Gloom, Despair, and Agony

By now, you're beginning to get the picture. The condemned, "suffering" half of the human motivational cycle is appealed to in harrowing detail at many, many points in the Koran.

> **Caution!**
>
> The punishments of disbelief are laid out in terrifying detail in the Koran. Hell's residents can look forward to a long list of torments: being burned continuously by flames more intense than those on earth, being attacked by animals, being scourged with flaming chains, and being forced to eat and drink a variety of loathsome substances. It's not a place anyone wants to end up.

Those who rejected the guidance of God will be chained and consumed with fire:

> On the day when the earth and the heavens will be replaced by another earth and heavens and everyone will be brought before the One Almighty God, you will see the guilty ones bound in chains, with garments of pitch and faces covered by fire. (14:48–50)

They will be dragged headlong into hell's fierce flames, and they will be forced to feed upon the tree of Zaqqum. This is the infamous tree of hell; it is incomparably bitter, and its foul odor is beyond description. Those who must select it for a main course, the Koran advises, are unlikely to enjoy the meal:

The tree of al-Zaqum is food for the sinner. It will be like molten brass, which will boil in the bellies like water. (It will be said of such sinners), "Seize them and drag them into the middle of hell. Then pour unto their heads the boiling water to torment them." They will be told, "Suffer the torment. You had thought yourselves to be majestic and honorable. This is the torment that you persistently doubted." (44:43–50)

The passage you just read stands as a good representative of the Koran's descriptions of the terror awaiting those who turn away from the instructions of God during earthly life. Notice that it features not only condemnation and physical torture ("Seize them and drag them into the middle of hell …") but a reminder that the pleasures chosen on Earth (in this case, majesty and honor) were not worth their consequences in the hereafter. Finally, notice the Koran's warning that many of the inmates of hell will have doubted its very existence while they were alive on Earth, and still had the chance to repent and turn to God.

Remember, too, that the Koran teaches that *all* of humanity will eventually repent and seek to submit to the will of Allah. For the residents of hell, however, that repentance will have come too late.

The Word

The Koran sets out God's plan:

> To be saved from the fire and admitted to Paradise is certainly a great triumph. The worldly life is no more than a deceitful possession. (3:185)

The Inhabitants of Paradise

Let's turn now to the joyous, "blessed" half of the Koran's teaching about the afterlife. It makes considerably more pleasant reading than what we've just seen, of course—but it must, believers hold, be taken in context with what the Koran has to say about the punishments for disobedience to God.

The Sensual Rewards of Paradise

We know what the Koran has to say about what will happen after death to those who reject the message of salvation. A very different fate awaits those who submit to the Lord and follow his instructions.

They will be granted entry to a permanent community of bliss:

> We shall remove all hatred from their breasts and make them as brothers reclining on thrones facing one another. No fatigue will touch them nor will they be expelled therefrom. (15:47–48)

They will enjoy the approving presence of the Lord:

> The righteously striving believers are the best of all creatures. Their reward from their Lord will be the gardens of Eden wherein streams flow and wherein they will live forever. God will be pleased with them and they will be pleased with Him. This (reward) is for those who fear their Lord. (98:7–8)

Passages like the one you just read—in which believers are rewarded with God's pleasure for their obedience—are often overlooked by non-Muslims who believe that the afterlife is regarded solely as a sensual paradise in Islam. There are, to be sure, Koranic assurances of what human beings would associate with physical pleasure for those who believe:

> These fruits are produced very much like them (those we had before)." They will have purified spouses and it is they who will live forever. (2:25)

In the passage above, "spouses" is translation of the Arabic word "azwaj," which can also be rendered as "pair." The idea seems to be that one of the rewards of Paradise is a mate, or match, of perfect virtue. There is no mention of reproduction in the Koran; the whole idea of "purified spouses" is probably best understood by means of a famous hadith, which informs us that "in paradise are things which no eye has ever seen or ears ever heard of."

In confirmation of this, believers are reminded in the third Sura that the experiences of Paradise will far surpass any experience of earthly life:

> (Muhammad), ask them, "Shall I tell you what is far superior to worldly pleasures? Those who have fear of God will have (as their reward) gardens wherein streams flow and wherein they will live forever with their purified spouses and with the consent of God. God knows all about His servants." (3:15)

Once again, the author of the Koran has demonstrated a deep knowledge of the motivational realities that so profoundly affects human learning and experience. The prospect of such a Paradise is certainly unlikely to be ignored!

But it is important not to focus too narrowly on these kinds of promises, or to distort them beyond recognition—by, for instance, assuming sensual rewards in Paradise will apply only to men. (This is a common error among non-Muslims; in fact, both men and women are promised "purified spouses" in the Koran.)

Back to the Garden

There are many other promises in the Koran to believers about Paradise, after all. There are promises about delicious food and drink, of safety, of reunions with loved ones that are completely consistent with the principle of divine justice, of beautiful gardens where eternal streams flow, and of peace incomprehensible to the human mind. Entry to this place, the Koran teaches, is a kind of success that surpasses every success of earthly life.

The Word

God's love and forgiveness is the ultimate reward:

(Muhammad), tell them, "If you love God, follow me. God will love you and forgive your sins. God is All-forgiving and All-merciful." (3:31)

In Paradise there is, the Koran assures us, the promise of a welcome from God Almighty:

> To those who have said, "God is our Lord, " and who have remained steadfast to their belief, the angels will descend saying, "Do not be afraid or grieved. Receive the glad news of the Paradise which was promised to you. We are your guardians in this world and in the life to come, where you will have whatever your souls will desire and whatever you call for, a hospitable welcome from the All-forgiving and All-merciful God." (41:30–32)

This welcome from Allah, the Koran seems to imply, is the most important of the rewards of Paradise. It is the ultimate pleasure to which believers should aspire.

Believers hold that both the torments of hell described in the Koran, and the rewards of heaven it outlines, far transcend the experiences of human beings on earth. They remind themselves that someone who experiences the greatest imaginable physical and emotional sufferings on Earth, and who turns away from Allah, thereby earning entry to hell, will long for the days when he suffered on Earth. By the same token, they believe that someone who experiences the highest possible level of physical, material, or social pleasure and success during earthly life, and who gains entry to heaven, would weep and wail in agony if he were somehow transported back to his life of earthly enjoyment.

The Word

The blessed ones will live in Paradise as long as the heavens and the earth exist, unless your Lord decides to grant endless rewards to whomever He wants. (11:108)

Certainty

In Islam, believers hold with certainty that there are two basic qualities that God will use to evaluate the events of one's life and determine whether or not one will earn his favor in the afterlife:

♦ Whether one searched earnestly for the truth to reach a state of belief, or faith.

♦ Whether one was obedient to this belief, or faith, once one discovered it.

Believers also maintain that there are also two ways of life that will result in being cast into hell:

♦ A careless or self-centered attitude in searching for the truth.

♦ Arrogance in the face of the truth once one has been exposed to it.

The Koran argues, at great length and with breathtaking eloquence, for the promotion of the first two values over the second two values. And in doing so, it brings a quiet certainty about death and its consequences to the daily lives of the believers.

The Least You Need to Know

♦ The Koran teaches that death is inevitable.

♦ It also teaches that there will be a reckoning after death.

♦ Horrific torments, we read, await those who turned away from the instructions of God during their lifetimes.

♦ Eternal pleasure, on the other hand, awaits those who faithfully submitted to the will of the Lord while they lived.

Part 6

The Holy Koran Today

The Koran's teachings transcend time, yet they are utterly relevant to modern life.

This section of the book explores contemporary issues and resources related to Koranic study.

Part

The Holy Koran Today

The Koran's teachings transcend time, yet they are utterly relevant to modern life.

This section of the book explores contemporary issues and respects related to Koranic study.

Chapter 20

Pursuing the Word

In This Chapter

- ♦ Simple guidelines for reading the Koran
- ♦ The Sunna's relationship to the Koran
- ♦ The importance of reading with deliberation
- ♦ Using the Holy Book as a guide in life
- ♦ Non-Muslims on the wisdom of the Koran

It has been said that the Koran offers something for even the nonbeliever ... and everything for the believer. Whether you're a believer or not, you may very well find great benefits from consulting the Koran directly.

In this chapter, you learn six simple guidelines for studying this remarkable book—and, perhaps, for applying its lessons to the challenges of modern life.

Something for Everyone

Regardless of whether one accepts the text of the Koran as the divinely revealed word of God, as believers do, it is hard to deny the Koran's status as one of the most influential books ever written.

Many in the West are relatively familiar with the other great religious texts that have influenced humanity—the Bible, the recorded sayings of the Buddha, the Hindu scriptures—but less familiar with the actual text of the Koran. Certainly, anyone interested enough in spirituality and the development of religious and social systems should also make a place for familiarity with the Islamic scripture.

True familiarity, of course, can only come with direct exposure to the text, either in its original Arabic form or (to a much lesser degree) in a responsible translation. Real familiarity with the Koran cannot, unfortunately, come from an analysis or overview of the book, like the book you're reading now.

When approached with an open mind, the Koran definitely has great gifts to bestow on Muslims and non-Muslims alike. Inquiring minds from both "sides" of this apparent divide have repeatedly cited the unique wisdom of its message, and the importance of its historic—and ongoing—influence on society.

Spotlight on Islam _____

I am not a Muslim in the usual sense—though I hope I am a "Muslim" as "one surrendered to God"—but I believe that embedded in the Quran and other expressions of the Islamic vision are vast stores of divine truth from which I and other occidentals have still much to learn, and Islam is certainly a strong contender for the supplying of the basic framework of the one religion of the future.

—W. Montgomery Watt, in his book, *Islam and Christianity Today*

Clearly, this is a book worth getting to know firsthand. Here then, are six important pieces of advice for those interested in pursuing the words of the Koran directly.

How the Sunna Helps Us Interpret the Koran

The Sunna, you'll recall, is the accumulated body of statements, actions, and silent approvals of the Prophet Muhammad. Because the Koran itself offers Muhammad as a model for humankind, believers look to the Sunna for detailed instructions on the Muslim deen, or way of life.

Practical Islam is easy. One's deeds fall under these categories:

◆ Obligatory

◆ Prohibited

◆ Desirable

- Detestable to do

- Permissible

Qualified experts in the Islamic practical laws publish their Fatwas (authentic opinions) on the status of a given action. To practice Islam properly one can follow existing Fatwas, one can become an expert capable of issuing Fatwas, or one can base one's practice purely on precaution (which is probably the hardest method). It's worth noting that Islamic communities that actually adhere to the standards of Islamic law enjoy (among many other benefits) a crime rate so low that they have no need for a police force!

However, one has to admit that to understand all of the potential Islamic responses to all of the questions that may arise in society is a task as difficult as mastering the curriculum of a great university. The Koran is regarded as the divine Word, but the Sunna, most believers would agree, is absolutely essential in interpreting that Word. And while the Koran occupies a single volume, the Sunna forms a small library. (Commentaries on and interpretations of the Koran and the Sunna constitute a *large* library!)

This is not, of course, a book about the Sunna, but it is meant to give you some idea of the tools Muslims use to evaluate and interpret their central text. Here, then, is a tiny representative sampling: four important ahadith. These are excerpted from the hundreds upon hundreds of authenticated sayings and actions of the Prophet—guideposts that believers have used for centuries to pursue the meaning of the Koran. If you're wondering what the Sunna looks and sounds like, and whether Muhammad's personal instruction is distinguishable in tone and outlook from that of the Koran, here's your answer.

The Supremacy of the Koran

The Prophet Muhammad on the supreme authority in human affairs:

> The Holy Prophet, has said, "Over every truth there is a reality and above every valid issue there is light. Whatever agrees with the Holy Koran you must follow it, and whatever does not agree disregard it." (Hadith No 196, Chapter 22, hadith No1 al-kafi, vol 1)

Moderation in Worship

The Prophet Muhammad warns against extremism in religion:

> The Messenger of Allah once said, "O Ali, this religion is strong (and vast). Follow it with care. Do not cause your soul to hate the worship of your Lord.

The extremist is like a person who during a journey destroys his riding animal and is left without any animal to ride before reaching his destination. Do good deeds like one who knows he will die very old and be cautious as one who is afraid of dying the next day." (Ibid Hadith No 1658, Chapter 41 hadith No 6, vol 2)

Importance of Following the Prophet's Example, Teachings, and Lifestyle

The Prophet Muhammad sets out the proper way of living:

The Messenger of Allah has said, "For every form of worship there is a strong desire and willingness, then it reduces. Whoever's worship falls within my tradition and practice, he has found the right guidance, and whoever is against my tradition is lost and his deeds are a total loss. I, however, pray, sleep, fast, eat, laugh and weep. Whoever dislikes my tradition and practice is not of my people." He has said, "Death is a sufficient preacher, certainty is enough wealth and worship is enough occupation." (Ibid Hadith No 1651, Chapter 40 hadith 1 vol. 2)

Allah and the Believer

The Prophet Muhammad on Allah's response to those who seek him:

The Holy prophet once said: "Whoever comes forward to accept what Allah, the Most Majestic, the Most Holy, loves, Allah comes forward with what he (the servant) loves. Whoever seeks protection with Allah, He protects him. To whoever's rescue Allah comes He will protect him even if the skies were to fall on earth or an incident involving all the inhabitants of earth were to befall them, but the person under the protection of Allah would be among the members of the party of Allah, well guarded against all misfortunes. Is it not that Allah, the Most Majestic, the Most Holy, says, 'the pious people live in a peaceful place'?" (44:51) (Ibid, Hadith No 1565, Chapter No 28, hadith No 4)

> **Spotlight on Islam**
>
> To learn more about the Sunna, you may wish to visit the As-Sunnah Foundation of America website (www.sunnah.org) or (www.al-islam.org) look for Hadith, which feature an extensive online collection of resources.

Take Your Time

The Prophet himself, believers hold, was instructed by Allah in the Koran not to rush through its text. The Prophet also appears, in the very same verse, to have been advised to approach the document as a whole:

God is the Most High and the True King. (Muhammad), do not be hasty in reading the Koran to the people before the revelation has been completed. "Say, My Lord, grant me more knowledge." (20:114)

This remains important advice to anyone who would consult the Koran for insight on dealing with problems or issues in contemporary life, on spiritual questions, on social interactions, or on any other topic. The request that a higher power guide one in the pursuit of wisdom has a long and glorious history in all religious traditions. It is particularly emphatic in Islam, and there the request is strongly associated with *slow* and measured study of the Koran.

Points to Ponder

The Prophet specifically advised his followers not to read the entire Koran over a period of a day or two, but to take more time in doing so.

Slow and purposeful study of the Koran's words is particularly important in understanding the many passages in which the Koran claims for itself the virtue of clarity. Here is one such passage:

> A light and a clarifying Book has come to you from God to show the way of peace to those who seek His pleasure, to bring them out of darkness into light through His will and to guide them to the right path. (5:15–16)

The Koran does not claim (as some who have read it hastily or with a closed mind often claim) that *all* of its verses are instantly comprehensible to a person reading or hearing it for the first time. This is clearly not the case!

Instead, it claims to guide people to important and abiding truths, assuming, of course, that those who consult it are interested in encountering those truths. Those who quickly scan its verses to prove or disprove a particular point of their own, by contrast, are unlikely to gain many meaningful insights on life.

Keep an Open Mind

In the seventh Sura, we read:

> Whenever the Koran is recited (to you), listen to it quietly so that you may receive mercy. (7:204)

That word "quietly" applies not only to the presence or absence of external sounds, but to a certain quietness of spirit and mind.

If you approach this text with preconceived notions about its meaning, or the structure you feel it should have, or its ability to conform with your own opinions of what Islam is or isn't, you may find yourself frustrated, baffled, or overwhelmed.

If, on the other hand, you leave grasping notions or preconditions aside, and simply follow the book wherever it goes, you may find that it offers you the insight you need to resolve a personal, professional, intellectual, or spiritual problem.

One of the reasons it's very important to read the Koran with an open mind is that many of its passages can be interpreted in a number of ways—and have, in fact, been the subject of intense debate for many centuries! Rather than jumping to conclusions about what such passages mean, we should evaluate them in the context of the Koran as a whole.

Interestingly, the Koran itself mentions this issue:

> It is God who has revealed the Book to you in which some verses are clear statements (which accept no interpretation) and these are the fundamental ideas of the Book, while other verses may have several possibilities. Those whose hearts are perverse, follow the unclear statements in pursuit of their own mischievous goals by interpreting them in a way that will suit their own purpose. No one knows its true interpretations except God and those who have a firm grounding in knowledge say, "We believe in it. All its verses are from our Lord." No one can grasp this fact except the people of reason. (3:7)

Determining which verses are "clear statements" and which verses have "several possibilities" may, of course, require years of study. This task should not ignore the significant contributions of fourteen centuries of Islamic scholarship on the Koran and the Sunna.

Turn to It for Guidance

It's not enough simply to approach the Koran with an open mind. Actively seeking guidance from it is an essential part of the process, too. Over and over again, the Koran reminds its readers and hearers that it is a guide to all of humanity, even—or especially—during troubled times in one's life. Sometimes it's hard to focus on the Koran's specific advice, especially if we're distracted with what we believe to be the specifics of difficulties in our career, our relationships, our families, or our communities. Even during such hard times, however, the Koran presents itself as a beacon to be followed through the darkness:

This (Koran) is a reminder for the people and a guide and advice for the pious. Do not be discouraged or grieved. You alone will have true dignity if you only are true believers. (3:138–139)

If we are reading in a way that consciously seeks guidance and help with the resolution of problems, we will learn that even the most grave challenge is part of a larger plan:

Points to Ponder

Among many other notable Westerners, Napoleon Bonaparte praised the wisdom of the Koran. He wrote:

> We shall test you through fear, hunger, loss of life, property, and crops. (Muham-mad), give glad news to the people who have patience and in difficulty say, "We are the servants of God and to Him we shall all return." It is they who will receive blessings and mercy from God and who follow the right guidance. (2:155–157)

> I hope the time is not far off when I shall be able to unite all the wise and educated men of all the countries and establish a uniform regime based on the principles of the Qur'an which alone are true and which alone can lead men to happiness.

> The Koran promises an increasing clarity to all those who earnestly seek its help. God further enlightens those who seek guidance. (19:76)

Those who consult the Koran regularly believe that this is not an idle promise. They claim that repeated consultation of the Koran has an uncanny way of placing one's face directly in front of verses that are relevant to the challenges currently at the forefront of one's life. You may be skeptical about this claim, but there is only one way to test it, and that is to read the Koran regularly yourself with an open mind and the expectation of receiving guidance … and see what happens.

Trust in the Guidance You Receive

Trust in Allah's plan is an essential component of the Koran's message to humanity. The Koran relates the following observation from the Prophet Jacob:

> Everyone's destiny is in His hands. I put my trust in Him. Whoever needs a trustee must put his trust in God. (12:67)

Elsewhere in the Koran, we read the simple but powerful words:

> God loves those who trust Him. (3:159)

Personal trust in the guidance of the Koran on social, political, spiritual, or personal matters usually does not come during the first few times one exposes oneself to it. However, continuous examination of the message has a way of strengthening one's trust in the text.

This has been the practical experience of many non-Muslims (among them Leo Tolstoy, Goethe, and H. G. Wells).

> **Spotlight on Islam** _____
>
> The Islamic teachings have left great traditions for equitable and gentle dealings and behavior, and inspire people with nobility and tolerance. These are human teachings of the highest order and at the same time practicable. These teachings brought into existence a society in which hard-heartedness and collective oppression and injustice were the least as compared with all other societies preceding it … Islam is replete with gentleness, courtesy, and fraternity.
>
> —H. G. Wells

Be Grateful

Finally, Muslims believe that it is important to be grateful for the guidance one eventually does receive from reading the Koran. Even a skeptic will usually admit that the "course corrections" one encounters from reading the Koran—whether they result in an improved business relationship, a stronger marriage, a solution for a social problem, or a more direct connection to Allah—would not have arisen from one's own insights. So simple logic dictates that one express gratitude for the guidance one receives.

The Koran predicts that, in Paradise, the believers will say:

> "God who guided us to this, deserves all praise. Had He not guided us, we would never have been able to find the right direction. The (angelic) Messengers of our Lord came to us with the Truth." They shall be told, "This is the Paradise which you have inherited because of your good deeds." (7:43)

If believers and nonbelievers alike put all of the ideas discussed in this chapter into practice—exploring the Sunna, perusing the Koran slowly and thoughtfully, approaching it with an open mind, actively seeking guidance during times of challenge, trusting in the guidance received, and expressing gratitude—we might all live in a very different world.

A Final Thought on Pursuing the Word

Before we close this discussion, we should address one more important point.

You may be curious about whether or not the benefits of consulting the Koran described in this chapter are real or imagined. There is only one way to know for sure, and that is to secure a responsible translation and take a look. If you wish, you can begin with an online version of the translation that is used in this book, which can be found at www.alshia.com/html/eng/p.php?p=quran&url=Translation.

The question may just change from "How does the Koran fit into modern life?" to "How does it fit into your life?"

The Least You Need to Know

- ◆ Learn the Sunna's role in the correct interpretation of the Koran.

- ◆ Explore the Koran slowly and thoughtfully.

- ◆ Keep an open mind.

- ◆ Actively seek guidance during times of challenge.

- ◆ Trust in the guidance you receive from the Koran.

- ◆ Be grateful for that guidance.

21

Exploring the Koran Online

In This Chapter

- ◆ Internet resources for newcomers to Islam
- ◆ Internet resources for advanced students
- ◆ Where to find translations of the Koran online

Muslims have taken advantage of the Internet to make a wealth of information and resources related to the Koran available to anyone who wants to point their browser to them. In this chapter, you'll learn about a few of the most interesting sites.

You should know, before we even begin, that what follows is a very selective overview of the available work, and that there are thousands upon thousands of excellent websites devoted to the Koran and Islam in general.

Al-Islam

A superb place to start. The site gives an authoritative overview of the Islamic faith, offers a responsible, easy-to-understand history of the Prophet and his message, and provides instruction in the Holy Koran. It is highly recommended.

You'll Be Particularly Impressed By ...

... the clear, simple, introductions and the uncluttered visual display, both of which are perfect for those without scholarly backgrounds.

Here's a brief extract from its excellent overview of the Koran:

> The Book of Allah is like an ocean. The less learned, like children, collect pebbles and shells from its shores. The scholars and thinkers, like pearl divers, bring out from it the highest philosophy, wisdom and rules of a perfect way of living.

Check It Out!

You can visit the Al-Islam site at www.al-islam.org.

eMuslim

The eMuslim site offers a variety of essential online resources related to Islam. (A directory of U.S. mosques, for instance.) It also issued the following eloquent condemnation of terrorist activity on behalf of mainstream American Muslims:

> American Muslims utterly condemn what are apparently vicious and cowardly acts of terrorism against innocent civilians. We join with all Americans in calling for the swift apprehension and punishment of the perpetrators. No political cause could ever be assisted by such immoral acts.

Points to Ponder

You can also point children who are interested in (or assigned to learn more about) Islam toward the Al-Islam site.

The Word

For this reason, We made it a law for the children of Israel that the killing of a person for reasons other than legal retaliation or for stopping corruption in the land is as great a sin as murdering all of mankind. However, to save a life would be as great a virtue as to save all of mankind. (5:32)

You'll Be Particularly Impressed By ...

... the link to a PDF file that provides a word-for-word translation of the Koran from Arabic to English. This can be an important tool for non-Arabic speakers who are eager to learn more about the specifics of the original text.

Check It Out!

For the main eMuslim page, visit www.emuslim.com, and for the link to the helpful word-for-word translation visit www.emuslim.com/Quran/Dictionary/_English.asp—the text is broken up into eight portions.

Qurantime

This can best be described as an exhaustively international site. It contains links to translations of the Koran in English, Turkish, Russian, Nederland, Bosnian, German, Spanish, Portuguese, Polish, and many other languages (not to mention, of course, the original Arabic).

You'll Be Particularly Impressed By ...

... the online Japanese-language Koran (assuming you are or know of a Japanese student of Islam who's been searching in vain for such a translation).

Check It Out!

You can visit the site at www.qurantime.com.

The Modern Religion

An extraordinary gathering-together of Muslim-related resources, The Modern Religion offers an exhaustive collection of articles, links, forums, debates, and old-fashioned good advice. It covers just about everything, and its only potential drawback is that there's so much to choose from that the site can be a little imposing to a newcomer.

Such misgivings are certainly worth overcoming, however, and with just a little practice one realizes how best to navigate the (extraordinary) wealth of offerings.

Here one will find advice on mastering the Arabic of the Koran:

> People are frequently scared away from learning Arabic because the script looks so different. Most agree that it is beautiful, especially in calligraphic form, but also find its looks intimidating. Those who are feeling that way may be encouraged by the fact that the Arabic language has an alphabet made up of twenty-eight letters that are connected to each other in a way similar to English cursive writing. A difference is that Arabic is written from right to left. Most students will tell you that the script is much easier to learn than it appears. Some will say that it is the least of their problems, and that the grammar is really tough. (From *This Darned Arabic Language* by Tatyana Krueger.)

And reminders about the importance of attending Friday prayers:

> Muslims should attend Juma'a (Friday) prayers because it is ordained on them by Allah. In Sura[h] #62 (Al_Juma'a) comes the clear order from Allah:
>
>> Believers, on Friday when the call for prayer is made, try to attend prayer (remembering God) and leave off all business. This would be better for you if only you knew it (62:9). (From *Khutba Rules* and *Guidelines* by Salman.)

And potent questions for Christians to consider:

> If Jesus was God, why did he tell the man who called him "good master" not to call him "good" because accordingly, there is none good but his God in Heaven alone?
>
> If belief in the Trinity was such a necessary condition for being a Christian, why didn't Jesus teach and emphasize it to the Christians during his time?
>
> How were those followers of Jesus considered Christians without ever hearing the term Trinity? (From *Sixty Questions for Christians* by Hussein Khalid Al-Hussein.)

And much, much more.

You'll Be Particularly Impressed By ...

... the section entitled "The Basics of Muslim Belief."

Check It Out!

Visit The Modern Religion at www.themodernreligion.com, and bookmark it, because you'll probably be coming back again and again.

Shialink

A comprehensive collection of World Wide Web resources related to the Shi'a movement. It offers over 500 links of interest to Shi'a Muslims and those studying this school of Islam.

You'll Be Particularly Impressed By ...

... the constantly updated collection of resources ... and the bulletin-board feature that allows users to post thoughts, questions, and concerns.

Check It Out!

Visit Shialink at www.shialink.org.

Quran MP3

This site offers audio feeds of an excellent recitation of the Koran in Arabic.

You'll Be Particularly Impressed By ...

... the tone and delivery of the recitations, which are by the late and highly esteemed Sheikh Mahmoud Khalil Al-Husary. The site's operators describe Sheikh Al-Husary as having "a clear yet beautiful voice and excellent rendition." Listening to the recitation, it's hard to disagree.

Check It Out!

You can visit Quran MP3 at www.ahlanbi.com/quran_mp3.htm.

100 Questions About the Quran

This site offers answers to 100 common questions about the Koran. If you're interested in learning who the Koran's first *hafiz* was, for instance, this concise, rapid-fire quiz will give you the correct answer in a hurry. (It was the Prophet Muhammad—but perhaps you knew that already.)

You'll Be Particularly Impressed By ...

... the site's pithy, accessible style.

> **What's It Mean?**
>
> *Islamic Dictionary*
>
> **Hafiz** means someone who has memorized the Koran in its entirety and is capable of reciting it.

Check It Out!

Visit 100 Questions About the Quran at

www.angelfire.com/il2/islamicpage/100questions.

The True Religion

An excellent—if occasionally overly-energetic—site. It is devoted "to introducing the reader to Islam, the natural religion of man."

The site has this to say about its mission and founding principles:

> As well as an overview of core beliefs, compelling evidence and rational arguments for the truth of Islam will be presented throughout these pages. We will also focus on clarifying the numerous misconceptions concerning Islam and refuting anti-Islamic allegations, God-Willing.

You'll Be Particularly Impressed By ...

... True Religion's unapologetic, no-holds-barred tone (if that's your taste). Consider the following borderline-confrontational extract from a recent article on Christianity:

> In the New Testament one reads:
>
> *And Jesus answered and said unto him, Get thee behind me, Satan: for it is written, Thou shalt worship the Lord thy God, and him only shalt thou serve. (Luke 4:8)*
>
> Surely, Jesus would have said, "Thou shalt worship *Me*," if that is what he really meant!

Check It Out!

Visit The True Religion at www.thetruereligion.com.

The Noble Quran

This site offers, among other resources, line-by-line translations of not one, but three respected translations of the Koran—Pickthall's, Shakir's, and Ali's. The line-by-line arrangement is particularly helpful for non-Arabic speakers interested in understanding the different approaches taken by the various translators to the Arabic text.

Spotlight on Islam

Mohammed Marmaduke Pickthall, an Englishman who converted to Islam, delivered what most consider the first top-flight English translation of the Koran in 1930; his work is elegant though now a little musty-sounding. Abdullah Yusuf Ali's translation, completed in 1937, is perhaps the most popular English version; Ali was an Arabic speaker whose command of English was extraordinary, and his vibrant, passionate translation has proved both enduring and influential. M.H. Shakir, an Iranian, completed a popular 1982 translation; it reflects both his Shi'a outlook and an occasionally convoluted style. (Shakir's translation, like Pickthall's, feels a little like the King James Bible.) All three translations are easily available via the World Wide Web.

Below, you'll find an example of the line-by-line translation. Note the parenthetical additions, which are different between Ali and Pickthall, and, in this case, are omitted entirely in the Shakir translation. Of course, no "definitive" translation of the Koran—in English or any other language—exists, but this approach of comparing English translations verse by verse can be helpful, and suggestive of the complexity of the original text.

Here, for the sake of comparison, is 2:62 as rendered by all three men:

- **Ali:** Those who believe (in the Qur'an), and those who follow the Jewish (scriptures), and the Christians and the Sabians,— any who believe in Allah and the Last Day, and work righteousness, shall have their reward with their Lord; on them shall be no fear, nor shall they grieve.

- **Pickthall:** Lo! Those who believe (in that which is revealed unto thee, Muhammad), and those who are Jews, and Christians, and Sabaeans—whoever believeth in Allah and the Last Day and doeth right—surely their reward is with their Lord, and there shall no fear come upon them neither shall they grieve.

- **Shakir:** Surely those who believe, and those who are Jews, and the Christians, and the Sabians, whoever believes in Allah and the Last day and does good, they shall have their reward from their Lord, and there is no fear for them, nor shall they grieve.

You'll Be Particularly Impressed By ...

... Syed Abu-Ala' Maududi's Chapter Introductions to the Koran, in-depth essays on each Sura that are available on the site.

Check It Out!

Visit The Noble Quran at www.usc.edu/dept/MSA/quran/—and be prepared to spend a while using its offerings! It's addictive.

"The Amazing Qur'an"

Dr. Gary Miller's comprehensive and spirited defense of the Koran as the literal word of God is among the most extraordinary Koran-related articles available on the Internet. If you have the time or inclination for only one online article, it should probably be this one.

> **Points to Ponder**
>
> If any religion had the chance of ruling over England, nay Europe, within the next hundred years, it could be Islam.
> —George Bernard Shaw

In what amounts to a 15-page legal brief that manages to be both thorough and accessible to the layman, Miller examines and overturns the most common preconceptions and stereotypes non-Muslims bring to the Koran. He also offers a series of extraordinary textual commentaries.

You'll Be Particularly Impressed By ...

... Miller's discussion of the Koran's enduring challenge to its readers. Here's an excerpt:

> A perfect example of how Islam provides man with a chance to verify its authenticity and "prove it wrong" occurs in the fourth chapter. And quite honestly, I was very surprised when I first discovered this challenge ...:
>
>> Do they not consider the Qur'an? Had it been from any other than Allah, they would surely have found therein much discrepancy. (4:82)
>
> This is a clear challenge to the non-Muslim. Basically, it invites him to find a mistake. As a matter of fact, the seriousness and difficulty of the challenge aside, the actual presentation of such a challenge in the first place is not even in human nature and is inconsistent with man's personality. One doesn't take an exam in school and after finishing it, write a note to the instructor reading: "This exam is perfect. There are no mistakes in it. Find one if you can!"

Check It Out!

You can find Dr. Miller's remarkable and inspiring article at users.erols.com/ameen/amazingq.htm

Spotlight on Islam

The Internet boasts many websites that claim to find contradictions in the Koran. Experience shows, however, that these "contradictions" overwhelmingly involve innocent (or perhaps not-so-innocent) misunderstandings of English versions of the Koran, rather than the Arabic text of the Koran itself. After sorting through 40 or 50 of these arguments (and their rebuttals from Muslim websites), you may well conclude that the whole exercise of searching for contradictions is indeed just as vain as the Koran suggests.

Al-Quran

The site provides an in-depth commentary for every verse of the Koran. It's indispensable for those who have read the work on their own (or perhaps completed an introductory book such as this one) and are looking for responsible, in-depth analysis.

You'll Be Particularly Impressed By ...

... the easy-to-use search features and simple, accessible interface. This site offers a near-perfect balance between ease of use and comprehensiveness of material.

Check It Out!

Visit Al-Quran at www.al-quran.org.uk.

Society for Quranic Studies

For the advanced student. The site offers a wealth of resources for in-depth study of the Koran, including a variety of scholarly articles. The organization describes itself as "dedicated to advancing the study of all accessible aspects of the Qur'an and disseminating knowledge about this unique Book." There is quite a lot to choose from here, but this site is probably best reserved for those who are approaching the Koran from a scholarly or research perspective.

You'll Be Particularly Impressed By ...

... the articles describing evidence for mathematical miracles in the Koran, which are dense but rewarding.

Also of interest here is another article by the gifted Gary Miller, "The Difference Between the Bible and the Qur'an," which features the following insightful passage:

> [T]he Qur'an does not demand belief—the Qur'an invites belief, and here is the fundamental difference (between the Qur'an and the Bible) ... Throughout the Qur'an the statements are always: Have you, O man, thought of such and such, have you considered so and so? It is always an invitation for you to look at the evidence (followed by a question:) "Now what do you believe?"

Check It Out!

Visit the Society for Quranic Studies at www.quranic-studies.com—and be ready to take plenty of notes!

Arabic Calligraphy

Long-standing custom severely limits figurative art within the Islamic tradition. Many believers regard the artistic representation of humans or animals as an unwelcome and inappropriate imitation of the creative powers of God Almighty.

(This is why you will find no images of people or animals in this book, or indeed in the vast majority of Islamic publications or websites.)

Some of the greatest genius of Islamic art, we find, lies not in the depiction of people, but in *calligraphy* and the decorative arts, especially as it is reflected in passages from the Koran.

There are dozens of excellent websites offering samples of breathtaking Islamic calligraphy.

What's It Mean?

Calligraphy is decorative lettering or writing by hand. Arabic calligraphy of Koranic verses is an extraordinary artistic legacy that has no close Western equivalent.

You'll Be Particularly Impressed By ...

... the diversity of calligraphic styles and schools represented.

Check It Out!

Visit Classical Calligraphy at piglet.ex.ac.uk/archive/1998-99/itp3002/calligraphy/—and prepare yourself to stare in wonder.

A breathtaking rendition of a passage of the Koran: "Against them make ready your strength to the utmost of your power." (8:60)

(Illustration [from traditional Arabic collections]: Judith Burros)

And here is a stark, angular rendition of this passage: "And say: Our Lord! Advance us in knowledge!" (20:114)

(Illustration [from traditional Arabic collections]: Judith Burros)

The Least You Need to Know

- There are many excellent websites devoted to Islam and the Koran; this chapter discusses a few of them.

- A good starting-point is www.al-islam.org.

- You'll find Gary Miller's remarkably well-argued defense of the Koran as the literal word of God at users.erols.com/ameen/amazingq.htm.

- There is an embarrassment of riches at www.themodernreligion.com.

- Three respected English translations of the Koran appear in line-by-line parallel form at www.usc.edu/dept/MSA/quran/.

The Least You Need to Know

- There are many excellent websites devoted to Islam and the Koran; this chapter discusses a few of them.

- A good starting-point is www.al-islam.org.

- You'll find Gary Miller's remarkably well-argued defense of the Koran as the literal word of God at these sites or by searching among them.

- There is an embarrassment of riches at www.themodernreligion.com.

- Three repeated English translations of the Koran appear in line-by-line parallel form at www.wsu.edu/dept/MSA/quran/.

22

Close Encounters of the Koran Kind

In This Chapter

◆ The self-conversion phenomenon

◆ Powerful encounters

◆ True stories

People from all conceivable nationalities, social backgrounds, and religious traditions have found themselves drawn to the Koran.

These people have brought their own unique perspectives, but have found themselves turning to the book, ultimately, in a very similar way ... in search of something beyond themselves, something beyond the familiar efforts to win favor from other people or collect possessions or secure sensual satisfaction. The journey of life proceeds for these people, but with a new direction and a new compass.

The "Self-Conversion" Phenomenon

There are many accounts—both ancient and modern—of conversions to Islam guided solely by a person's own evolving, self-guided search for wisdom

What's It Mean?

Proselytizing means trying to convert someone else to your religion.

within the Koran. This search, and the resulting gradual, personal change of viewpoint, is the motivating factor behind many conversions. Such life changes are *not* the *proselytizing* efforts of individual Muslims, although they are sometimes assumed to be so.

The Koran itself, when approached with respect, deliberation, and thoughtfulness, turns out to be the best advocate of all for Islam. The book carries a remarkable persuasive force that brings about this phenomenon of "self-conversion," which is rare in many other religious traditions.

In this chapter, you'll read true first-hand stories of a handful of such self-conversion experiences. There are thousands more such contemporary stories waiting to be discovered on the Internet, and many more ancient ones that have been documented over the centuries. Islam has always had extraordinary "self-conversion" narratives.

Each of the accounts that appears here was composed by the person whose experiences they describe (although we've edited them slightly), and each was offered freely and openly to the world at large as evidence of a close—and life-changing—encounter with the Koran.

Soft Laughter—and a Suggestion for Further Reading

At the age of 20 I began talking religion with a cab driver, and heard the term "Islam" for the first time from a real person. The nightly news talked about Islam and the Muslims—sure, they were called terrorists. I mentioned this to my driver, Alhamdulillah, who laughed softly and suggested I read the Koran. Actually, I read a few books on Islam first, then the Koran. This is when I knew I could have both my faith and logic ... It took another two years before I took *Shahada*, and another two before *hijab*.

—Ms. Amal

(from www.usc.edu/dept/MSA/newmuslims/amal.html)

What's It Mean?

Shahada is a ceremony of formal conversion to Islam. Hijab means covering the head and the body in accordance with God's instructions.

The Children of Freedom

Regarding my Jewish background: I read in our generous Koran the beautiful, beautiful Sura 28, about the life of Moses. I cried when I read the Koran's description of Moses' life, because although the account in Torah, in Jewish scripture, is very beautiful and moving—it also makes me cry—the Koran has something extra: that when Moses had killed the Egyptian oppressor, and was then forgiven by Allah, that he said to Allah. "Oh my Lord! For that thou hast bestowed Thy Grace on me, never shall I be a help to those who sin!" That is, as Muslims, we must never aid oppressors; we are, as Muslims, the children of freedom.

—Suleyman Ahmad Stephen Schwartz

(from www.naqshbandi.org/events/articles/conversion_schwartz.htm)

The Word

Once the Koran touches a person in a profound way, it is difficult to even think of going back to life like it was before:

> When they hear what is revealed to the Messenger, you can see their eyes flood with tears, as they learn about the Truth. They say, "Write our names down as bearing witness to it. Why should we not believe in God and the Truth that has come to us and hope that the Lord will admit us into the company of the righteous people?" (5:83–84)

A Christian Minister Changes Course

In 1952 I got my M.A. from Princeton University and was appointed as a teacher in the Faculty of Theology in Asiut (Egypt). I used to teach Islam as well as the faulty misconceptions spread by its enemies and the missionaries against it. During that period I decided to enlarge my study of Islam, so that I should not read the missionaries' books on it only. I had so much faith in myself that I was comfortable reading the other point of view. Thus I began to read books written by Muslim authors. I also decided to read the Koran and understand its meanings both because of my love of knowledge and my desire to add more proofs against Islam. The result was, however, exactly the reverse ....

Points to Ponder

I would like to stress that I did not come into contact with any Muslim before I embraced Islam. I read the Qur'an first and realized that no person is perfect.

—Yusuf Islam (formerly known as Cat Stevens)

(Eventually) I made my final decision to convert to Islam. In the morning I spoke with my wife with whom I have three sons and one daughter … She cried and asked for help from the head of the mission …. He was a very cunning man. When he asked me about my true attitude, I told him frankly what I really wanted and then he said, "Regard yourself out of a job until we discover what has befallen you." Then I said, "This is my resignation from my job." He tried to convince me to postpone it, but I insisted. So he made a rumor among the people that I became mad. Thus I suffered a very severe test and oppression until I left Aswan for good and returned to Cairo.

—Ibrahim Khalil, former Egyptian Coptic priest

(from: www.islamfortoday.com/khalil.htm)

Sister Khadijah Changes Her Faith

I had just graduated with my Master's degree of Divinity from an elite seminary five months before. It was at that time I met a lady who had worked in Saudi Arabia and had embraced Islam. Of course I asked her about the treatment of women in Islam. I was shocked at her answer; it wasn't what I expected so I proceeded to ask other questions relating to Allah and Muhammad. She informed me that she would take me to the Islamic Center where they would be better able to answer my questions ….

Having taught Evangelism I was quite shocked at their approach; it was direct and straightforward. No intimidation, no harassment, no psychological manipulation, no subliminal influence! None of this, "let's have a Koranic study in your house," like a counterpart of the Bible study. I couldn't believe it!

They gave me some books and told me if I had some questions they were available to answer them in the office. That night I read all of the books they gave me. It was the first time I had ever read a book about Islam written by a Muslim; in school I had studied and read books about Islam only written by Christians. The next day I spent three hours at the office asking questions. This went on every day for a week, by which time I had read 12 books and knew why Muslims are the hardest people in the world to convert to Christianity. Why? Because there is nothing to offer them! [In Islam] there is a relationship with Allah, forgiveness of sins, salvation, and promise of Eternal Life ….

At the end of that week, after having spent eight years in formal theological studies, I knew intellectually that Islam was true. But I did not embrace Islam at that time because I did not believe it in my heart. I continued to pray, to read the Bible, to attend lectures at the Islamic Center. I was in earnest asking and seeking God's direction. It is not easy to change your religion. I did not want to loose my salvation if there was salvation to lose. I continued to be shocked and amazed at what I was learning because it was not what I was taught about Islam. In my graduate courses, the professor I had was respected as an authority on Islam, yet his teaching and that of Christianity in general was full of misunderstanding. He and many Christians like him are sincere, but they are sincerely wrong.

Two months later after having once again prayed seeking God's direction, I felt something drop into my being! I sat up, and it was the first time I was to use the name of Allah, and I said, "Allah, I believe you are the One and Only True God." There was peace that descended upon me and from that day four years ago until now I have never regretted embracing Islam. This decision did not come without trial …

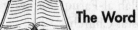

The Word

Truly, my prayer, my service of sacrifice, my life and my death are all for God the Cherisher of the Worlds. No partner has He, this I am commanded. And I am the first of those who bow to Allah in Islam. (6:162–163)

—Sister Khadijah Watson

(from www.islamfortoday.com/khadijah_sue_watson.htm)

A New Beginning for a Pentecostal Minister

It was not long after arriving in Saudi Arabia that I saw an immediate difference in the lifestyle of the Muslim people. They were different from the followers of Elijah Muhammad and Minister Louis Farrakhan (of the U.S. group known as the Nation of Islam) in that they were of all nationalities, colors, and languages. I immediately expressed a desire to learn more about this peculiar brand of religion. I was amazed by the life of Prophet Muhammad and wanted to know more. I requested books from one of the brothers who was active in calling people to Islam. I was supplied with all of the books that I could possibly want. I read each and every one. I was then given the Holy Koran and read it completely several times within four months.

I asked question after question and received satisfactory answers. What appealed to me was that the brothers were not keen on impressing me with their knowledge. If a brother didn't know how to answer a question, he would tell me that he simply didn't know and would check with someone who did. The next day he would always bring the answer. I noticed how humility played such a great role in the lives of these mysterious people of the Middle East.

I was amazed to see the women covering themselves from face to foot. I did not see any religious hierarchy. No one was competing for any religious position. All of this was wonderful, but how could I entertain the thought of abandoning a teaching that had followed me since childhood? What about the Bible? I knew that there is some truth in it even though it had been changed and revised countless numbers of times. I was then given a video cassette of a debate between (Muslim apologist) Shaykh Ahmed Deedat and (Christian evangelist) Reverend Jimmy Swaggart. After seeing the debate I immediately became a Muslim.

—Abdullah al-Faruq, (formerly Kenneth L. Jenkins, minister and elder of the Pentecostal Church)

(from www.themodernreligion.com/convert/convert_KLJ.htm)

A Very Special Ramadan

After I had my second child my husband … said that the following Ramadan we would begin to pray salat and read the Koran translation tapes his father had given us a couple of years ago.

I tried to make excuses and claimed that I couldn't remember to pray. But when I put the cassette on and began to listen to the Koran, I cannot explain what effect it had on me—my body started to tremble with fear and tears were flowing from my eyes. I felt like I was the worst person on earth for not living the way Allah has told us. I began to pray five times a day and read all the Koran. I will never forget that Ramadan, as it changed my life and my husband's forever.

—Anonymous

(from www.convertstoislam.com/Stories/anonymous2.html)

Her Mother-In-Law Made Her Do It

In a conversation with my mother-in-law, we began to discuss Islam. She made the comment "All Muslims, by the very nature of their religion, are violent." Let me say, and I say this as fact, not as insult, that she is a very closed-minded person and does not educate herself on religions outside her narrow view of Protestant Christianity. So when she made the comment, I didn't believe what she said. But it did occur to me that I was unable to agree or disagree based on my own knowledge. I felt the need to change that. In classes in college I had learned the Five Pillars of Islam, and that Muslims prayed toward Mecca because Muhammad was from there (textbooks don't have to be correct, do they?).

> **CAUTION**
>
> **Caution!**
>
> Remember that Muslims pray toward Mecca because the Koran tells them to and because it is the site of the ancient monotheistic shrine known as the Ka'ba. They do not pray to Mecca because the Prophet was a native of the city.

Soon after I had the chance to receive some free pamphlets about Islam from a website. I sent for them, thinking that if we were going to be at war with these people, I should know something about them.

The pamphlets came. I read them and was amazed. This religion was nothing like what I had previously thought! A volunteer from the website e-mailed me and offered me an English translation of the Koran. I thought "Why not?" I had read the Bible, some of the Hindu Vedas, much of the Talmud, and the Book of Mormon. So in the interest of education, I accepted the offer.

When the book came, I found that he had generously sent me two other books. *An Illustrated Guide to Islam* and *Towards Understanding Islam*. I read them first. Then I began *The Meaning of the Qur'an*. It was if scales had fallen off my eyes, and off of my heart. I felt in my heart that I had found how to please God.

I promised myself I would not take shahada until I had read the entire Koran. Even though I spent hours studying other aspects of Islam on the Internet, there was nothing that I learned that turned me off the faith. Instead, there were so many ideas that I had believed already. It was if Allah had been leading me to Islam all of my life.

—Heather (Khadija)

(from www.geocities.com/plantgirl848/conversion.html)

An Unwanted Gift

In 1997 my fiancee gave me the Koran as a gift, simply because I loved to read. Just to show you how much I hated the Muslims … Well, when she gave me the Koran it caused a fight between us and we separated for quite some time. Eventually, however, I picked up the book and began reading it.

I can remember that very day. The house was crystal clean, the air was soft and sweet, and the lighting was dim and perfect for reading. It was the translation from Abdullah Yusuf Ali. I read his introduction, the first three pages, and I began to cry like a baby. I cried and cried and I couldn't help myself. I knew that this was what I was looking for and I wanted to beat myself to death for not finding it earlier. I just knew in my heart how magical it was. This was not the Islam I knew. This was not the Arab thing I was taught to think was dirty. This was my life wrapped up in a few pages. Every page told my life. I was reading my soul and it felt good, but regretful.

—James Farrell

(from www.utm.thaqalayn.org/files/converts.pdf)

Spotlight on Islam

Muslims believe that Allah uses the Koran to summon people to the Islamic way of life, and to strengthen the faith of the worldwide community of believers. The Koran offers the parable of the tree to describe the enduring effect of its words on those who heed them:

Consider (Muhammad) how God (in a parable) compares the blessed Word to that of a blessed tree which has firm roots and branches rising up into the sky and yields fruits in every season, by the permission of its Lord. God sets forth parables for people so that they may take heed. An evil word is compared to an evil tree with no firm roots in the land and thus has no stability. God strengthens the faith of the believers by the true Words in this world and in the life to come. He causes the unjust to go astray and does whatever He pleases. (14:24–27)

The Least You Need to Know

◆ "Close encounters" with the Koran are common.

◆ The self-conversion experience has been reported by people of many different nationalities and social backgrounds.

◆ The encounter has a way of leaving one permanently changed.

◆ Muslims believe that Allah uses the Koran to call humankind and strengthen the faith of the believers.

Chapter 23

A Book for Yesterday, Today, and Tomorrow

In This Chapter

- ◆ The Koran and "modern" values
- ◆ Returning to the timeless word of God
- ◆ The challenge of da'wah

In this final chapter, you'll see why millions of people around the world see the Koran's message as timeless—that is, both old and new—and how it supports the continuing propagation of the faith.

Of Timelines, Human and Divine

Non-Muslims often refer to Islam as though it were a fairly recent development in human religious practice. They speak of its having "originated" in the seventh century C.E., or of its strong historical association with the Prophet, or even of the cultural and social influences that are thought to have "inspired" it. Muslims, however, view their faith in a very different way.

They see the Koran as the final expression of the plan set out for humanity by Allah Almighty—a plan that has been in place since the moment the Creator established humankind on Earth. As a result, Muslims see themselves not as the practitioners of something "invented" or "created" in seventh-century Arabia, but as the practitioners of the world's most ancient—and inspiring—faith.

An Enduring Message

The Koran itself supports this view.

It sets out a vision of history as transitory—as beginning and ending not with human chronicles or movements or ideas, but with God himself:

> (This will happen) on the day when We roll up the heavens as if it were a written scroll and bring it back into existence just as though We had created it for the first time. This is what We have promised and We have always been true to Our promise. (21:104)

It sets out an extraordinary vision of a judgment whose ramifications echo into eternity.

> On the day when We shall gather you all together (for the Day of Judgment), all cheating will be exposed. Those who believe in God and act righteously will receive forgiveness for their sins. They will be admitted into Paradise wherein streams flow and they will live forever. This certainly is the greatest triumph. (64:9)

It speaks movingly of human life as something that is both sacred and transitory, a journey from birth to death to judgment. This, the Koran tells us, is a journey we all must make:

> I was born with peace and I shall die and be brought to life again with peace. (19:33)

And, in words that are impossible to forget, it sets out a vision of mankind as, ultimately, a single unit. Islam asks us to see humanity as one nation—a massive grouping that transcends all geographical, political, or historical distinctions, one that has been blessed, as a whole and in its various subdivisions, with the messages of God's warning Prophets:

> At one time all people were only one nation. God sent Prophets with glad news and warnings. He sent the Book with them for a genuine purpose to provide the people with the ruling about disputed matters among them. No one disputed this matter except those who had already received evidence before. Their dispute was only because of their own hostility. To deal with this dispute, God, through His will, sent guidance to the believers. God guides to the right path whomever He wants. (2:213)

A Common Mistake

This ideal of a universal world-view—and universal accessibility—is extremely important to the religion that claims the Koran as its holy scripture.

It may be tempting for outsiders to view the Koran as an ancient document, or to consider the text as somehow limited to experiences and cultures of the Middle East, or even to view Islam as an outdated faith. But doing this is a great mistake.

This mistake is quite common, and it is similar to the one of assuming that all Muslims are Arabs when, in fact, the vast majority are not. The faith set out in the Koran, and supported in the Sunna, is not a regional faith, but a worldwide one. It is not a limited historical message, but a timeless one with endless applications to human life in the twenty-first century and beyond.

As long as humanity must face life, death, and the challenge of coming to terms with God, the Koran will remain both old and new—a supremely modern document of truly ancient origin.

Points to Ponder

One might expect a religious document of seventh-century Arabia to contain (for instance) superstitious or legendary explanations for natural events, or claims of supernatural power for prominent contemporary people of the time. The Koran, however, resolutely avoids such explanations and claims, focusing with relentless energy on the question of humanity's submission to God.

Returning to the Word of God

Today, human society faces many daunting challenges, including environmental, political, and social problems.

The most alarming challenge, however—at least to Muslims—may well be the tendency, evident in so many corners of the world, to denigrate God, to worship things in his place, or even to imagine that he does not exist.

Islam teaches that we are all mortals, and that we must all be prepared to offer an accounting to the Creator for the way we have spent our lives. These are teachings that have endured for centuries and are timeless.

Muslims believe that guidance to deal with all human problems that could possibly be encountered is available from Allah Almighty, that the Koran offers such divine guidance, and that the most serious human problem of all is the failure to submit to the will of God. With God, they believe, the most important problems people face today can all be navigated. Without God, people are certain to be among the losers—if not in this life, then in the next.

Focusing on Self to the Exclusion of God

And yet *atheism* has somehow become fashionable in many corners of contemporary life; so has a strange brand of *nihilism* that seems to be particularly attractive to young people in the West between the ages of about 14 and 24. Equally distressing to people of faith is a total apathy, or failure to care about, religious matters—an attitude that is often categorized under the popular label *agnostic*. These are distinctly "modern" outlooks.

What's It Mean?

Atheism describes a person's belief that God does not or cannot exist (this is so-called "strong atheism") or that the case for his existence is unpersuasive (this is the so-called "weak atheism"). **Agnosticism** describes the belief of a person who is not sure whether or not God exists. **Nihilism** is the belief that nothing, ultimately, matters. Islam rejects all of these schools of thought.

Devout Muslims believe that all of these ways of thinking can be seen as forms of self-obsession and self-delusion—a focusing on one's own negative perceptions or preconceptions that is so intense that they exclude Allah from one's life, perhaps in the name of personal freedom. The Koran clearly rejects this way of life when it gives us Joseph's words:

> I do not think that I am free from weakness; all human souls are susceptible to evil except for those to whom my Lord has granted mercy. My Lord is certainly All-forgiving and All-merciful. (12:53)

A Problem ... and a Solution

Millions upon millions of people in the modern world have—consciously or unconsciously—rejected God. Muslims believe that the result of this rejection is a society rife with social problems: drug and alcohol abuse, state-sponsored gambling, adultery and other forms of sexual immorality, and pornography, to name just a few.

On the individual level this trend presents a serious problem. And on the social level, there are some grave implications as well.

A hardening of atheism, agnosticism, and nihilistic attitudes—and a cycle of ever-deepening cynicism about core human values—is not hard to detect in many corners of today's media-saturated society. Thirty years ago, children were not exposed to profanity in movies and television shows. Today they are, and most parents do nothing about it. Thirty years ago, a nationally broadcast shampoo commercial that consciously echoed soft-core pornography would have been something unthinkable. Today, such a commercial is hardly noticed. Thirty years ago, a couple's intimate marital problems were considered an inappropriate topic for public conversation. Today, the detailed discussion of such problems is the subject of highly-rated talk shows.

There is a word for the sensationalist trend of today's media, and for activities like promiscuity, adultery, alcohol abuse, drug abuse, and atheism—a word that many in the West, it seems, have grown frightened of even pronouncing. The word is "wrong."

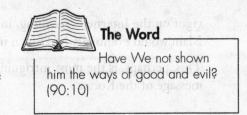

The Word
Have We not shown him the ways of good and evil? (90:10)

Yet many people have come to accept these grave social challenges as not wrong, but as normal or acceptable—at least, as far as they form part of the daily routine. People may even see serious social problems like the ones just cited as evidence of a society's commitment to tolerance or freedom of expression. But the Koran emphasizes the overriding importance of following God's direction, and on his knowledge of who actually does so:

> Your Lord knows best who has gone astray from His path and who is rightly guided. Do not yield to those who reject the Truth. (7–8)

Yet somehow "yielding to those who reject the Truth" is a very common activity!

Another Kind of Modern Message

The Koran rejects some of the supposedly "modern" attitudes of secular society. For example:

- Public displays of drug addiction and alcoholism must be part of how an open society operates; and anyway, use of alcohol and drugs may not be that bad after all. Who can really say what's right and what's wrong?

- It must be simply in the course of things that 70 to 80 percent of the customers at the average convenience store are there to purchase lottery tickets and play Keno games; and anyway, lotteries may not be that bad after all. Who can really say what's right and what's wrong?

- Sex is on display everywhere; and anyway, public depiction of sensuality to sell shampoo or cars or cheese puffs or beer may not be that bad after all. Who can really say what's right and what's wrong?

In North America and Europe, particularly, a strong consumer culture, a tradition of inebriation and self-medication, and an exploitative media all seem to amplify a profound sense of spiritual emptiness today, particularly among young people.

Interestingly, however, it is in these very parts of the world that interest in Islam—and specifically in the Koran—is growing most rapidly. And it is growing with particular vigor on the Internet—fulfilling, in a truly striking way, the Prophet's prediction that Islam would eventually be known in every corner of the globe.

This, perhaps, is the most intriguing modern message on the World Wide Web: the message of the Koran.

The Antidote to Today's Heart Disease

The Koran, Muslims believe, is the timeless antidote to the epidemic of heart disease that so often afflicts "modern" society.

It is the document, Islam holds, to which all people should devote their attention—even, perhaps, their skeptical attention. Those who are concerned not only about where they are and what they are experiencing now—but also where they are going *next* and what they will experience when they get there—will certainly find food for thought in the Koran.

By consulting the Koran, Muslims believe, we will regain purpose and meaning in our lives, and we will once again, and with very little effort, recall the difference between right and wrong in the life of an individual.

This is because each and every line of the Koran speaks to each individual human being about the most important subject of all: his or her relationship with the Creator.

Whether we hear and act upon that message is up to us—but Muslims believe that the Koran is in fact *calling* each of us as an individual ... and by extension each community, and the total human population of this planet. It is calling us to consult its words closely.

It asks us simply to listen.

Two Outcomes

Two things can happen when one consciously exposes oneself to the message of the Koran. One of them, the rejection of the text, is inherently cynical and self-centered. The other, the acceptance of the text, is joyful, and likely to cause one to re-evaluate one's entire life. Today, in the West, there are more and more stories of the second reaction to the Koran.

For You or Against You

The Prophet Muhammad said, "The Koran is (either) a proof for you or against you." (This comes from the collection known as *Muslim*.)

Practitioners of Islam interpret this saying to mean that one of two things will happen after we die. Either the word of God will stand as our witness, or it will stand against us as the deeds of our lives are evaluated.

Once we have been exposed to the Koran, it is up to us to determine what role it will actually play in our self-definition during our time on Earth.

Spotlight on Islam

It was in fact the Sura called "The Poets" which made me stop and evaluate my life and abandon the music business when I embraced Islam 20 years ago. Toward the end of the chapter, Allah, the Almighty, says:

> Should I tell you to whom the satans come? They come to every sinful liar. The satans try to listen to the heavens but many of them are liars. Only the erring people follow the poets. Have you not seen them wandering and bewildered in every valley and preaching what they themselves never practice. The righteously striving believers among them who remember God very often and use their talent to seek help after they have been wronged are the exceptional. The unjust will soon know how terrible their end will be. (26:221–227)

> ... I realized that this was the true religion; religion not in the sense the West understands it, not the type for only your old age. In the West, whoever wishes to embrace a religion and make it his only way of life is deemed a fanatic. I was not a fanatic; I was at first confused between the body and the soul. Then I realized that the body and soul are not apart, and you don't have to go to the mountain to be religious. We must follow the will of God.

–Yusuf Islam (the former Cat Stevens), in a message about his faith posted on www.catstevens.com.

The Challenge of Da'wah

Da'wah is the practice of inviting non-Muslims to Allah. It is the act of calling those unfamiliar with the message of the Koran to become familiar with it.

And it is with a verse about da'wah that this book offers its final passage from the Koran:

> A Book has been revealed to you, (Muhammad), so that, by the permission of their Lord, you would be able to lead people from darkness into light along the path of the Majestic, Praised One. (14:1)

If *this* book (lower-case "b") has left you more inclined to consult *that* Book (upper-case "B")—whether out of religious faith or out of simple curiosity—then our project has served its purpose.

Let's close with the words that began the Koran, and that began this book, the words that translate as "In the Name of Allah, the Compassionate, the Merciful":

Bismillahir Rahmanir Raheem!

The Least You Need to Know

- ◆ Muslims regard Islam as a faith with a history as long as God's relationship to humanity.

- ◆ The Koran is not limited by regional or historical preconceptions.

- ◆ It is simultaneously ancient and modern.

- ◆ Its messages concerning life, death, and salvation are profoundly relevant to contemporary people.

- ◆ Once we have encountered the Koran, it is up to us to decide what role it will play in our lives.

Chapter 24

Epilogue

In This Chapter

- Giving the Koran the last word
- The Koran on the Koran

It has been said that the Koran is its own best interpreter.

We decided to let the Koran have the last word in this book. Here are just a few of the more memorable passages from the holy book of Islam about ... the holy book of Islam.

Authoritative Guidance Meant to Be Followed

We have made the Koran easy to understand, but is there anyone who would pay attention? (54:17)

There is no doubt that this Book is revealed by the Lord of the Universe. (32:2)

Truth and Falsehood

Say, "Truth has come and falsehood has been banished; it is doomed to banishment." We reveal the Koran which is a cure and mercy for the believers but does nothing for the unjust except to lead them to perdition. (17:81–82)

Attentive Meditation

Whenever the Koran is recited (to you), listen to it quietly so that you may receive mercy. Remember your Lord deep within yourselves, humbly and privately, instead of shouting out loud (in prayer) in the mornings and evenings, and do not be of the heedless ones. (7:204–205).

Is it that they do not think about the Koran—or are their hearts sealed? (47:24)

Conquering Evil, Earning the Great Reward

When you recite the Koran, seek refuge in God from the mischief of Satan. (16:98)

This Koran shows the way to that which is the most upright and gives to the righteous believers the glad news of a great reward. (17:9)

Uncorrupted and Authentic

We Ourselves have revealed the Koran and We are its Protector. (15:9)

No one could have composed this Koran besides God. This confirms previous revelations and explains itself. There is no doubt that it is from the Lord of the Universe. (10:37)

Revealed as a Blessing

This Book which We have revealed is a blessed one. Follow its guidance and have piety so that you perhaps may receive mercy. (6:155)

The Least You Need to Know

- The Koran has been called its own best interpreter.
- It assures its audience that it offers authoritative guidance worth following.
- It offers vivid distinctions between truth and falsehood.
- It encourages humanity to meditate attentively on its message.
- It urges people to turn away from evil and toward righteousness in order to win a great reward.
- It presents itself as uncorrupted and authentic.
- It holds that its teachings are revealed as a mercy to mankind.

Appendix A

A Concise Islamic Timeline

Date	Event
circa 570 C.E.	Muhammad is born in Mecca.
595	Muhammad marries Khadija.
610	The Prophet receives his first revelation at Mt. Hira.
622	In response to persecution and assassination plots, he organizes a hijra (exodus) to Yathrib (later Medina), establishing the first Muslim community there.
630	He returns triumphantly to Mecca with a large number of followers and captures it without bloodshed.
630–632	Establishment of a Muslim community in Mecca; consolidation of control of Arabia; cleansing of the Ka'ba (shrine of Abraham) of idols.
632	Death of the Prophet. Abu Bakr, his father-in-law, is selected as first caliph (successor).
632–656	Period marked by extraordinary military, religious, and social expansion of Islam.
661	Death of Imam Ali. (His caliphate was marred by civil war.) Beginning of Umayyad rule. Objections to the legitimacy of this rule eventually leads to the formation of the Shi'a sect of Islam (contrasting with the Sunni sect).
711	Islam expands to Spain to the west and India to the east.
750	Abbasids assume control of the empire; capital shifted to Baghdad.

continues

(continued)

Date	Event
780–1031	Period of the Western caliphate (based in Spain), founded by a surviving member of the Umayyad family.
909–1171	Period of the Fatimid caliphate (based in Africa).
1000	Islam spreads rapidly through Africa; Nigeria established as important Islamic cultural and trading center.
1099	Christian Crusaders mount a successful assault on Jerusalem. (After a long and extremely bloody series of conflicts, Muslim forces eventually repel all the Crusaders from the region.)
1120	Islam spreads rapidly through Asia.
1175–1203	Islamic authority expands in India.
1258	Baghdad falls to the Mongols; Abassids flee.
1299	First Ottoman state founded in Turkey.
1345	Initial Ottoman military campaigns in Europe.
1369	Timur (Tamburlaine) conquers central Asia.
1453	Ottomans conquer Constantinople, rename it Istanbul.
1517	Ottomans conquer Mamluk region.
1517	Capture of Egypt by the Ottomans; Selim I is proclaimed caliph. A long period follows during which Ottoman sultans retain the title of caliph.
1575	Conclusion of Ottoman period of military ascendance.
circa 1600–1800	Roughly one third of all slaves kidnapped in Africa and forced into slavery in the United States are Muslim.
Early 1700s	Wahhabi movement gains strength in eighteenth century Arabia. The movement promotes a campaign of intolerance against those elements of Islam deemed "unorthodox," or "unfaithful," including the Shi'ite minority.
1798	Napoleon in Egypt.
1815	Muhammad Ali leads a successful movement for an independent Egypt.
1918	Ottoman Empire dissolved with the conclusion of the First World War. In the years following, many Islamic regions are colonized by Europeans, often with little or no regard for existing religious traditions.
1924	Title of caliph abolished.

Date	Event
1930	"Nation of Islam" founded in Detroit. The American movement incorporates some Islamic ideas, but designates the movement's founder, Elijah Muhammad (a.k.a. Wallace Fard), as a Prophet. (The Koran states clearly that Muhammad was the Final Prophet.)
1979	Iranian revolution leads to the founding of the Islamic Republic of Iran, the first modern-day Islamic state.

Date	Event
1930	Nation of Islam founded in Detroit. The American movement incorporates some Islamic ideas, but designates the movement's founder, Elijah Muhammad (a.k.a. Wallace Fard), as a Prophet. (The Koran states clearly that Muhammad was the Final Prophet.)
1979	Iranian revolution leads to the founding of the Islamic Republic of Iran, the first modern-day Islamic state.

Recommended Reading

The Koran

Ali, A. Yusuf, trans. and comm. *The Holy Qur'an: English Translation of the Meanings and Commentary*. Medina, Saudia Arabia: Complex for the Printing of the Holy Qur'an, 1983.

Arberry, Arthur J., trans. *The Koran Interpreted*. New York, NY: Macmillan Pub. CO., 1986.

Asad, Muhammad, trans. and expl. *The Message of the Qur'an*. Lahore: Maktaba Jawahar, 1992.

Ayoub, Mahmoud M. *The Qur'an and Its Interpreters*. 2 vols. Albany: State University of New York Press, 1984.

Cleary, T. *The Essential Koran*. San Francisco: HarperSanFrancisco, 1993.

Cook, M. *The Koran: A Very Short Introduction*. Oxford, UK: Oxford UP, 2000.

Mir, Mustansir. *Dictionary of Qur'anic Terms and Concepts*. New York: Garland, 1987.

Rahman, Fazlur. *Major Themes of the Qur'an*. 2nd ed. Minneapolis: Bibliotheca Islamica, 1989.

Shakir, M. H., trans. *The Qur'an*: Elmwood, NY: Tahrike Tarsile Qur'an, Inc., 2001.

Tabataba'i, Allamah Sayyid Muhammad Husayn. *The Quran in Islam: Its Impact and Influence on the Life of Muslims*. London: Zahra Trust, 1987.

Other Books

Armstrong, K. *Islam, A Short History*. Modern Library Edition, Random House, 2000.

Chittick, W. C. *Faith and Practice of Islam*. Albany, NY: State University of New York Press, 1992.

Esposito, J. L., ed. *The Oxford History of Islam*. Oxford, UK: Oxford University Press, 2000.

Lapidus, I. M. *A History of Islamic Societies*. Cambridge, UK: Cambridge University Press, 1989.

Le Gai, C. *Islam and the Destiny of Man*. Albany, NY: State University of New York Press, 1985.

Lewis, B. *Islam and the West*. Oxford, UK: Oxford University Press, 1993.

Murata, S. and Chittick, W. C. *The Vision of Islam*. New York, NY: Paragon House, 1994.

The Muslim Almanac. Gale Research, 1996.

Nasr, S. H. *Science and Civilization*. Cambridge, MA: Harvard University Press, 1968.

The Oxford Encyclopedia of the Modern Islamic World. Oxford: Oxford University Press, 1995.

Renard, J. *Seven Doors to Islam: Spirituality and the Religious Life of Muslims*. Berkeley, CA: University of California Press, 1996.

Sachedina, A. *The Islamic Roots of Democratic Pluralism*. Oxford, UK: Oxford University Press, 2001.

Mosques, Educational Institutions, and Community Centers in Your Area

As we mentioned in the first chapter, this book can only provide an overview of the Koran and Islam. If you wish to find out more, we encourage you to contact one of the local Islamic groups or organizations listed here. Reaching out to these places will help you connect with believers—and find out more about the Koran, as well as about Islamic communities and study resources in your area.

Alabama

Muslim American Society-Huntsville, AL
3612 Greenbriar Dr. NW
Huntsville, AL 35810
Phone: 256-851-6642
Fax: 256-858-3896
Website: www.mashuntsville.20m.com

Huntsville Islamic Center
1645 Sparkman Dr.
Huntsville, AL 35816
Phone: 256-721-1712
Fax: 256-721-1752
Website: www.islam.org/hic

MCA—Auburn and Opelika
338 Armstrong St.
Auburn, AL 36830
Phone: 334-821-7301
Website: www.auburn.edu/~ahmadha

Arizona

Islamic Center of Yuma
781 2nd Ave.
Yuma, AZ 85364
Phone: 520-539-5301
Fax: 520-539-5301

Almahdi Islamic Center
753 S. Alma School Rd.
Mesa, AZ 85210
Website: www.almahdi.net

Islamic Center of Tucson
901 E. 1st St.
Tucson, AZ 85719
Phone: 520-624-3233
Website: www.ictucson.com

Islamic Community Center of Phoenix
7516 N. Black Canyon Hwy.
Phoenix, AZ 85051
Phone: 602-249-0496
Fax: 602-249-0554
Website: www.islamcenter.com/iccp/index.htm

Islamic Cultural Center
131 E. Sixth St.
Tempe, AZ 85281
Phone: 602-894-6070
Fax: 602-894-6070
Website: www.tempemasjid.com

Arkansas

Islamic Center of Little Rock
3224 Anna Rd.
Little Rock, AR 72205
Phone: 501-565-4930
Website: www.iclrnet.org

California

Muslim Community Association of San Francisco Bay Area
P.O. Box 180
Santa Clara, CA 95052
Phone: 408-970-0647
Fax: 408-246-0244
Website: www.mca-sfba.org

Muslim Community Center of Greater San Diego
12788 Rancho Penasquitos Blvd.
San Diego, CA 92129
Phone: 858-484-0074
Website: www.mcc-gsd.org

IMAN, Iranian Muslim Organization of North America
3376 Motor Ave. Box 25941
Los Angeles, CA 90024
Phone: 310-202-8181
Fax: 310-202-0878
Website: www.iman.org

Muhammad's Mosque #27
8713 S. Vermont
Los Angeles, CA 90044
Phone: 323-751-1283
Website: www.noi.org

Mosque Al Noor
3004 16th St. #102
San Francisco, CA 94103
Phone: 415-552-0366
Fax: 415-552-4737
Website: www.islamicbulletin.com

Shia Muslim Association of Bay Area
2725 S. White Rd.
San Jose, CA 95148
Phone: 408-238-9496
Website: www.saba-igc.org

Masjid Annur
6990 65th St.
Sacramento, CA 95823
Phone: 916-392-6687
Fax: 916-42-ANNUR
Website: www.masjidannur.com

Muslim Community Center
850 Divisadero
San Francisco, CA 94117
Phone: 415-563-9397
Website: www.sfmuslim.org

Masjid Al Islam
8210 MacArthur Blvd.
Oakland, CA 94605
Phone: 510-638-9541
Website: www.sabiqun.com

Islamic Cultural Center of Northern California
1433 Madison St.
Oakland, CA 94612
Phone: 510-832-7600
Website: www.iccnc.org

Islamic Center of Southern California (ICSC)
434 S. Vermont Ave.
Los Angeles, CA 90020
Phone: 213-382-9200
Fax: 213-384-4572
Website: www.islamctr.org/icsc

Shia Ithna-Asheri Jamaat of Los Angeles
7925 Serapis Ave.
Pico Rivera, CA
Phone: 562-942-7442
Website: www.lajamaat.org

Colorado

Imamia Education Society of Colorado
P.O. Box 262112
Highlands Ranch, CO 80163-2112
Phone: 303-782-6944
Website: www.iesdenver.org

Muslim Students Association
Box 204, Lory Student Center, Colorado State University
Fort Collins, CO 80524
Website: www.colostate.edu/Orgs/MSA

MSAA-Univ. of Colo.-Denver
Tivoli Student Union, Auraria Campus, Downtown Denver
Denver, CO 80217
Phone: 303-556-4537
Website: www.cudenver.edu/msaa

Islamic Center of Boulder
1530 Culver Ct.
Boulder, CO 80303
Phone: 303-444-6345
Website: www.islamicsupport.net/ICB

Connecticut

Yale Muslim Students' Association
Yale University
New Haven, CT
Phone: 203-436-1201
Website: www.yale.edu/msa

Islamic Center of New London
16 Fort St.
Groton, CT 06320
Phone: 860-442-6321
Website: www.icnl.freeservers.com

Daar Ul Ehsaan USA
739 Terryville Ave.
Bristol, CT 06010
Phone: 860-585-9742
Fax: 860-589-4512
Website: www.daar-ul-ehsaan.org

District of Columbia

Masjid Al-Shura
3109 Martin Luther King Jr. Ave. S.E.
Washington, DC 22032
Phone: 202-547-8417
Fax: 561-431-0789
Website: www.salaam.net

Masjid Al-Islam
4603 Benning Road, S.E.
Washington, DC 20019
Phone: 202-581-1616
Fax: 202-581-0004
Website: www.sabiqun.com

Ivy City Educational Center and Masjid
2001 Galludet St., N.E.
Washington, DC 20002
Phone: 202-529-3100
Website: www.ivycitymasjid.com/index1.html

American Muslim Council (AMC)
1212 New York Ave., N.W., Suite 400
Washington, DC 20005
Phone: 202-789-2AMC
Fax: 202-789-2550
Website: www.amconline.org/newamc

Delaware

Masjid Al-Amaanah (Wilmington Islamic Da'wa Center)
2215 Washington St.
Wilmington, DE 19802
Phone: 302-661-1611
Fax: 302-429-1824
Website: www.naifinc.com

Masjid Ibrahim
28 Salem Church Rd.
Newark, DE 19713
Phone: 302-733-0373
Fax: 302-733-0311
Website: www.isdonline.org

Florida

Husseini Islamic Center
5211 Hester Ave.
Sanford, FL 32773
Phone: 407-320-7006
Website: www.husseini-islamic.org

Darul Uloom Masjid
7050 Pines Blvd.
Hollywood, FL 33024
Phone: 954-963-9514
Fax: 954-963-4902
Website: www.alhikmat.com

Islamic Center of Boca Raton
141 N.W. 20th St., Suite #A-7
Boca Raton, FL 33431
Phone: 561-395-7221
Fax: 561-395-7229
Website: www.icbr.org

Muslim Social Services
1320 N. Semoran Blvd., Suite 112
Orlando, FL 32807
Phone: 407-273-3995
Fax: 407-273-0266
Website: www.muslimsocialservices.org

Muslim Academy of Central Florida
1021 N. Goldenrod Rd.
Orlando, FL 32807
Phone: 407-382-9900
Fax: 407-277-4190
Website: www.macf.net

Masjid Al-Haq
545 W. Central Blvd.
Orlando, FL 32801
Website: www.islam.org/iscf

Islamic Education Center of Tampa
6450 Rockpoint Dr.
Tampa, FL 33634
Phone: 813-884-0847
Fax: 813-886-5286
Website: www.iecflorida.org

Masjid Al-Ansar
5245 N.W. 7th Ave.
Miami, FL 33127
Phone: 305-757-8741
Fax: 305-757-9768
Website: www.masjidalansar.8m.com

Georgia

Masjid Al-Hedaya
968 Powder Springs St.
Marietta, GA 30064
Phone: 770-795-9391
Website: www.alhedaya.com

Sahebozzaman Islamic Center of Atlanta
P.O. Box 671001
Marietta, GA 30066
Phone: 770-642-9411
Website: www.sicoa.org

Spencer-Majeed, Ltd.
P.O. Box 11041
Atlanta, GA 30310
Phone: 404-366-6610
Website: www.angelfire.com/home/spencermajeed/index.htm

Al-Farooq Masjid of Atlanta
442 14th St. N.W.
Atlanta, GA 30318
Phone: 404-874-7521
Fax: 404-874-7764
Website: www.alfarooqmasjid.org

Sahebozzaman Islamic Center of Atlanta
4853 Old Mountain Park Rd.
Roswell, GA 30075
Phone: 770-642-9411
Fax: 404-728-3792
Website: www.sicoa.org

Zainabia Islamic Educational Center
1100 Hope Rd.
Atlanta, GA 30350
Phone: 770-645-5413
Website: www.zainabia.comAtlanta Masjid of Al-Islam

Iowa

Islamic Center of Des Moines
6201 Franklin Ave.
Des Moines, IA 50322
Phone: 515-255-0212
Website: www.icodm.org

Idaho

Pocatello Mosque
343 S. 4th St., Apt. #3
Pocatello, ID 83201
Website: www.isu.edu/departments/idmosque

Illinois

Islamic Foundation of Peoria
2200 W. Altorfer Dr.
Peoria, IL 61615
Phone: 309-243-1082
Website: www.islamicfoundationofpeoria.org

United Muslims Moving Ahead (UMMA)
2320 N. Kenmore Ave.
Chicago, IL 60614
Phone: 312-325-2592
Website: www.depaul.edu/~umma

Tawheed Islamic Center
8607 1/2 S. Ashland Ave.
Chicago, IL 60620
Phone: 773-298-1976
Website: www.angelfire.com/il/sadaqa/tawheed.html

MSA Masjid at Illinois Institute of Technology
3300 S. Michigan Ave.
Chicago, IL 60616
Website: www.iit.edu/~msa

Mahdavia Islamic Center Chicago (MICC)
7419 N. Western Ave.
Chicago, IL 60645
Phone: 773-262-6680
Website: www.promisedmehdi.com

Baitu-Salaam Masajid
1058 W. Loyola
Chicago, IL 60626
Phone: 312-508-8548
Website: www.luc.edu/orgs/msa

Midwest Association of Shia Organized Muslims (MASOM)
6111 W. Addison
Chicago, IL 60634
Phone: 773-283-9718
Website: www.masom.com

Indiana

Islamic Center of Bloomington
1925 E. Atwater Ave.
Bloomington, IN 47401
Phone: 812-333-1611
Website: www.indiana.edu/~msaweb

Islamic Society of Evansville
1332 Lincoln Ave.
Evansville, IN 47716
Phone: 812-425-9801
Website: www.islamtomorrow.com

Kansas

Islamic Center of Lawrence
1917 Naismith Dr.
Lawrence, KS 66044
Phone: 785-749-1638
Website: www.ukans.edu/~msa

Masjid An-Noor/Islamic Society of Wichita
3104 E. 17th St.
Wichita, KS 67214
Phone: 316-687-4946
Fax: 316-682-4594
Website: www.noornet.com/isw

Kentucky

Islamic Society of Central Kentucky
4580 Nicholasville Rd.
Lexington, KY 40515
Phone: 859-245-5749
Website: www.isck.org

Louisiana

Islamic Society of Central Louisiana
2232 Worley Dr.
Alexandria, LA 71301
Phone: 318-442-0401
Website: www.iscla.org

Massachusetts

Islamic Society of Boston
204 Prospect St.
Cambridge, MA 02139
Phone: 617-876-3546
Fax: 617-576-6268
Website: www.imagineer-web.com/isb

Masjid Al-Quran
35 Intervale St.
Dorchester, MA 02121
Phone: 617-445-8070
Website: www.masjidalquran.org

Islamic Center of Boston
126 Boston Post Rd.
Wayland, MA 01778
Phone: 508-358-5885
Website: www.icbwayland.org

Islamic Society of Western Massachusetts
377 Amostown Rd.
West Springfield, MA 01090
Phone: 413-788-7546
Fax: 413-788-4949
Website: www.masjidma.com

Maryland

Islamic Society of Baltimore
6631 Johnnycake Rd.
Windsor Mill, MD 21244
Phone: 410-747-4869
Website: www.isb.org

IMAAM (Indonesian Muslim Association in America)
13113 Holdridge Rd.
Silver Spring, MD 20906
Phone: 301-949-4020
Fax: 301-949-3945
Website: www.imaam.org

Muslim Community Center Masjid (MCC)
15200 New Hampshire Ave.
Silver Spring, MD 20905
Phone: 301-384-3454
Fax: 301-384-6281
Website: www.mccmd.org

Michigan

Flint Islamic Center
9447 Corunna Rd.
Flint, MI 48532
Phone: 810-635-9099
Website: www.flintislamiccenter.com

Masjid Mu'ath Bin Jabal
6096 Dorothy St.
Detroit, MI 48211
Phone: 313-571-9502
Website: www.muathbinjabal.com

Attawheed Masjid
18624 W. Warren Ave.
Detroit, MI 48228
Phone: 313-492-8880
Fax: 313-582-1436
Website: www.tawheed.net

Islamic Center and Mosque of Grand Rapids
1301 Burton St. S.E.
Grand Rapids, MI 49507
Phone: 616-247-8786
Website: www.icgr.homestead.com

Islamic Association of Greater Detroit (IAGD)
865 W. Auburn Rd.
Rochester, MI 48307
Phone: 248-299-9866
Website: www.iagd.net

Masjid Abdur Rahman
114 N. 4th St.
Saginaw, MI 48601
Phone: 517-790-4473
Fax: 517-249-1666
Website: www.svsu.edu/msa

Islamic Center Lansing
920 S. Harrison Rd.
East Lansing, MI 48823
Phone: 517-351-4309
Website: www.mainnet.com/icl

Tawheed Center
29707 W. 10 Hills Rd.
Farmington, MI 48336
Phone: 313-581-2404
Fax: 419-730-6190
Website: www.angelfire.com/mi/tawheed

Masjid Wali Muhammad
11529 Linwood Ave.
Detroit, MI 48206
Phone: 313-868-2131
Website: www.masjidwalimuhammad.org

Islamic Center of America
15571 Joy Rd.
Detroit, MI 48228
Phone: 313-582-7442
Website: www.icofa.com

Ahlebait Association of MI
2230 Crumb Rd.
Walled Lake, MI 48390-2807
Phone: 248-669-5740
Website: www.geocities.com/majalis.geo/cal

Minnesota

Dar Al-Farooq
983 17th Ave. S.E.
Minneapolis, MN 55414
Phone: 612-331-1234
Fax: 612-331-8888
Website: www.alfarooq.org

Anjaman-e-Ásghari
10301 Jefferson Hwy.
Brooklyn Park, MN 55444
Phone: 763-424-4909
Website: www.mnjamat.org

Missouri

Islamic Society of Greater Kansas City
8501 E. 99th St. Box 410891
Kansas City, MO 64141
Phone: 816-763-2267
Fax: 816-763-6468
Website: www.isgkc.org

Mississippi

Islamic Center of Mississippi
204 Herbert St.
Starkville, MS 39759
Phone: 662-323-6559
Website: www.msstate.edu/org/msa/msa.html

North Carolina

Islamic Association of Raleigh
3020 Ligon St.
Raleigh, NC 27607
Phone: 919-834-9572
Website: www.islam1.org

Islamic Center of Morganton
203 Bethel St.
Morganton, NC 28655
Phone: 828-439-9487
Website: www.masjidmorganton.uni.cc

Islamic Center of the Sunnah
2911 E. Market St.
Greensboro, NC 27402
Phone: 336-273-0897
Website: www.tcfb.com/imranet

Islamic Center of Charlotte (ICC)
1700 Progress Ln.
Charlotte, NC 28205
Phone: 704-537-9399
Fax: 704-537-1577
Website: www.iccharlotte.com

Nebraska

Masjid Alnoor
P.O. Box 667
Dakota City, NE 68731
Website: www.masjidalnoor.20m.com

Islamic Center of Omaha
3511 N. 73 St.
Omaha, NE 68134
Phone: 402-571-0720
Website: www.ico-ne.org

New Hampshire

Islamic Society of Greater Manchester
P.O. Box 16363
Hooksett, NH 03106
Phone: 603-644-0939
Website: www.isgm.net

Islamic Society of Seacoast Area (ISSA)
13 Jenkins Ct. P.O. Box 52
Durham, NH 03824
Phone: 603-868-5937
Website: www.issa-nh.org

New Jersey

Muslim Community Of New Jersey
P.O. Box 865
Woodbridge, NJ 07095
Phone: 732-726-1244
Website: www.mcnjonline.com

Islamic Center of Ocean County
2116 Whitesville Rd. Box 473
Toms River, NJ 08754
Website: www.prontomail.com/Prontomail/Users/ICOC

Masjid Altaqwah
3536-38 Atlantic Ave.
Atlantic City, NJ 08401
Phone: 609-344-1786
Website: www.taqwah.tsx.org

Masjid Al-Salaam
2824 Kennedy Blvd.
Jersey City, NJ 07306
Phone: 201-798-9653
Website: www.masjidassalam.org

Nevada

Islamic Training Foundation
P.O. Box 204
Sparks, NV 89432
Phone: 702-784-6824
Fax: 702-355-0393
Website: www.islamist.org

New York

Masjid Fatih/United American Muslim Association NY, Inc.
59-11 8th Ave.
Brooklyn, NY 11220
Phone: 718-438-6919
Website: www.fatihcami.org

Masjid Musab Bin Omayer
6807 5th Ave.
Brooklyn, NY 11220
Phone: 718-680-0121
Fax: 718-493-4992
Website: www.almuslimnews.com

Muslim Center of Manhattan, Inc.
36 W. 44th St., Suite 311
New York, NY 10036
Phone: 212-302-5347
Website: www.MuslimCenterofManhattan.com

Jafria Association of North America
124 Third St.
Brentwood, NY 11717
Phone: 1-800-273-1201
Website: www.jana.org/index

Masjid Daru-as-Salaam
75 E. Parade
Buffalo, NY 14211
Phone: 716-896-0725
Fax: 716-896-1164
Website: www.muslims.net/MDS

Flatbush Islamic Center
1288 Nostrand Ave.
Brooklyn, NY 11226
Website: www.fic.4t.com

Ohio

Islamic Foundation Of Central Ohio
1428 E. Broad St.
Columbus, OH 43205
Phone: 614-253-3251
Website: www.ifco-columbus.org

Masjid Islam
4600 Rocky River Dr.
Cleveland, OH 44135
Phone: 216-676-9177
Fax: 216-941-3557
Website: www.emuslim.com

Akron Masjid
1145 (Old) S. Main St.
Akron, OH 44301
Phone: 330-374-9799
Website: www.uakron.edu/msa/message.htm

Islamic Society of Greater Columbus
580 Riverview Dr.
Columbus, OH 43202
Phone: 614-262-1310
Fax: 614-262-0263
Website: www.isgc.org

Islamic Center of Dayton
26 Josie St.
Dayton, OH 45403
Phone: 937-228-1503
Website: www.muslims.net/ISGD

First Cleveland Mosque
3613 E. 131st St.
Cleveland, OH 44120
Phone: 216-283-9027
Website: www.firstclevelandmosque.com

Toledo Islamic Academy
4404 Secor Rd.
Toledo, OH 43623
Phone: 419-292-1491
Website: www.toledomuslims.com

Oklahoma

Islamic Society of Tulsa
4630 S. Irvington Ave.
Tulsa, OK 74136
Phone: 918-665-2024
Fax: 918-665-2023
Website: www.istulsa.org

Masjid An-Nur
420 W. Lindsey St.
Norman, OK 73069
Phone: 405-364-5341
Website: www.muslims.net/ISN

Oregon

Masjed As-sabr
10323 S.W. 43rd
Portland, OR 97219
Phone: 503-293-6554
Website: www.assaber.com

Islamic Center of Portland
4420 S.W. 110th Ave.
Beaverton, OR 97005
Phone: 503-526-9305
Website: www.icop.org

Pennsylvania

Islamic Center of As-Sabereen
1403 S. Cameron St.
Harrisburg, PA 17105
Phone: 717-238-8313
Fax: 717-238-3599
Website: www.as-sabereen.com

The Foundation for Islamic Education/Al-Aqsa Islamic Center
1860 Montgomery Ave.
Villanova, PA 19085
Phone: 610-520-9624
Website: www.fiesite.org

Islamic Society of Greater Harrisburg (ISGH)
407 N. Front St. P.O. Box 7463
Steelton, PA 17113
Phone: 717-939-3107
Website: www30.brinkster.com/isghpa

Mahdieh
P.O. Box 1485
Havertown, PA 19083
Phone: 215-871-7656
Website: www.mahdieh.org

Rhode Island

Masjid Al-Razzaq, Muslim Community Center of Rhode Island
234 Pavilion Ave.
Providence, RI 02905
Phone: 401-467-0011
Website: www.mccri.org

South Carolina

Islamic Society of Greenville
P.O. Box 25721
Greenville, SC 29616
Phone: 864-292-2219
Fax: 803-292-1326
Website: www.greenvillemasjid.com

Masjid Al-Muslimiin
1929 Gervais St.
Columbia, SC 29201
Phone: 803-254-7242
Website: www.microbyte.net/icc

South Dakota

Mosque & Dawah Center of East Central South Dakota
P.O. Box 284
Brookings, SD 57006
Website: www.geocities.com/rural_islam

Islamic Society of Brookings
803 13th Ave.
Brookings, SD 57006
Phone: 605-697-6187
Fax: 605-693-3936
Website: www.angelfire.com/sd/Islam

Tennessee

Al Rasool Islamic Center
5311 Stage Rd.
Memphis, TN 38134
Phone: 901-380-9002
Website: www.alrasoolcenter.org

Masjid as-Salaam/Muslim Society of Memphis
1065 Stratford Rd.
Memphis, TN 38122
Phone: 901-685-8906
Website: www.masjiidassalam.com

Islamic Center of Nashville
2512 12th Ave. S.
Nashville, TN 37204
Phone: 615-385-9373
Website: www.muslimeen.org

Masjid Al-Mu'minun
4412 S. Third St.
Memphis, TN 38109
Phone: 901-789-1904
Fax: 901-789-4556
Website: www.islam.org/al-muminun

Texas

Dallas Central Mosque
Islamic Association of North Texas
840 Abrams Rd.
Richardson, TX 75081
Phone: 972-231-5698
Website: www.iant.com

Islamic Center of Irving
P.O. Box 154401
Irving, TX 75015-4401
Phone: 972-721-9136
Fax: 972-579-3309
Website: www.irvingmasjid.org

Islamic Education Center of Houston, Texas
2313 S. Voss Rd.
Houston, Texas 77057
Phone: 713-787-5000
Website: www.iec-houston.org

Al-Murtaza Organization of Muslims Inc
6274 Hwy. 6 S.
Houston, TX 77083
Phone: 832-328-1400
Website: www.al-murtaza.org

Utah

Alrasool Islamic Center
470 E. Stanley Ave. (3182 South)
Salt Lake City, UT 84115
Phone: 801-467-3978
Website: www.al-rasool.org

Islamic Discovery
470 E. Stanley Ave.
Salt Lake City, UT 84158
Phone: 801-467-3978
Website: www.islamicdiscovery.com

Virginia

Masjid Abdul Aziz of Williamsburg
2692A John Tyler Hwy.
Williamsburg, VA 23185
Phone: 757-564-1659
Fax: 757-564-1659
Website: www.masjid-abdulaziz.org

Kufa Center of Islamic Knowledge (KCIK)
2319 10th St., N.W.
Roanoke, VA 24012
Phone: 540-563-8471
Fax: 540-563-8471
Website: www.geocities.com/eureka/plaza/7288

Norfolk Masjid
898 Lexington Ave.
Norfolk, VA 23504
Phone: 757-627-1646
Website: www.norfolkmasjid.org

Islamic Society of Greater Richmond (ISGR)
6324 Rigsby Rd.
Richmond, VA 23226-2915
Phone: 804-673-4177
Fax: 804-750-1147
Website: www.isgr.org

Idara Dawat-o-Irshad, USA Inc.
P.O. Box 22885
Alexandria, VA 22304
Phone: 703-256-8622
Fax: 703-256-8624
Website: www.irshad.org

Islamic Center of Virginia
1241 Buford Rd.
Richmond, VA 23235
Phone: 804-796-6479
Website: www.islamiccenterva.org

Vermont

Islamic Society of Vermont Inc.
P.O. Box 476
Essex Junction, VT 05453
Phone: 802-388-3227
Website: www.middlebury.edu/~islamic/ISVI.html

Washington

Zainab Organization of Greater Seattle
14327 Sunnyside Ave. N.
Seattle, WA 98133
Website: www.zainab.org

Islamic Center of Kent, Washington
10820 S.E. 211th Pl., #1102
Kent, WA 98031
Phone: 253-223-2096
Website: www.ickent.com

Wisconsin

Islamic Center of Milwaukee
4707 S. 13th St.
Milwaukee, WI 53221
Phone: 414-282-1812
Fax: 414-282-9329
Website: www.expinc.net/Islam

West Virginia

Islamic Society of Appalachian Region
247 Frontage Rd.
Princeton, WV 24740
Website: www.isar-mosque.com

Islamic Assoc. of West Virginia
P.O. Box 8414
Charleston, WV 25303
Phone: 304-744-1031
Website: www.iawv.org

Washington

Zainab Organization of Greater Seattle
14322 Sunnyside Ave. N.
Seattle, WA 98133
Website: www.zainah.org

Islamic Center of Kent, Washington
10820 S.E. 211th Pl. #107
Kent, WA 98031
Phone: 253-222-2006
Website: www.ickent.com

Wisconsin

Islamic Center of Milwaukee
4707 S. 13th St.
Milwaukee, WI 53221
Phone: 414-282-1812
Fax: 414-282-8229
Website: www.icmwi.net

West Virginia

Islamic Society of Appalachian Region
247 Frontage Rd
Princeton, WV 24740
Website: www.isar-mosque.com

Islamic Assoc. of West Virginia
P.O. Box 8414
Charleston, WV 25303
Phone: 304-744-1031
Website: www.iawv.org

The Suras (Chapters) of the Koran

In this part of the book, you'll find a short overview of each of the 114 Suras, or chapters, of the Koran. There is no replacement for reading the original in its entirety, of course, but if you're looking for an English-language sampling that will give you some sense of the depth and breadth of the material, this appendix can serve as a starting point.

The "Meccan" Suras are those delivered before the Prophet's hijrah (migration) to the city eventually known as Medina—the first Muslim community. "Medinan" Suras are those delivered after the hijrah. The designation of a Sura as "Meccan" or "Medinan" is sometimes a matter of scholarly controversy; the identifications below are intended as a rough guide only. The sequence of Suras as they appear in the Koran does *not* reflect the order of their revelation.

Sura #1

Arabic Name: Fatehah
English Name: The Opening
Period of Revelation: Meccan
Representative Passage (The "Seven Oft-Repeated Verses," which form the whole of the Sura):

In the Name of Allah, the Beneficent, the Merciful
All praise belongs to God, Lord of the Universe,
the Beneficent, the Merciful
and Master of the Day of Judgment.
(Lord), You alone We do worship and from You alone we do seek assistance
(Lord), guide us to the right path,
the path of those to whom You have granted blessings, those who are neither subject to Your
anger nor have gone astray. (1:1–7)

Sura #2

Arabic Name: Al-Baqarah
English Name: The Cow
Period of Revelation: Medinan
Representative Passage:

Say, "Belief in God and following the guidance of Islam are God's means of purification for us. Islam is the baptism of God. No one is a better baptizer than He and we Muslims worship Him." (2:138)

Sura #3

Arabic Name: Al-Imran
English Name: The Imrans
Period of Revelation: Medinan
Representative Passage:

There is no Lord but God. It is God who is Majestic and All-wise.

If they turn away (from the Truth, let it be known that) God knows well the evil-doers. (3:62–63)

Sura #4

Arabic Name: Al-Nisa
English Name: The Women
Period of Revelation: Medinan
Representative Passage:

God wants to guide you, explain to you the customs of those who lived before you, and grant you forgiveness. He is All-knowing and All-wise.
God wants to be merciful to you but those who follow their evil desires seek to lead you astray.
God wants to relieve you of your burden; all human beings were created weak. (4:26–28)

Sura #5

Arabic Name: Al-Maidah
English Name: The Table
Period of Revelation: Medinan
Representative Passage:

God does not want you to suffer hardship. He wants you to be purified. He wants to complete His favors to you so that perhaps you would give Him thanks. (5:6)

Sura #6

Arabic Name: Al-Anam
English Name: The Cattle
Period of Revelation: Meccan
Representative Passage:

Only those who have understanding will accept your faith. (Those who have no understanding) are like the dead whom God will resurrect and to Him will all return. (6:36)

Sura #7

Arabic Name: Al-A'Raf
English Name: The Heights
Period of Revelation: Meccan
Representative Passage:

They ask you (Muhammad), "When will the Day of Judgment be?" Tell them, "My Lord knows best. It is He who has appointed its time. It will be a grave hour both in the heavens and the earth. It will only approach you suddenly." They say, "It seems that you know about the coming of the Day of Judgment." Tell them, "Only God knows about it, and most people do not know." (7:187)

Sura #8

Arabic Name: Al-Anfal
English Name: The Spoils
Period of Revelation: Medinan
Representative Passage:

Mobilize your (defensive) force as much as you can to frighten the enemies of God and your own enemies. This also will frighten those who are behind them whom you do not know but God knows well. Whatever you spend for the cause of God, He will give you sufficient recompense with due justice. If they (the unbelievers) propose peace, accept it and trust in God. God is All-hearing and All-knowing. (8:60–61)

Sura #9

Arabic Name: Al-Taubah
English Name: The Repentance
Period of Revelation: Medinan
Representative Passage:

Believers, do not accept your fathers and brothers as your guardians if they prefer disbelief to faith, lest you be unjust. (9:23)

Sura #10

Arabic Name: Yunus
English Name: Jonah
Period of Revelation: Meccan
Representative Passage:

No one could have composed this Quran besides God. This confirms the existing Book (the Bible) and explains itself. There is no doubt that it is from the Lord of the Universe. (10:37)

Sura #11

Arabic Name: Hud
English Name: Hud
Period of Revelation: Meccan
Representative Passage:

The righteously striving believers who are humble before their Lord, will be the dwellers of Paradise wherein they will live forever. Can the two groups, the blind and the deaf, be considered equal to those who have vision and hearing? Will you then not take heed? (11:23–24)

Sura #12

Arabic Name: Yusuf
English Name: Joseph
Period of Revelation: Meccan
Representative Passage:

Yusuf (Joseph) said, "Lord, prison is dearer to me than that which women want me to do. Unless You protect me from their guile, I shall be attracted to them in my ignorance." His Lord heard his prayers and protected him from their guile; He is All-hearing and All-knowing. (12:33–34)

Sura #13

Arabic Name: Al-Ra'd
English Name: The Thunder
Period of Revelation: Meccan
Representative Passage:

In (God's) plans everything has been designed proportionately. He knows all the unseen and seen. He is the most Great and High. It is all the same to Him whether you speak in secret or out loud, try to hide in the darkness of night or walk in the brightness of day. (13:8–10)

Sura #14

Arabic Name: Ibrahim
English Name: Abraham
Period of Revelation: Meccan
Representative Passage:

God guides or causes to go astray whomever He wants. He is Majestic and All-wise. (14:4)

Sura #15

Arabic Name: Al-Hijr
English Name: The Rocky Tract
Period of Revelation: Meccan
Representative Passage:

God said (to Satan), "The path which leads to Me is straight, and you have no authority over My servants except the erring ones who follow you. (15:41–42)

Sura #16

Arabic Name: Al-Nahl
English Name: The Bee
Period of Revelation: Meccan
Representative Passage:

We have sent you the Book which clarifies all matters. It is a guide, a mercy, and glad news to the Muslims. (16:89)

Sura #17

Arabic Name: Al-Isra'
English Name: The Night Journey
Period of Revelation: Meccan
Representative Passage:

Do not follow what you do not know; the ears, eyes, and hearts will all be held responsible for their deeds. (17:36)

Sura #18

Arabic Name: Al-Kahf
English Name: The Cave
Period of Revelation: Meccan
Representative Passage:

Read whatever is revealed to you from the Book of your Lord. No one can change His words and you can never find any refuge other than Him. (18:27)

Sura #19

Arabic Name: Marium
English Name: Mary
Period of Revelation: Meccan
Representative Passage:

The human being says, "Shall I be brought to life again after I will die?" Does he not remember that We created him when he did not exist? (19:66–67)

Sura #20

Arabic Name: Ta Ha
English Name: Ta Ha
Period of Revelation: Meccan
Representative Passage:

Instruct your family to pray and to be steadfast in their worship. We do not ask any sustenance from you; it is We who give you sustenance. Know that piety will have a happy end. (20:132)

Sura #21

Arabic Name: Al-Anbiya
English Name: The Prophets
Period of Revelation: Meccan
Representative Passage:

Have the unbelievers not ever considered that the heavens and the earth were one piece and that We tore them apart from one another. From water We have created all living things. Will they then have no faith? (21:30)

Sura #22

Arabic Name: Al-Hajj
English Name: The Pilgrimage
Period of Revelation: Medinan
Representative Passage:

God will admit the righteously striving believers to the gardens wherein streams flow. God has all the power to do whatever He wants. (22:14)

Sura #23

Arabic Name: Al-Muminun
English Name: The Believers
Period of Revelation: Meccan
Representative Passage:

Every nation has an appointed life span. (23:43)

Sura #24

Arabic Name: Al-Nur
English Name: The Light
Period of Revelation: Medinan
Representative Passage:

Believers, do not follow the footsteps of Satan; whoever does so will be made by Satan to commit indecency and sin. Were it not for the favor and mercy of God, none of you would ever have been purified. (24:21)

Sura #25

Arabic Name: Al-Farqan
English Name: Discernment
Period of Revelation: Meccan
Representative Passage:

They worship besides God things that can neither benefit nor harm them. The unbelievers are defiant against their Lord. (25:55)

Sura #26

Arabic Name: Ash-Shuara
English Name: The Poets
Period of Revelation: Meccan
Representative Passage:

On the Day of Judgment Paradise will be brought near the pious and hell will be left open for the rebellious ones who will be asked, "What did you worship besides God? Will the idols help you? Can they help themselves?" (26:91–93)

Sura #27

Arabic Name: Al-Naml
English Name: The Ant
Period of Revelation: Meccan
Representative Passage:

They ask, "When the Day of Judgment will come, if it is true at all?" Say, "Perhaps some of the things which you wish to experience immediately are very close to you." (27:71–72)

Sura #28

Arabic Name: Al-Qasas
English Name: The Story
Period of Revelation: Meccan
Representative Passage:

(Some of) the followers of the Bible believe in the Quran. When it is recited to them, they say, "We believe in it. It is the Truth from our Lord. We were Muslims before it was revealed." These will receive double reward for their forbearance, replacing evil by virtue, and for their spending for the cause of God. When they hear impious words, they ignore them, saying, "We shall be responsible for our deeds and you will be responsible for yours. Peace be with you. We do not want to become ignorant." (28:52–55)

Sura #29

Arabic Name: Al-Ankabut
English Name: The Spider
Period of Revelation: Meccan
Representative Passage:

Do people think they will not be tested because they say, "We have faith?" (29:2)

Sura #30

Arabic Name: Al-Rum
English Name: The Romans
Period of Revelation: Meccan
Representative Passage:

Those who disbelieve do so against their own souls. Those who do good pave the way for their own benefit. (30:44)

Sura #31

Arabic Name: Luqman
English Name: Luqman
Period of Revelation: Meccan
Representative Passage:

If they try to force you to consider things equal to Me, which you cannot justify, equal to Me, do not obey them. Maintain lawful relations with them in this world and follow the path of those who turn in repentance to Me. To Me you will all return and I shall tell you all that you have done. (31:15)

Sura #32

Arabic Name: As-Sajdah
English Name: Prostration
Period of Revelation: Meccan
Representative Passage:

The only people who believe in Our revelations are those who, when reminded about them, bow down in prostration and glorify their Lord with His praise without pride. (32:15)

Sura #33

Arabic Name: Al-Ahzab
English Name: The Confederate
Period of Revelation: Medinan
Representative Passage:

God has promised forgiveness and great rewards to the Muslim men and the Muslim women, the believing men and the believing women, the obedient men and the obedient women, the truthful men and the truthful women, the forbearing men and the forbearing women, the humble men and the humble women, the alms-giving men and the alms-giving women, the fasting men and the fasting women, the chaste men and the chaste women, and the men and women who remember God very often. (33:35)

Sura #34

Arabic Name: Al-Saba
English Name: Sheba
Period of Revelation: Meccan
Representative Passage:

Say, "It is my Lord who determines and increases the sustenance of whomever He wants. He will replace whatever you spend for His cause, and He is the best Sustainer." (34:39)

Sura #35

Arabic Name: Al-Fatir
English Name: The Originator
Period of Revelation: Meccan
Representative Passage:

People, you are always in need of God and God is Self-sufficient and Praiseworthy. (35:15)

Sura #36

Arabic Name: Ya'sin
English Name: Ya'sin
Period of Revelation: Meccan
Representative Passage (The exquisite thirty-sixth sura is traditionally held to be the "heart of the Koran."):

Is the One who has created the heavens and the earth not able to create another creature like the human being? He certainly has the power to do so. He is the Supreme Creator and is All-knowing. Whenever He decides to create something He has only to say, "Exist," and it comes into existence. All glory belongs to the One in whose hands is the control of all things. To Him you will all return. (36:81–83)

Sura #37

Arabic Name: As-Saffat
English Name: The Ranks
Period of Revelation: Meccan
Representative Passage:

(Zaqqum) is a tree which grows from the deepest part of hell, and its fruits are like the heads of devils. The dwellers of hell will eat that fruit and fill up their bellies. Then they will have on top of it a mixture of boiling water. They can only return to hell. (37:64–68)

Sura #38

Arabic Name: Sad
English Name: Sad
Period of Revelation: Meccan
Representative Passage:

We have not created the heavens and the earth and all that is between them without purpose, even though this is the belief of the disbelievers. Woe to the disbelievers; they will suffer the torment of fire. (38:27)

Sura #39

Arabic Name: Az-Zamar
English Name: The Hordes
Period of Revelation: Meccan
Representative Passage:

(Muhammad), give the glad news to those of Our servants who listen to the words and only follow the best ones. Tell them that they are those whom God has guided. (39:18)

Sura #40

Arabic Name: Al-Ghafir
English Name: The Forgiver
Period of Revelation: Meccan
Representative Passage:

Every soul will be recompensed for its deeds on this Day. There will be no injustice. Certainly God's reckoning is swift. (40:17)

Sura #41

Arabic Name: Al-Fusillat
English Name: Expounded Revelations
Period of Revelation: Meccan
Representative Passage:

(Muhammad), say, "I am a mere mortal like you. I have received a revelation that your Lord is the only One. So be up-right and obedient to Him and seek forgiveness from Him. (41:6)

Sura #42

Arabic Name: Ash-Shura
English Name: The Counsel
Period of Revelation: Meccan
Representative Passage:

Do they say that he, (Muhammad), has invented falsehood against God? Had God wanted, He could have sealed up your heart. God causes falsehood to vanish and, by His words, firmly establishes the truth. He has full knowledge of what the hearts contain. (42:24)

Sura #43

Arabic Name: Al-Aukhruf
English Name: The Ornament
Period of Revelation: Meccan
Representative Passage:

The pagans say, "Had the Beneficent God wanted, we would not have worshipped them (idols)." Whatever they say is not based on knowledge. It is only a false conjecture. (43:20)

Sura #44

Arabic Name: Al-Dukhan
English Name: Smoke
Period of Revelation: Meccan
Representative Passage:

We have not created the heavens and the earth and all that is between them for Our own amusement. We have created them for a genuine purpose, but most people do not know. (44:38–39)

Sura #45

Arabic Name: Al-Jathiyah
English Name: The Kneeling
Period of Revelation: Meccan
Representative Passage:

God has created the heavens and the earth for a genuine purpose so that every soul will be duly recompensed for its deeds without being wronged. (45:22)

Sura #46

Arabic Name: Al-Ahqaf
English Name: The Sandhills
Period of Revelation: Meccan
Representative Passage:

On the day when the disbelievers will be exposed to the fire, they will be told, "You have spent your happy days during your worldly life and enjoyed them. On this day you will suffer a humiliating torment for your unreasonably arrogant manners on earth and for the evil deeds which you have committed." (46:20)

Sura #47

Arabic Name: Muhammad
English Name: Muhammad
Period of Revelation: Meccan
Representative Passage:

Are they waiting for the Hour of Doom to suddenly approach them? Its signs have already appeared. How will they then come to their senses when the Hour itself will approach them? (47:18)

Sura #48

Arabic Name: Al-Fath
English Name: The Victory
Period of Revelation: Medinan
Representative Passage:

Those who pledge obedience to you are, in fact, pledging obedience to God. The hands of God are above their hands. As for those who disregard their pledge, they do so only against their own souls. Those who fulfill their promise to God will receive a great reward. (48:10)

Sura #49

Arabic Name: Al-Hujurat
English Name: The Chambers
Period of Revelation: Medinan
Representative Passage:

(Muhammad), say, "Do you teach God about your religion? God knows whatever is in the heavens and the earth. He has the knowledge of all things." (49:16)

Sura #50

Arabic Name: Qaf
English Name: Qaf
Period of Revelation: Meccan
Representative Passage:

We swear that We have created the human being and We know what his soul whispers to him. We are closer to him than even his jugular vein. (50:16)

Sura #51

Arabic Name: Al-Dhariyat
English Name: The Winds
Period of Revelation: Meccan
Representative Passage:

We have made the heavens with Our own hands and We expanded it. (51:47)

Sura #52

Arabic Name: Al-Tur
English Name: Mt. Sinai
Period of Revelation: Meccan
Representative Passage:

Do they have another god besides God? God is too exalted to be considered equal to the idols. (52:43)

Sura #53

Arabic Name: Al-Najm
English Name: The Star
Period of Revelation: Meccan
Representative Passage:

To your Lord will all things eventually return. (53:42)

Sura #54

Arabic Name: Al-Qamr
English Name: The Moon
Period of Revelation: Meccan
Representative Passage:

The pious ones will live in Paradise wherein streams flow, honorably seated in the presence of the All-dominant King. (54:54–55)

Sura #55

Arabic Name: Ar-Rahman
English Name: The Benificent
Period of Revelation: Medinan
Representative Passage:

Blessed is the Name of your Lord, the Lord of Glory and Grace. (55:78)

Sura #56

Arabic Name: Al-Waqiah
English Name: The Event
Period of Revelation: Meccan
Representative Passage:

Have you seen the water which you drink? Is it you who sent it down from the clouds or is it We who have sent it down? (56:68–69)

Sura #57

Arabic Name: Al-Hadid
English Name: The Iron
Period of Revelation: Medinan
Representative Passage:

Know that the worldly life is only a game, a temporary attraction, a means of boastfulness among yourselves and a place for multiplying your wealth and children. It is like the rain which produces plants that are attractive to the unbelievers. These plants flourish, turn yellow, and then become crushed bits of straw. In the life hereafter there will be severe torment or forgiveness and mercy from God. The worldly life is only an illusion. (57:20)

Sura #58

Arabic Name: Al-Mujadila
English Name: She Who Pleaded
Period of Revelation: Medinan
Representative Passage:

Those who oppose God and His Messenger will be humiliated like those who lived before. We have sent illustrious revelations and those who disbelieve will suffer a humiliating torment. (58:5)

Sura #59

Arabic Name: Al-Hashr
English Name: The Exile
Period of Revelation: Medinan
Representative Passage:

He is the only Lord, the King, the Holy, the Peace, the Forgiver, the Watchful Guardian, the Majestic, the Dominant, and the Exalted. God is too exalted to have any partner. (59:23)

Sura #60

Arabic Name: Al-Mumtahana
English Name: To Verify Faith
Period of Revelation: Medinan
Representative Passage:

Believers, do not choose My enemies and your own enemies for friends, and offer them strong love. They have rejected the Truth which has come to you, and have expelled the Messenger and you from your homes because of your belief in your Lord. When you go to fight for My cause and seek My pleasure, you secretly express your love of them. I know best what you reveal or conceal. Whichever of you does this has indeed gone astray from the right path. (60:1)

Sura #61

Arabic Name: As-Saff
English Name: The Battlefield Formations
Period of Revelation: Medinan
Representative Passage:

Believers, be the helpers of God just as when Jesus, the son of Mary, asked the disciples, "Who will be my helpers for the cause of God?" and the disciples replied, "We are the helpers of God." A group of the Israelites believed in him and others rejected him. We helped the believers against their enemies and they became victorious. (61:14)

Sura #62

Arabic Name: Al-Jumah
English Name: Day of Assembly
Period of Revelation: Medinan
Representative Passage:

When they see some merchandise or some sport, they rush towards it and leave you (Muhammad) alone standing. Say, "(God's rewards for good deeds) are better than merriment or merchandise; God is the best Sustainer." (62:11)

Sura #63

Arabic Name: Al-Munafiqun
English Name: The Hypocrites
Period of Revelation: Medinan
Representative Passage:

God will never grant respite to any soul when its appointed time has come. God is Well-Aware of what you do. (63:11)

Sura #64

Arabic Name: Al-Taghabun
English Name: Cheating Exposed
Period of Revelation: Medinan
Representative Passage:

On the day when We shall gather you all together (for the Day of Judgment), all cheating will be exposed. Those who believe in God and act righteously will receive forgiveness for their sins. They will be admitted into Paradise wherein streams flow and they will live forever. This certainly is the greatest triumph. (64:9)

Sura #65

Arabic Name: Al-Talaq
English Name: Divorce
Period of Revelation: Medinan
Representative Passage:

God will make a way (out of difficulty) for one who has fear of Him and will provide him with sustenance in a way that he will not even notice. God is Sufficient for the needs of whoever trusts in Him. He has full access to whatever He wants. He has prescribed a due measure for everything. (65:3)

Sura #66

Arabic Name: Al-Tahrim
English Name: Prohibition
Period of Revelation: Medinan
Representative Passage:

Believers, turn to God in repentance with the intention of never repeating the same sin. (66:8)

Sura #67

Arabic Name: Al-Mulk
English Name: The Kingdom
Period of Revelation: Meccan
Representative Passage:

(Muhammad), say, "It is God who has brought you into being and made ears, eyes, and hearts for you, but you give very little thanks." Say, "It is God who has settled you on the earth and to Him you will be resurrected." (67:23–24)

Sura #68

Arabic Name: Al-Qalam
English Name: The Pen
Period of Revelation: Meccan
Representative Passage:

Do not yield to one persistent in swearing, back-biting, gossiping, obstructing virtues, a sinful transgressor, ill-mannered, and morally corrupt, or because he may possess wealth and children. When Our revelations are recited to him, he says, "These are ancient legends." We shall brand him on his nose. We have tested them in the same way as we tested the dwellers of the garden (In Yemen) when they swore to pluck all the fruits of the garden in the morning, without adding ("if God wills."). (68:10–18)

Sura #69

Arabic Name: Al-Haqqah
English Name: The Inevitable
Period of Revelation: Meccan
Representative Passage:

On that day (the Day of Judgment), all your secrets will be exposed. (69:18)

Sura #70

Arabic Name: Al-Maarij
English Name: High Ranks
Period of Revelation: Meccan
Representative Passage:

A sinner will wish that he could save himself from the torment of that day by sacrificing his children, his wife, his brother, his kinsmen who gave him refuge (from hardship) and all those on earth. By no means! (70:11–15)

Sura #71

Arabic Name: Nuh
English Name: Noah
Period of Revelation: Meccan
Representative Passage:

Lord, forgive me, my parents, the believers who have entered my home and all believing men and women. Give nothing to the unjust but destruction. (71:28)

Sura #72

Arabic Name: Al-Jinn
English Name: The Jinn
Period of Revelation: Meccan
Representative Passage:

Say, "No one can protect me from God, nor can I find any place of refuge but with him. My only (means of protection) is to convey the message of God. Whoever disobeys God and His Messenger will go to hell, wherein he will live forever." (72:22–23)

Sura #73

Arabic Name: Al-Muzammil
English Name: The Mantled One
Period of Revelation: Meccan
Representative Passage:

Prayer at night leaves the strongest impression on one's soul and the words spoken are more consistent. During the day, you are preoccupied with many activities. Glorify the Name of your Lord, the Lord of the eastern and western regions, with due sincerity. He is the only Lord, so choose Him as your guardian. (73:6–9)

Sura #74

Arabic Name: Al-Mudashir
English Name: The Cloaked One
Period of Revelation: Meccan
Representative Passage:

Would that you really knew what hell is! It leaves and spares no one and nothing. It scorches people's skin and it has nineteen angelic keepers. (74:27–30)

Sura #75

Arabic Name: Al-Qiyamah
English Name: The Resurrection
Period of Revelation: Meccan
Representative Passage:

The human being does not want to believe the Truth, nor does he want to pray. He rejects the faith, turns away and haughtily goes to his people. Woe to you! Woe to you! For you, the human being of such behavior, will certainly deserve it. Does the human being think that he will be left uncontrolled? Was he not once just a drop of discharged sperm. Was he not turned into a clot of blood? God then formed him and gave him proper shape. From the human being, God made males and females in pairs. Does He then not have the power to bring the dead back to life? (75:31–40)

Sura #76

Arabic Name: Al-Dahr
English Name: The Human Being
Period of Revelation: Disputed
Representative Passage:

The servants of God fulfill their vows and are afraid of the day in which there will be widespread terror. They feed the destitute, orphans, and captives for the love of God, saying, "We only feed you for the sake of God and we do not want any reward or thanks from you. We are afraid of our Lord and the bitterly distressful day." God will certainly rescue them from the terror of that day and will meet them with joy and pleasure. (76:7–11)

Sura #77

Arabic Name: Al-Mursalat
English Name: Angels Sent Forth
Period of Revelation: Disputed
Representative Passage:

In which word other than the Quran will they believe? (77:50)

Sura #78

Arabic Name: Al-Naba
English Name: The News
Period of Revelation: Meccan
Representative Passage:

That will be the Day of the Truth. So let those who want seek refuge from their Lord. (78:39)

Sura #79

Arabic Name: Al-Naziat
English Name: Soul Snatchers
Period of Revelation: Meccan
Representative Passage:

By the angels who violently tear out the souls of the disbelievers from their bodies,
by the angels who gently release the souls of the believers,
by the angels who float (in the heavens by the will of God),
by the angels who hasten along
and by the angels who regulate the affairs, (you will certainly be resurrected).
On the day when the first trumpet sound blasts.
and will be followed by the second one,
hearts will undergo terrible trembling,
and eyes will be humbly cast down. (79:1–9)

Sura #80

Arabic Name: Abasa
English Name: He Frowned
Period of Revelation: Meccan
Representative Passage:

He frowned and then turned away from a blind man who had come up to him. You never
know. Perhaps he (the blind man) wanted to purify himself, or receive some (Quranic) advice
which would benefit him. Yet you pay attention to a rich man, though you will not be ques-
tioned, even if he never purifies himself. As for the one who comes to you earnestly (striving
for guidance), and who has fear of God, you ignore him! (80:1–10)

Sura #81

Arabic Name: Al-Takwir
English Name: The Cessation
Period of Revelation: Meccan
Representative Passage:

Your companion (Muhammad) does not suffer from any mental illness. He certainly saw him
(Gabriel) high up on the horizon in his original form. He (Muhammad) is not accused of
lying about the unseen. The Quran is not the word of condemned Satan. Where then will you
go? (81:22–26)

Sura #82

Arabic Name: Al-Infitar
English Name: The Cataclysm
Period of Revelation: Meccan
Representative Passage:

On that day, no soul will be of any benefit to any other soul. On that day, all affairs will be in the hands of God. (82:19)

Sura #83

Arabic Name: Al-Tatfif
English Name: The Defrauders
Period of Revelation: Meccan
Representative Passage:

Woe to those who are fraudulent in (weighing and measuring), those who demand a full measure from others but when they measure or weigh, give less. (83:1–3)

Sura #84

Arabic Name: Al-Inshiqaq
English Name: (Heavens) Rendered Apart
Period of Revelation: Meccan
Representative Passage:

Human being, you strive hard to get closer to your Lord, and so you will certainly receive the recompense (of your deeds). (84:6)

Sura #85

Arabic Name: Al-Bhruj
English Name: The Constellations
Period of Revelation: Meccan
Representative Passage:

Those who persecute the believing men and women without repenting will suffer the torment of hell and that of the burning fire. (85:10)

Sura #86

Arabic Name: Al-Tariq
English Name: The Nightly Rising Star
Period of Revelation: Meccan
Representative Passage:

They (disbelievers) plot every evil plan, but I too plan against them. (86:15–16)

Sura #87

Arabic Name: Al-A'la
English Name: The Most High
Period of Revelation: Meccan
Representative Passage:

(Muhammad), glorify the Name of your Lord, the Most High, Who has created (all things) proportionately, decreed their destinies, and provided them with guidance. (87:1–3)

Sura #88

Arabic Name: Al-Ghashiya
English Name: The Overwhelming Event
Period of Revelation: Meccan
Representative Passage:

(Muhammad), preach; you are only a preacher. You do not have full control over them. (88:21–22)

Sura 89

Arabic Name: Al-Fajr
English Name: The Dawn
Period of Revelation: Meccan
Representative Passage:

As for the human being, when his Lord tests him, honors him, and grants him bounty, he says, "God has honored me." However, when his Lord tests him by a measured amount of sustenance , he says, "God has disgraced me." (Since wealth does not necessarily guarantee everlasting happiness) then why do you not show kindness to the orphans, or urge one another to feed the destitute? (89:15–18)

Sura #90

Arabic Name: Al-Balad
English Name: The Town
Period of Revelation: Meccan
Representative Passage:

Would that you knew what Aqaba (the uphill path) is! It is the setting free of a slave or, in a day of famine, the feeding of an orphaned relative and downtrodden destitute person, (so that he would be of) the believers who cooperate with others in patience (steadfastness) and kindness. (90:12–17)

Sura #91

Arabic Name: Al-Shams
English Name: The Sun
Period of Revelation: Meccan
Representative Passage:

By the sun and its noon-time brightness,
by the moon when it follows the sun,
by the day when it brightens the earth,
by the night when it covers the earth with darkness,
by the heavens and that (Power) which established them,
by the earth and that (Power) which spread it out
and by the soul and that (Power) which designed it
and inspired it with knowledge of evil and piety,
those who purify their souls will certainly have everlasting happiness
and those who corrupt their souls will certainly be deprived (of happiness). (91:1–10)

Sura #92

Arabic Name: Al-Leyl
English Name: The Night
Period of Revelation: Meccan
Representative Passage:

I have warned you about the fierce blazing fire in which no one will suffer forever except the wicked ones who have rejected the (Truth) and have turned away from it. The pious ones who spend for the cause of God and purify themselves will be safe from this fire. (92:14–18)

Sura #93

Arabic Name: Al-Duha
English Name: Daylight
Period of Revelation: Meccan
Representative Passage:

Did He not find you (Muhammad) as an orphan and give you shelter? Did He not find you wandering about and give you guidance? (93:6–7)

Sura #94

Arabic Name: Al-Inshira
English Name: The Comfort
Period of Revelation: Meccan
Representative Passage:

Certainly, after every difficulty there comes relief. (94:6)

Sura #95

Arabic Name: Al-T'in
English Name: The Fig
Period of Revelation: Meccan
Representative Passage:

Is God not the best of the Judges? (95:8)

Sura #96

Arabic Name: Al-Alaq
English Name: The Clot of Blood
Period of Revelation: Meccan
Representative Passage (This was the first Sura revealed to the Prophet):

(Muhammad), read in the name of your Lord who created (all things). He created man from a clot of blood. Recite! Your Lord is the most Honorable One, who, by the pen, taught the human being: He taught the human being what he did not know. Despite this, the human being still tends to rebel because he thinks that he is independent. However, (all things) will return to your Lord. (96:1–8)

Sura #97

Arabic Name: Al-Qadr
English Name: Destiny
Period of Revelation: Meccan
Representative Passage:

We revealed the Quran on the Night of Destiny. (97:1)

Sura #98

Arabic Name: Al-Beyinnah
English Name: The Testimony
Period of Revelation: Disputed
Representative Passage:

The righteously striving believers are the best of all creatures. (98:7)

Sura #99

Arabic Name: Al-Zilzal
English Name: The Earthquake
Period of Revelation: Disputed
Representative Passage:

When the earth is shaken by a terrible quake, and it throws out its burden, the human being will say (in horror), "What is happening to it?" On that day the earth will declare all (the activities of the human being) which have taken place on it, having been inspired by your Lord. (99:1–6)

Sura #100

Arabic Name: Al-Aadiyat
English Name: The Chargers
Period of Revelation: Disputed
Representative Passage:

(I swear) by the snorting chargers (of the warriors), whose hoofs strike against the rocks and produce sparks while running during a raid at dawn, and leave behind a cloud of dust which engulfs the enemy, The human being is certainly ungrateful to his Lord. (100:1–6)

Sura #101

Arabic Name: Al-Qariah
English Name: The Crash
Period of Revelation: Meccan
Representative Passage:

*On that day, people will be like scattered moths and mountains will be like carded wool.
(101:4–5)*

Sura #102

Arabic Name: Al-Takatur
English Name: Worldly Gains
Period of Revelation: Meccan
Representative Passage:

*The desire to have more of the worldly gains have pre-occupied you so much (that you have
neglected remembering God), until you come to the graves. You shall know. (102:1–3)*

Sura #103

Arabic Name: Al-Asr
English Name: The Time
Period of Revelation: Meccan
Representative Passage:

*By the time (of the advent of Islam), the human being is doomed to suffer loss, except the
righteously striving believers who exhort each other to truthful purposes and to patience.
(103:1–3)*

Sura #104

Arabic Name: Al-Humazah
English Name: The Slanderer
Period of Revelation: Meccan
Representative Passage:

*Woe to every slanderer and backbiter who collects and hordes wealth, thinking that his prop-
erty will make him live forever. (104:1–3)*

Sura #105

Arabic Name: Al-Fil
English Name: The Elephant
Period of Revelation: Meccan
Representative Passage:

Did He not cause their evil plots to fail? (105:2)

Sura #106

Arabic Name: Al-Qureysh
English Name: The Qureysh
Period of Revelation: Meccan
Representative Passage:

For God's favors to them during their summer and winter journeys, (the) Qureysh should worship the Lord of this House. (106:1–2)

Sura #107

Arabic Name: Al-Ma'un
English Name: Cooperation
Period of Revelation: Medinan
Representative Passage:

Have you seen the one who calls the religion a lie? It is he who turns down the orphans and never encourages the feeding of the destitute. (107:1–3)

Sura #108

Arabic Name: Al-Kauthar
English Name: Abundant Virtue
Period of Revelation: Meccan
Representative Passage:

(Muhammad), We have granted you abundant virtue! (108:1)

Sura #109

Arabic Name: Al-Kafirun
English Name: The Unbelievers
Period of Revelation: Meccan
Representative Passage:

You follow your religion and I follow mine. (109:6)

Sura #110

Arabic Name: Al-Nasr
English Name: The Help
Period of Revelation: Medinan
Representative Passage:

Glorify your Lord with praise and ask Him for forgiveness. He accepts repentance. (110:3)

Sura #111

Arabic Name: Al-Lahab
English Name: Condemnation
Period of Revelation: Meccan
Representative Passage (a curse against an uncle of the Prophet Muhammad, who was an unyielding enemy of Islam):

May the hands of Abu Lahab perish! (111:1)

Sura #112

Arabic Name: Al-Iklas
English Name: The Purity
Period of Revelation: Meccan
The Sura: (This is a concise affirmation of the unity of God that the Prophet reportedly referred to as "one-third of the Koran"; it is reproduced here in its entirety.)

In the Name of God, the Beneficent, the Merciful:(Muhammad), say, "He is the only God. God is Absolute. He neither begets nor was He begotten. There is no one equal to Him." (112:1–4)

Sura #113

Arabic Name: Al-Falaq
English Name: The Daybreak
Period of Revelation: Meccan
Representative Passage:

(Muhammad), say, "I seek protection from the Lord of the Dawn, against the evil of whatever He has created." (113:1–2)

Sura #114

Arabic Name: Al-Nas
English Name: Mankind
Period of Revelation: Meccan
Representative Passage:

(Muhammad), say, "I seek protection from the Cherisher of mankind, the King of mankind, the Lord of mankind ..." (114:1–3)

Sura #113

Arabic Name: Al-Falaq
English Name: The Daybreak
Period of Revelation: Meccan
Representative Passage

(Muhammad), say, "I seek protection from the Lord of the Dawn against the evil of what He has created." (113:1-2)

Sura #114

Arabic Name: Al-Nas
English Name: Super/Mankind
Period of Revelation: Meccan
Representative Passage

(Muhammad), say, "I seek protection from the Cherisher of mankind, the King of mankind, the Lord of mankind, ..." (114:1-3)

Index

X-Y-Z

CHECK OUT THESE BEST-SELLERS

More than 450 titles available at booksellers and online retailers everywhere!

978-1-59257-115-4

978-1-59257-900-6

978-1-59257-855-9

978-1-59257-222-9

978-1-59257-957-0

978-1-59257-785-9

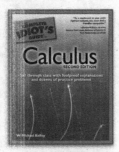

978-1-59257-471-1

978-1-59257-483-4

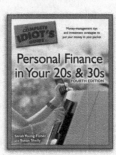

978-1-59257-883-2

978-1-59257-966-2

978-1-59257-908-2

978-1-59257-786-6

978-1-59257-954-9

978-1-59257-437-7

978-1-59257-888-7

ALPHA   idiotsguides.com